"Frank Joseph's book on synchronicity demonstrates, with research and understanding, how truly harmonious and balanced every act and event in our lives is --- not just coincidence. It proves how we are all part of a fabric of which we should be made more aware."
—**Shirley MacLaine**, actress, author, hostess of *Independent Expression Radio*, www.ShirleyMacLaine.com

Readers applaud Frank Joseph's earlier book on the subject, *Synchronicity & You* ---

"Joseph here presents a way for individuals to find ultimate meaning within the juxtaposition of apparently unrelated events. "Synchronicity" or meaningful coincidence" is the long-lost, direct experience with God." Such an experience, Joseph contends, is at once individual and a "materialization of the organizational will of the universe. Joseph provides seventeen categories for such experiences and offers meditation as a technique for reflecting on their meaning."

—*Library Journal*

"From Etruscan to Jungian, a long tradition of monistic esotericism is summoned to support Joseph's teaching: 'Synchronicity...is the golden key, searched for by generations of thinkers, to unlock the reality of spiritual existence.... It is our individual lifeline to that Compassionate Mystery that speaks its care to us in symbols meant specifically for us'."

—*John R. Leech*, *New York Reed Business Information, Inc.*

"Frank Joseph and his work on synchronicity is powerful and insightful. *Synchronicity & You* is an absolutely wonderful book....
I highly recommend it to anyone interested in meaningful coincidences."

—**Patricia Upczak,** author *Synchronicity, Signs & Symbols*

"This book was great; really enjoyed it; some parts were very deep and had to be read over and over again to understand the point, but highly recommend it."

—**Roxana L Cruz,** amazon.com reviewer

"Frank Joseph and his work on synchronicity is powerful and insightful. *Synchronicity & You* is an absolutely wonderful book.... I highly recommend it to anyone interested in meaningful coincidences. We have all experienced inexplicable coincidences – such as thinking about an old friend before the phone rings and it happens to be that old friend. A valuable guide book that... leads us, step by step, into communication with our deeper subconscious nature and nudges open the gate to our inner self."

—**Dale Graff,** author *Tracks in the Psychic Wilderness*

"An engrossing, thorough and well-researched examination of the phenomenon of 'coincidences' accessible to layman and scholar alike. A wonderful read and valuable contribution to the growing body of literature on this ever-fascinating subject."

—**Yeti Halberstam,** author, *Small Miracles*

"In *Synchronicity & You*, Frank Joseph takes us beyond the sensational stories and the scientific debates into the very heart and soul of synchronicity. This is a masterpiece of a book written with the profound insight, clarity and awe that can only come from first-hand personal experience. Joseph weaves together hundreds of striking synchronicity examples along a series of recognizable themes selected to astonish, fascinate, move and amuse us. A first-class book for anyone who wants to widen horizons and deep self-discovery!"

—**Suzanne V. Brown**, Ph.D., Editor, *The Synchronicity Connection*

"Frank Joseph boldly and eloquently connects us to a larger world."

—**Thomas Ropp**, *The Arizona Republic*

"I became interested in the subject of meaningful coincidences or synchronicities following a series of unexplainable occurrences in my own life. David Ricoh's book by the same title is also outstanding for a deeper understanding of these events and their significance. But it is Joseph who provides a scientific approach to record and analyze these events through the use of two journals, one to record random minor and major coincidences that we see in our everyday lives and a second to immediately record our dreams. He also recommends daily meditation to enhance focus on these events and their patterns in our lives. His discussion of Moira or life passion is also illuminating and will enhance your personal appreciation for pursuing your bliss."

—**Ross Reller** amazon.com reviewer

"Is there more to interpreting reality than just the perceptions of your five senses? Is there indeed a "cosmic trickster" who decides to send you signals with irregular patterns about your own life? In this fascinating book it is a reevaluation of older principles (the ancient Greek belief about lower and higher destiny for one) connected with modern psychology (Carl Jung primarily) that leads to a mesmerizing study of the phenomenon of synchronicities: events that we today tend to describe as "incredible coincidences" or Déjà Vu moments without actually realizing that there could be a meaning, a "code", which can reveal to us either things about to happen or can function as warnings about the future, or even, 'messages' about ourselves and what we can do to alter the 'higher destiny,' which is the part of fate we actually can manipulate.

"In the hi-tech, fast paced and materialistic modern world, all this may sound like another book for 'weirdoes,' but it can't be dismissed as others in its genre exactly because synchronicities are something mostly everyone notices at one point of life or another, and the more aware you are about them the more apparent they become. Being a natural skeptic, the first time I picked up this book I abandoned it after only being one-third into it, because I felt it wasn't compatible with my own personal system of beliefs and understanding. It was only after I started noticing some startling synchronicities myself that I read it (through this time) again, only to realize that there's way more to synchronicities than, well, meets not only the eye but any of our senses.

"I tend to think that the 'truth' (whatever that may be) is not only something one can "learn" but it's also something one can feel and I consider both processes equally important. The author divides synchronicities into seventeen categories and studies them providing in the process numerous truly incredible examples about them. At certain parts of the book it's the examples themselves that steal the show and you may find yourself recognizing situations that are in one way or the other familiar to you but you hadn't paid attention when they happened. Attention is of primary importance, as you will find out if you go ahead and read it.

"Frank Joseph attempts to find what most of us would call a "rational explanation" about synchronicities. He's never dogmatic (to his credit) about his own thoughts and his book reads like a conversation with the reader making it one definite *can't-put-downer*.

"In the end what he proposes is essentially that the reader examines this his/herself and explain it in his/her terms. It doesn't actually matter how one decides to explain synchronicities he muses, what matters is that there is a different dimension of reality present for everyone waiting to be explored, discovered and deciphered. Put this book in your bag of valuable tools."

—amazon.com reviewer

Synchronicity as Mystical Experience

Applying Meaningful Coincidence in Your Life

by Frank Joseph

Shanti Publishing
PO Box 6252
Pine Mountain Club, CA 93222

Synchronicity as Mystical Experience

Applying Meaningful Coincidence in Your Life

Joseph, Frank, 1944–

Synchronicity as Mystical Experience Applying Meaningful Coincidence In Your Life/ Frank Joseph

Includes bibliographical references and index.

Paperback ISBN: 978-1-942171-02-7
Library of Congress Control Number: 2017959584

Published in the United States of America
by Shanti Publishing

" ... the essence of mysticism is a belief in the underlying unity of all things that otherwise appear

distinct." ——Mark Thurston, Ph.D. *The Essential Edgar Cayce.* NY: Jeremy P. Tarcher/Penguin, 2004

Table of Contents

Foreword:
Synchronicity, the Key
to Understanding

by Von Braschler, Minneapolis Regional Director of The Theosophical Society, author of *Seven Secrets of Time Travel* (VT: Destiny Books, 2012) and *Confessions of a Reluctant Ghost Hunter* (VT: Destiny Books, 2014).

I have known Frank Joseph for more than twenty years. His drive to discover and reveal the great mysteries in our world still astound me. I first met him in 1991, while working at Llewellyn Publications, in St. Paul, Minnesota, on his first book, *Sacred Sites*. Since then, he's written some thirty more books on a variety of fascinating, baffling subjects that hold mystery and intrigue for all of us. He seems driven to delve into the deeper mysteries about who we are, our hidden roots, and why we are here. As an enterprising journalist with a news writing background, Frank has produced more books that explore the mysteries of Atlantis than anyone dead or alive. And that's just one subject that motivates him.

What impresses me most is that Frank is always digging, researching, and personally exploring the bigger mysteries of human experience. One of his pet projects with immense personal attachment involves his fascination with synchronicity, or meaningful coincidence, as psychologists call it. In the area where I live, Frank's lectures and workshops have drawn many people into his ongoing study of synchronicity. He has thrilled our Minneapolis Theosophical Society group locally with his stories along these lines. He even taught a popular series of local Open U classes on the subject, which many people still discuss in depth.

Through the years, Frank has interviewed more than a hundred people about synchronicity in their personal lives. He has kept a daily journal for many years that lists meaningful coincidences that he has observed. He has maintained a running record of meaningful coincidences that he has read or heard about.

So, an index for his new, in-depth book on synchronicity should read like a Who's Who of people and events that pose compelling arguments for the importance of synchronicity in the world and in our lives. He has examined famous persons, historical figures, and everyday people in the news who have experienced bizarre coincidences of significance. *Synchronicity As Mystical Experience* is loaded with them; and in the end, their stories will leave you convinced.

It's important to recognize synchronicity. Meaningful coincidences in our lives need to be carefully observed. We need to be more than wowed by these coincidences, and should pay close attention to them, because they have something important to say. They speak to us on many levels.

On one level, Frank Joseph considers how meaningful coincidences impact seven distinct personality types. They are determined by which of the seven major chakras is dominant in a person's life and defines that life. And this makes great sense when you consider the seven rays of light that ushers in seven different types of people. The seven rays can be determined by the fragmented colors of light, the spectrum that is refracted from the one Ray of Life or divine source. These seven colors of light energy correspond to the seven different colors that are associated with the major seven chakras of our bodies. And the chakras exist on all levels of being from our physical body to our emotional body, our mental bodies, our causal body, and our spiritual bodies. Some of us are simply stuck in the root chakra, the red-colored chakra. In other people, another chakra is dominant in their development, as that color from that energy vortex pours forth in greater abundance. Frank's analysis of the seven different chakra types with regard to synchronicity is ground-breaking material, worthy of deep study and contemplation.

The meaningful significance of repetitive patterns of numbers is also fascinating material in this new book about synchronicity. Frank Joseph analyzes the Pythagorean theory of numbers and their mystical significance through the lens of synchronicity. He shows that recurring numbers can hold meaningful significance. This treatment should appeal to historians and psychologists, as well as mathematicians, numerologists, and musicians. Numbers don't lie.

Supplementing this detailed treatment of meaningful patterns of coincidences and the preponderance of historical evidence of synchronicity at work, Frank Joseph relates his own true-life accounts with this mystical experience. Here is a talented and serious writer, who recognizes cosmic coincidence when it speaks to him. We are indebted to him for sharing what he has come to know so deeply in *Synchronicity as Mystical Experience.*

Introduction:
Are We Beneficiaries or Victims of Meaningful Coincidence?

"In the City of God there will be a great thunder. Two brothers are torn apart by chaos, while the fortress endures. The great leader will succumb. The third, big war will begin when the New City is burning. In the year of the new century and nine months, from the sky will come a great King of Terror. The sky will burn at forty-five degrees. Fire approaches the great New City" (Quatrains X.72, VI.79). [1]

These words seem to describe the destruction that hit New York City on 11 September 2001. The "two brothers torn apart by chaos" appear to be the twin towers of the World Trade Center which collapsed in the attack. "The fortress endures" might be the Pentagon Building, which sustained heavy damage during the terrorist operation. "The great leader" could refer to Osama bin Laden, "wanted dead or alive", according to U.S. President George Bush, who blamed the prominent Islamic figure for terrorism against America. In September 2001, "the year of the new century and nine months", the sky-jacked airliners come "from the sky", and "fire approaches the New City". New York City?

The extraordinary feature of this quotation is that it was spoken nearly half a millennium before the event it portrayed. In fact, the forty-five "degrees" might actually refer to the number of years separating it from a later time when "the sky will burn." In any case, the source for this exceptional prediction was a most remarkable man. Born Michel de Nostredame in Saint-Remy, on 14 December 1503, Nostradamus is history's most famous seer. During his mid-forties, the French apothecary began making grand predictions that were published for the first time in 1555. *Les Propheties* is composed of rhymed quatrains, or four-lined stanzas, grouped in hundreds; each set of a hundred quatrains was identified as a "century". The popularity of this work was so widespread, especially in high places, he dedicated an enlarged, second edition to the King. Having thus gained royal favor, Nostradamus was everywhere in demand. Catherine de Medici invited him to cast the horoscopes of her children, and he became the personal physician to Charles IX, who ascended the French throne in 1560.

Because of these important political contacts, Vatican hostility was temporarily avoided, but nonetheless inevitable. By 1781, the Roman Catholic Church had officially condemned Nostradamus, his prophecies and any Catholics who read them under the inquisitorial Congregation of the Index. This was a body of bishops and cardinals who busied themselves with rooting out perceived heresies. Since then, the "centuries" of Nostradamus have gained international attention for many prognostications that have apparently come to pass, and especially because those which are yet unfulfilled seem strangely relevant to our time. His prophetic statement about the September 2001 terrorist attack on New York City forms the first half of its own meaningful coincidence. Such a phenomenon occurs when two or more apparently disconnected events cross paths to create a previously unsuspected, significant relationship.

According to a report in *The Southern Illinoisian*, three days after the World Trade Center disaster, David Severin, the owner of a display store in the Illinois town of Benton, received an order for forty small American flags. Due to patriotic fervor in wake of the attack, however, flags were nowhere to be obtained, and he was unable to fill the purchase request. Soon after reluctantly turning down the order, Severin got another phone call, this time from his mother. "It was strange that I had just hung up the phone with somebody that was looking for flags," he said, "and she calls asking if I know anybody looking for flags." [2] She had forty of them, the precise number requested by Severin's customer. His mother had been going through the personal effects of her late husband, when she found the flags. Despite their age of more than three decades, they had never been unwrapped and were in pristine condition. Remarkably, their sales ticket, likewise preserved, indicated that the flags had been sent from New York City on 11 September 1970 --- thirty-one years to the day that New York's Twin Towers were destroyed. No less incredibly, the customer who ordered the forty flags resided at the same house address where Severin's late father lived at the time he received the package of flags he never opened.

Destruction of New York's World Trade Center has sometimes been compared to its 20th Century counterpart, the Japanese attack on Pearl Harbor, which had its own prophetic synchronicity. The words, later to become an American rallying cry, "Remember Pearl Harbor!", appeared in paint on a sidewalk in front of the entrance to a grammar school in Owensville, Indiana on 7 December 1939, two years to the day before the event took place.[3]

During the war, on 18 April 1942, Tokyo staged its first ever, full-dress air-raid rehearsal drill. Unbeknownst to its civil defense organizers, on that same day the Americans launched their premiere air-raid against Japan. When U.S. Colonel James Doolittle's carrier-based B-25 "Mitchell" medium bombers appeared overhead, the people of Tokyo were already safely ensconced in underground shelters. Thus, casualties were very low. It was as though a divine providence had spared untold numbers of non-combatant men, women and children from what would have otherwise been a terrible slaughter, when a military hospital, six schools and other civilian buildings were bombed during the attack.

In spring 2001, I was writing about B-17 "Flying Fortresses" and B-24 "Liberators," bomber-planes of the United States Army Air Force during World War II. My identification with the subject at the time was personal and intense, as I described their life-and-death struggles in the skies over Europe, sixty years before. Taking a break from my exhilarating work, I stepped outside my office to breathe in the afternoon sunlight. Looking up at the sky, I heard the droning of unusual aircraft engines. They sounded deep and ominous. Moments later, I was astounded to behold a "Flying Fortress" coming in at low altitude, allowing me to see that the aircraft was painted in wartime colors and camouflage. Recovering from the visual impact in this meaningful coincidence, I could hardly believe my eyes as another old bomber, this time a B-24 "Liberator," likewise in Second World War insignia, followed behind the B-17 a few minutes later. I never saw these rare, vintage aircraft in flight before or since.

Such mystically orchestrated dramas do not only take place on a historic scale, but more commonly inter-weave human life on a personal level. In 1932, Peg Entwistle climbed to the top of the fifty-foot-high letter "H" in the world-famous "Hollywood" sign raised on Mount Lee's steep slopes overlooking California's movie Mecca. A formerly successful Broadway stage-actress, she found no work in films after weeks of inquiry, and became deeply depressed. Leaving behind a note in which she apologized for her decision, she threw herself from the sign. At the moment of her suicide on 18 September, a notice was on its way to her from the Beverly Hills Community Players offering Entwistle an important part role in a new play. The part called for the heroine to kill herself at the close of the third act.

These were the kinds of inexplicable, although common events investigated by the great Swiss psychologist, Carl Jung. He devoted the last twenty-five years of his life to the research of meaningful coincidences --- those always unexpected, apparently random moments in which we find ourselves at the crossroads of two or more seemingly disconnected events that suddenly flash with personal significance. Synchronicity implies that our linear concept of time is only relative to our earthly existence. The universe runs on a different timetable and breaks through to or interfaces with our human realm only in instances of meaningful coincidence.

Jung found that incorporating such incidents into therapy generated invariably positive, sometimes transforming results for his patients. At this early stage of his investigation into the phenomena, he might have agreed with the observation of author John Anthony West that "a determination to see connections everywhere may be absurd, but it is no more absurd than the equal and opposite determination to see connections nowhere."[4] Jung's aptly titled book, Synchronicity, described some of his cases, in which meaningful coincidence was used as a tool for providing his clinically depressed clients with feelings of connectedness to something significant and compassionate more experienced than seen.

In his last recorded dream before he died, Jung told how he found himself wandering through different spaces, trying to find a mathematical formula that would explain synchronicity. He dreamed he was walking forward while holding a mirror in which he could simultaneously look backward. His "psycho-drama" revealed a wonderful truth about meaningful coincidence; namely, that it transcends time, in which past, present and future are merely points of reference.

French astronomer, Camille Flammarion's famous 1888 engraving illustrates that breakthrough moment, when meaningful coincidence reveals a fleeting glimpse of otherwise unseen, spiritual forces driving our day-to-day world of appearances, not unlike machinery hidden behind a theater curtain moving the scenery of a live stage play.

This fresh view of the subject follows Jung's lead in recognizing meaningful coincidence as a kind of modern-day enlightenment or emotional therapy that everyone, not only sufferers from chronic neuroses, may use to connect with the spiritual basis of being. *Synchronicity as Mystical Experience* defines the phenomenon in abundant anecdotal material, such as related accounts of the *Titanic* disaster, which attracted a constellation of synchronicity never described so thoroughly before, and informs readers how they may interpret the often puzzling elements in meaningful coincidence. These details include the significance of recurring numbers, and personal discovery of our parallel lives. The intimate secret of synchronicity and its fundamental mechanism lie inside every human being; this is the chakra system, comprising seven major energy-centers rising along the human spinal column. Re-examining them in the context of meaningful coincidence reveals that each one corresponds to a human personality type. In fact, they are nothing more than expressions of the chakras themselves.

Synchronicity as Mystical Experience examines each one, defines its personality, and associates it with a particular deity and gemstone that best exemplifies its qualities. The natural, spiritual organization that thus emerges demonstrates a fundamental connectedness underpinning not only all mankind, but beyond to a spiritual reality linking every individual human being to the illimitable organizing power of existence.

Scholars knew of the chakras for thousands of years before the name was first used in ancient India. In Babylon, and even earlier, in Sumer, the oldest known civilization, going back five thousand, five hundred years, the chakras were described in a dramatic myth still told today. It is the story of Inanna, the ravishingly beautiful love-goddess, who was saddened by the passing of her mortal paramour. She went down to the gates of the Underworld, where his soul was imprisoned, and beseeched the lord of Death to free her lover. "Only on the condition that you reveal to me all your naked loveliness," he replied. "My realm has seven levels, and you wear seven veils. With each veil you remove, you will be allowed to descend another grade. But to reach him, you will have to stand nude in the lowest layer of my kingdom." Inanna agreed, correspondingly disrobing through the seven levels of the Underworld, until she reached her lover, and brought him back to the world of the living.

Her myth (better known thanks to Oscar Wilde and Richard Strauss, as Salome's "Dance of the Seven Veils") is an analogy of the major chakras that make up the human energy centers. By "unveiling" or revealing their tremendous potential, even death may be overcome and life itself regained. This is the ultimate meaning and goal of integrating our spiritual vortexes with mystical experiences through synchronicity. "It is this experience of the infinite that cuts through every moment in time," according to Mark Thurston, biographer of Edgar Cayce, the previous Century's most famous psychic. "Once we perceive that unity links the apparent differences in life, then it's our challenge to return to the world of distinctions and apply what we have learned as practical mystics. We can bring this sense of oneness to everything we do ... We are born to bring the creative, spiritual world into the daily material world --- 'making the infinite finite'. ... each of us is born with a personal mission, a 'soul purpose' ... There is an aspect of service to soul-purpose, a sense of making a contribution to the world." [5]

The current, or fourteenth Dalai Lama likewise believes that the perception of the underlying inter-relatedness of the universe is the key to fulfilling our true purpose in life, and, through and beyond that, to attaining spiritual illumination. "Whoever sees the interdependent nature of reality," he says, "sees the *dharma*. And whoever sees *dharma*, sees Buddha. The universal truth is interconnectedness." [6] *Dharma* is Sanskrit signifying a kind of work most appropriate for a particular human being. It is the path, task, or mission that is uniquely true for him or her in the service of their own inner truth. For Tibetan Buddhists like the Dalai Lama, "seeing the Buddha" is a manner of saying that they have "seen the light;" i.e., achieved enlightenment. To be sure, anyone who experiences synchronicity and fully appreciates its mystery will "see Buddha," the "Awakened or Enlightened One."

As described in the final chapters, that enlightenment is associated with the *chakras*, vortexes of spiritual energy, inflections of the human personality, each with its own color. In sum, they make up our immortal soul, just as they comprise the colors of the rainbow. When light passes through droplets of water, its seven component parts become visual to the eye in the form of a rainbow. When they are unseparated, we experience light. So too, a combination of the seven major *chakra*s generates enlightenment. Awareness of synchronicity reveals the diverse but related aspects of our being, and their potential for illumination through balancing, harmonizing and energizing these "wheels" of divine light.

Chapter 1

Applying the Mystery of Synchronicity

"So much of the future hangs upon the most ephemeral of webs spun by the Fates, the remote likelihood that one of a thousand possible results will be chosen by the deities. If a man were ever able to unravel such threads, he would have finally solved the mystery of the universe and attained the wisdom of the gods."

—Michael Curtis Ford, *The Ten Thousand* [1]

Synchronicity is the most mysterious thing in the world. It is the term parapsychologists use for "meaningful coincidence." It happens to everyone, more often than we may realize. But synchronicities are not "mere" coincidences, random accidents without significance.

At the beginning of his international career, long before he became "Sir" Anthony Hopkins, he got on a subway in London after a fruitless search for his missing copy of George Feifer's novel, *The Girl from Petrovka*. The actor looked down, and there on the seat was the book. It was Hopkins' own, which had been stolen two years earlier.

The phenomenon is universal enough to be commonplace. Going through a half-forgotten collection of old photographs, you are surprised to find the snap-shot of a friend you lost contact with years ago. Just then the telephone rings and the voice on the other end of the line belongs to the same person in the photo.

You are desperate to find a parking place because you have simply got to be on time for a crucial appointment. There is not an open spot as far as the eye can see. Suddenly, a car pulls out in front of you, leaving you a space right in front of the address where you are expected.

You have just finished reading a book about hummingbirds, when the first hummingbird you've ever seen in your back yard comes to drink nectar from a nearby flower.

These are typical incidents of synchronicity. And while most people brush them aside as insignificant happenstance, some of the greatest minds in history have grappled with these strange enigmas. "Synchronicity" was coined by this century's leading psychologist, Carl Gustav Jung. Fascinated as he was by it, even Albert Einstein could not understand how it worked. The purpose here is not to succeed where he failed, but to describe synchronicity primarily through examples, and, more importantly, how --- surprisingly perhaps --- to improve one's life with it.

Meaningful coincidences are not the inevitable quirks of living. Most people pay little attention to them, ordinarily dismissing such events as amusing instances of statistical probability. But as numerous experiences presented in the following pages demonstrate, the apparent and assumed separateness of things in the so-called "real world" momentarily yields during a meaningful coincidence. Then the frayed curtain of consensus reality parts, if only momentarily, and we personally glimpse a vast, otherwise unseen network of inter-connecting unity beyond, behind, within, and at the same time supporting our existence.

But the objective here is less concerned with plumbing the deepest mystery of synchronicity, than embracing it as a means of defining the Seven Human Types --- fundamental human personalities, as expressions of those spinal vortexes identified in Eastern mysticism as chakras, or "wheels" of subtle energy connecting mind with the body. Cases presented in the following chapters demonstrate that meaningful coincidences do indeed occur. Like dreaming, synchronicity is irrational, but real. The following anecdote serves to illustrate.

While struggling to make a living through sales of his paintings, Dennis Rhoidt was virtually penniless. Eventually, however, he was offered a generous price for one of his canvases, but only if he could additionally provide a rare and very specific kind of frame for it within the next twenty-four hours, before the buyer left town. The impoverished Wisconsin artist searched frantically, high and low, for such a frame, without success. None of his friends, local art supply stores or even pawn shops could help. The hour was getting late. Soon the waiting buyer would board his train for parts unknown, taking with him Rhoidt's chance to make a desperately needed sale.

But he was unexpectedly distracted from his despair by some general commotion down the street in the city where he lived, Madison, the state capitol. A large crowd was gathering to watch the conflagration of an old warehouse. As flames leapt up through the roof of the building, firemen with their trucks and equipment arrived in a tumult of sirens and lights. Dennis, one of several hundred spectators, watched as high arcs of streaming water began to play over the doomed building. Suddenly, a large dog ran from the smoke-filled entrance bearing something in its jaws. Even at a distance, Dennis noticed that it seemed to resemble a picture frame. He ran from the crowd, chasing the dog for almost a full city block before it dropped what it was carrying.

When Dennis caught up with the fallen object, he was astounded to see that it was precisely the type of unusual frame his would-be buyer required before making a purchase. No less incredibly, it matched the dimensions of the painting for sale. Dennis rushed home with the frame, quickly and easily repaired its fire damage, then sold it and his artwork for a lucrative fee just as his patron was about to leave Madison.

Trying to explain such irrational experiences with the rational mind --- or subconscious experiences with the conscious mind --- is hazardous, at best. Instead, the purpose here is to show readers how to interpret meaningful coincidence by themselves, and use it to enrich and guide their lives toward a higher good. As Goethe observed, "we murder when we dissect."[2] Employing, rather then dismantling synchronicity, will make it work for us. Properly nurtured, synchronicity is the true mystical experience of our times, that personal connection between us and the creative consciousness that pervades everything --- from our unspoken thoughts to the swirl of whole galaxies.

Meaningful coincidence can put us in sync with that universally inclusive power, with which all things are possible. According to the German mythologist, Heinrich Zimmer, "the most important things cannot be explained; the second most important things are misunderstood."[3] Synchronicity is an extra-rational revelation to be experienced, not a factual event that can yield to rational explanations. At the very least, acknowledging synchronicity improves our perception of the world around and within us, making us alert to its subtleties we otherwise missed. There is, after all, far more to be perceived than we usually perceive.

During the course of my synchronicity research, I learned that certain qualities distinguished persons who paid very close attention to meaningful coincidences from most people for whom such events are insignificant. Individuals following the guidance implicit in synchronicity occasionally suffered difficulties and sorrow, just like everyone else. But what set them apart was their superior resilience and ability to recover from misfortune. They felt inwardly strengthened and reassured through their appreciation of numerous meaningful coincidences. As the poet says, "the universe is unfolding the way it should," even if sometimes things seem quite the opposite.[4] They have faith that a direction nevertheless exists, and that it leads toward an ultimate, so far undisclosed good, because innumerable synchronicities already revealed the organized pattern of all existence. Far from being the slaves to superstition, such persons have a heightened sense of meaning. They possess an inner calm manifesting itself as strengthened character when confronted by adversity.

Most powerful of all, synchronicities are sometimes epiphanies, our personal experience of spiritual vitality and reality. This was the function of the Ancient World's so-called "mystery cults," where would-be adherents were brought along an initiating path toward achieving genuine mystical experience. Growing disenchantment with institutionalized religions, together with popular cynicism fueled by a mechanistic science and dead-end materialism have stolen any capacity for encountering such an experience from millions of people around the planet.

We may read volumes on theology, but unless our senses are moved somehow, we are not really convinced of the existence of some godhood. Not the mind, but the soul must be touched. Synchronicity is that missing link between man and divinity. What we feel when we are contacted by a meaningful coincidence is the reflex action of our spirit. In other words, synchronicity is the viable mystical experience of our times.

A case in point was a synchronicity I experienced during the early fall of 2009, while asleep in a rented cabin at Estes Park, Colorado. A dream that night was so powerful, it startled me awake --- luckily, because all its vivid details were still fresh in my awakening mind. I recalled being almost eyeball to eyeball with a Native American shaman, his intently serious countenance decorated with face-paint: white, horizontal stripes beneath the man's dark eyes. A single, white feather stood perfectly vertical from his coal-black hair, as he spoke to me emphatically in a tribal language. Somehow, I knew another, adult, male presence was nearby. "I cannot understand him," I said without looking away from the intense, almost urgent Indian. A voice slightly above, off to my right, spoke, "He says tomorrow you will see God."

Remarkable as this psycho-drama may have been, it was blocked from my memory for the rest of that morning and into the early afternoon by the spectacular distractions of Rocky Mountain State Park that monopolized my attention, until around 3:00 p.m. Hiking westward through a broad valley, I gazed up at the otherwise clear sky to see a large, lone cloud shaped into an absolutely symmetrical, pure-white, delta formation, its two, base points resting precisely on equally tall mountain peaks flanking either side of the valley. The triangle has always been associated in cultures worldwide with divinity, from ancient Egypt's Great Pyramid to the Christian

Trinity. This awareness combined with recollection of the previous night's dream to make an almost overwhelming impression. I stared fixedly at the appropriately configured cloud for about ten minutes, when it began to break up.

The meaningful coincidence connecting my prophetic dream with the delta-shaped cloud was appropriate at the time I experienced it, because, in recent months, I had become increasingly interested in possibilities (or impossibilities) for the reality of God, questions that bedeviled me since childhood. The Rocky Mountain synchronicity made a galvanizing impact on a lifetime of speculations, fusing them into a hypothesis bordering on conviction; namely, that a universal, unifying consciousness appears to interpenetrate not only every cell of all living matter everywhere --- nor even each sub-atomic particle of matter --- but additionally the so-far-unknown substance of time itself, plus every form of energy, including human thought.

In other words, "God" (for lack of a better term to describe some kind of omnipresent awareness) is the aggregate of existence present everywhere, in everything, at all times. "God" is not, therefore, some anthropomorphic supreme being removed from nature, but inhabits every inflection of the entire universe. There is no "Creator" standing outside "His" creation. Instead, He/She/It (an identity beyond all categories of thought) is eternally self-creating, manifesting His/Her/Itself in every inflection of being. This interpretation allows meaningful coincidence to establish organic interconnections through matter, space, time or energy, because they are all aspects of a universal consciousness that expresses itself to humans in synchronicity.

The same phenomenon, as demonstrated by my predictive Estes Park dream, shows that our divisions of time into past, present, and future are mere conveniences allowing us to get our bearings in the course of living. Time is actually something entirely different from our daily perception of it. For example, an astronaut traveling round-trip for two weeks through outer space near the speed of light returns fourteen days older than the moment he departed, while everyone else on Earth has aged four years. Similar examples of "time dilation" are not theoretical, but have been repeatedly verified experimentally by precise measurements of atomic clocks flown in aircraft and satellites.

This temporal elasticity is the stuff of synchronicity, as exemplified by another prophetic dream experienced by Samuel Clemens. In early June, 1858, twenty-three-year-old Mark Twain and his younger brother, Henry, were serving together aboard a Mississippi river-boat, the *Pennsylvania*, steaming between New Orleans and St. Louis, where they over-nighted at their sister's home. It was there that Twain dreamt he saw Henry's corpse lying in an open, metal coffin, a bouquet of white flowers with a single, red rose at the center, placed on his chest.

Illustration of Henry and Samuel Clemens aboard the ill-fated *Pennsylvania*. From Albert Bigelow Paine's *Mark Twain, A Biography*. (NY: Harper & Brothers, 1912).

Several days later, Twain got into an argument with the Pennsylvania's captain, resigned his commission as steersman, and transferred to another steamboat, the A.T. Lacey, while Henry remained with the Pennsylvania for his return voyage north. On June 13, as the Pennsylvania passed Memphis, Tennessee, her boilers exploded, killing most of the crew and half of the five hundred passengers aboard. Blasted into the river, Henry swam back to the sinking vessel, despite having been severely scalded, to save as many survivors as possible, before he, too, eventually succumbed of his injuries and over exertion, one week later.

When his grieving, elder brother went to pay last respects, Twain was shocked to see Henry's body laid in an expensive, metal coffin, a gift from the people of Memphis in honor of the heroic youth. All the other hundreds of coffins pertaining to the *Pennsylvania* disaster were made of pine. As Twain looked on, an elderly woman entered the funeral parlor to place a bouquet of white flowers with a single, red rose at its center, on his Henry's chest. Following this prophetic synchronicity, Mark Twain became a member of the American branch of the Society for Psychical Research.

A synchronous event of my own in 1991 prompted me to interview, over the next six years, eventually one hundred persons about their feelings concerning this elusive enigma. The meaningful coincidences they shared with me proved more illuminating than anything I ever read on the subject. Collecting them into a loose order, I was somewhat astounded to see that these synchronous events experienced by my friends and acquaintances arranged themselves into repeating categories. Although many of the persons interviewed differed widely in age, spiritual beliefs or education, the meaningful coincidences they recounted all belonged to specific groups of common experience.

Widening my research, I found that persons belonging to other cultures, sometimes long dead ---

often many hundreds or even thousands of years ago --- fell into the same categories of experience that emerged from the men and women who told me of their own fortuitous occurrences. Their often dramatic, occasionally funny, always numinous testimony formed the basis for my first book on the subject, *Synchronicity & You, Understanding the Role of Meaningful Coincidence in Your Life.* Since its first release through Boston's Element Books in 1999, I have been interviewed on dozens of radio shows across the United States and overseas. Many of these programs allowed listeners to telephone me while I was on the air.

The callers invariably confessed that the synchronous events they encountered felt very significant, but were usually incomprehensible, and asked me to interpret these personal experiences for them. I explained that only individuals who actually lived through meaningful coincidences were really capable of understanding them, because such phenomena are deeply personal. All I could do was point out the significance of certain motifs common to human beings everywhere. Persons who examined their synchronicities in the light of these universal themes might then be able to find a meaning.

After my book was published in the United States, I was asked to teach a "learning annex" class in synchronicity at Minnesota's Open U, in Minneapolis. But here, too, my students always wanted to know the ultimate meaning of their coincidences. I told them that most individual synchronous events do not lend themselves to interpretation. More usually, the coincidences that happen to us make little or no sense --- in themselves, that is.

When seen in the context of the coincidences which took place before and after, however, the significance of individual synchronicities began to emerge --- like the single notes of a song. When sounded, just one note may bc pretty, but only when it is heard in relationship to the notes which precede and follow it may the melody be understood. So too, our individual coincidences. In and of themselves, they are often, if not usually, inscrutable. But seen in their place among other synchronicities before and after them, they begin to reveal themselves. That is why I urge interested persons to keep a diary of their meaningful coincidences. In making a record of them, we are able to trace the themes and patterns that intersect our destiny.

Even so, it was apparent that both my readers and students were more interested in deciphering synchronicity and applying it to their daily lives, than to understanding its place of origin. Indeed, there is no general consensus for the source of this phenomenon. Some speculate it emanates from the human subconscious. Others believe synchronicity is personal guidance from God in the form of subtle messages --- warps in the fabric of time. "God," according to the great American mythologist, Joseph Campbell, is a name for a power beyond our understanding, a concept excelling all categories of thought. He also likened "God" to a sphere, whose circumference is everywhere but extent is nowhere.

In earthly existence, we live in the field of time. Events happen, we experience life now, and anticipate what is to come. We absolutely need this clear division of past, present and future to get though daily life in the work-a-day world of physical reality. But science has revealed that this concept of time is not the only one. An astronaut who travels near the speed of light will return to find that the planet he left behind five of his years ago has changed five thousand Earth years. Synchronicity is part of this so-called "Theory of Relativity." When we have a meaningful coincidence, time seems to have stopped or been suspended, because we temporarily move out of our usual field of time, into the field of eternity; that is why synchronicities feel so strange. It is the so-called "wisdom body," our natural, supra-rational spiritual instincts, which are reacting to the presence of the divine.

If time can speed up or slow down, it can also organize itself occasionally into meaningful coincidences. Although it has not yet sunk into the general awareness of humankind, for almost one hundred years physicists have known that all things --- even the densest matter --- are only different arrangements of energy. In other words, there is nothing essentially different between my fingers and the keys they are pushing to write these words. Both myself and the computer keyboard I am using are differentiated only through their separate composition of molecules. If this is true (and it is), then such a realization tends to merge science with spirituality, and admits more than the possibility of unconventional events like telepathy, psychokinesis, time travel, and synchronicity. This concept of time as distinguished only through our circumscribed notions of past, present and future was prefigured and intuited by Edgar Cayce, as long ago as the early 20th Century. "All time is one time, see?" he asked. "That is a fact." [5]

Jung considered meaningful coincidence a mystical key to the workings of the cosmos and our interrelationship with it, both as species and individual. He believed it defined "the unitary aspect of being, which can very well be described as the *Unus Mundus*, or One World," in which all things seen and unseen are fundamentally connected.[6] His contemporary, Albert Einstein, thoroughly disagreed, concluding that synchronicity had "no significance," because the same event that appears to be a meaningful coincidence to one observer will not seem equally extraordinary to another from a different perspective. [7]

But Einstein did not grasp the obvious core-significance of synchronicity, the effectiveness of which depends on the vantage point of a particular viewer or experiencer at a specific time and place coordinated with a particular event --- unlike a comet seen more or less simultaneously and the same by everyone. As Arnold Mindell writes in his book, *Quantum Mind,* synchronicity "does not exist in an absolute sense. Coincidence thus implies that two events correspond to one another as far as their meaning is concerned for the individual who is experiencing both events. I prefer to redefine synchronicity as the non-consensus reality experience of a connection between two or more events, at least one of which occurs in consensus reality." [8]

Synchronicity occurs in a broad variety of media. Such disparate elements as license plates, the weather, names, art --- anything and everything can connect a human observer to meaningful coincidence. They all serve as vehicles for the Compassionate Intelligence that makes its guidance known to individuals through any number of perceptible things. By whatever means this information appears to us during a synchronous event, it opens profound pathways toward deeper understanding of our personal destinies.

Chapter 2

The Synchronicity of Numbers

"There are occasions and causes, why and wherefore, in all things."
—William Shakespeare, *Henry V*

Numbers are not lifeless concepts contrived for computation purposes alone. They were not invented by humans, but discovered by them in nature. As John Anthony West, a leading authority on ancient Egyptian mysticism, points out, "numbers are not mere inventions of man allowing him to make purely quantitative distinctions, but rather the symbolic keys to qualitative laws that govern the coherent universe."[1] Their extra-mathematical implications have been known at least since the time of the Greek philosopher, Pythagoras, more than two thousand five hundred years ago. According to one of his most important followers, the Greek philosopher, Philolaus, "Number is great, perfect, omnipotent, or having virtually unlimited authority or influence, and the guiding principle of divine and human life."[2] Patricia Upczak, a modern authority on synchronicity, writes, "Pythagoras taught that numbers represented spiritual qualities and processes. The meanings of figures are exoteric, or easily understood, and that numbers are esoteric, with hidden meanings. He felt that the numbers one through nine symbolized the underlying structure and orderly progression of life, and the number ten completed the cycle."[3]

In the *Epinomis* (991e, 992a), Plato carried on and expanded the Pythagorean concept of numbers as keys to the Ultimate Mystery, the synchronous interconnectedness as the supreme revelation: "To the man who pursues his studies in the proper way, all geometric constructions, all systems of numbers, all duly constituted melodic progressions, the ordered scheme of all celestial revolutions, should disclose themselves through the revelation of a single bond of natural interconnection."[4] Peter Tompkins, in his exhaustive study of Egyptian mathematics applied to sacred architecture, concluded that "numbers are but names applied to the functions and principles upon which the universe is maintained. The interplay of numbers causes the phenomena of the physical world."[5]

But only traumatic, universally recognized events of numerical significance are potent enough to compel a popular awareness of the relationship between destiny and number. The most recent example was the destruction of New York's Trade Center, in 2001. It took place on the eleventh day of the ninth month, or, as is commonly expressed: 9-11. This is the same sequence of digits used as a general emergency telephone number throughout the United States. Whether or not the attackers deliberately chose these numbers is unimportant. No one escaped the parallel between the date of the event, its disastrous character, and the emergency number. Synchronicity is that significance connecting two or more elements in a shared meaning which somehow comments on them all. And numbers encode all energies that drive the universe. The more familiar we become with them, the better our appreciation of their symbolic meanings, which can forewarn us of imminent dangers, if we regard them in the context of our own situation.

Persons sometimes experience the recurrence of specific numbers in patterns which elucidate particular aspects of their lives. The relationship between human destiny and numbers was recognized as long ago as the 550 B.C.E., when Pythagoras observed, "all is number."[6] This dictum means that all existing things can be ultimately reduced to number relationships. He regarded numbers as the expression of those relationships and the universal spiritual force connecting every one of them in a network of energy laid over the whole breadth of creation. His observation has been born out in the meaning of numbers as they continue to be applied to human destiny and personality, both of which are the same: destiny is personality. "You can observe the power of number not only in the affairs of demons and gods," observed Philolaus, "but in all the thoughts and acts of men."[7] Behind the quantitative description of things, numbers express a mystical dimension in the will to organize that networks throughout all existence.

As an illustrative example, music results from the organization of numbered notes with different vibrations. So too, numbers express cosmic and spiritual harmony. These observations by 6th Century B.C.E. Pythagoreans were verified two thousand five hundred years later by the renowned Russian chemist, Dimitri Mendeleev. When he ranked the known chemical elements according to their atomic weights (or their identifying numbers), distinct patterns emerged. All the known elements fit perfectly into the periodic table. No less amazing, gaps in the table indicated the existence of elements unknown in Mendeleev's time, now known to chemistry.

Numbers have their behavioral and metaphysical equivalents in human society, as well as the natural world. Their recurrence in synchronous events corresponds to important themes coursing through our lives. To understand what numbers imply when they appear to us in purposeful sequences, their associated meanings are listed from one through ten. These are the numbers that most frequently emerge in synchronicity. The majority of other numbers are largely variations on the first ten, usually serving to intensify their original purport. For example, the coincidental recurrence of Six, if repeated as Sixty-Six or Six Hundred Sixty-Six, does not alter its meaning, but simply stresses it with increasing emphasis.

Nor does the synchronistic emergence of a number suggest, in itself, a specific moral judgment. If a particular numeral is encountered in meaningful coincidence, its appearance may either mean that the person experiencing it should continue in the number's implied direction, or is lacking in its specific quality. Synchronicity always indicates that whenever something needful is lacking, the experiencer will always be able to acquire it; the potential for arriving at it exists, but only if the will and energy of the person in question can determine if the desired quality is indeed obtained. The experiencer alone is able to make the correct interpretation, given the context of his or her own situation.

The sacred character of number synchronicity was recognized by ancient Egyptian sages, who "considered the universe a whole, in which every part is related to every other part. To them the universe was, in its entirety, conscious. This consciousness manifested itself in the hierarchy of levels which man observes as diversity. What Man regards as 'matter' is a manifestation of consciousness, and what he regards as 'mind' is consciousness at a higher level. The key to understanding of the laws that govern the universe lay in number. They regarded the universe as number, insofar as number is the expression of function."[8]

Accordingly, the natural progression of numbers from One through Ten suggests a cosmological evolution: One, the original spiritual totality, divides in Two, creating multiplicity, or pairs of opposites struggling for possession of the material world in compensation for the loss of spiritual wholeness (One). They resolve in the divinity of Three, and achieve balance in Four (the harmonization of Two's duality). The offspring from this merging of spirit and matter are male consciousness (Five) and female intuition (Six). They eventually complete their destined cycle (Seven), die (Eight), and are transformed into goddesses (Nine) and Lords of the Earth (Ten). In this Pythagorean scheme is very broadly sketched out the development and destiny of all Nature itself.

Numerical meaningful coincidence is an expression of the observer's contemporary condition. In other words, the occurrence of a particular number in synchronous events is simultaneously generated by and comments on something important in the experiencer's life at the time it appears. I suddenly begin seeing the Number Three in a significant context at the same time I start reading the Bible; Three is associated with godhood. This example is too simplistic, however, because the number arises from and poses an inner challenge that must be properly interpreted in order to be successfully met. So, being synchronistically confronted by Three may signify various implications: I am reading the Bible because I lack and need spiritual energy, or I already have spiritual energy, but am following the right course in reading the Bible, because my higher destiny is part of its study. Additionally, every number has two sides: Seeing Three in meaningful coincidence implies either that I am deficient in godliness at this time, or that I have just embarked, or am considering embarking on a course to increase my godliness. The individual to whom instances of numerical synchronicity occur will know what the number is trying to convey, if he or she compares his/her present state of mind or personal circumstances with that number's timely appearance.

The significance of each numeral is described here, together with its alternative implications. People who encounter them in personally meaningful circumstances should, therefore, be able to understand what the universe is trying to tell them.

One --- Horik Svensson, who studied Tibetan Buddhism under the Dalai Lama, writes that One "is the primal force, the seed from which everything springs, the undifferentiated, single, unitary force."[9] It signifies the field of eternity, timelessness, non-materiality, the condition of the universe prior to the introduction of the relative moral concept of good versus evil; wholeness, unity, perfection, spiritual essence, a fundamentally moral or ethical purpose, being "centered," at peace with oneself. If this number appears in your life, it means you have arrived or are arriving at completeness in something, or are properly striving to achieve it. Conversely, One might indicate a need for totality, integrity, meditation, inner peace or maturity on some important level.

When One calls attention to itself in our daily life, we are either engaged in something that is delivering or magnifying our sense of wholeness, or we lack wholeness in our lives at this moment, or we are in danger of losing that sense of completeness.

Two --- The field of time; duality; materialism; pairs of opposites: truth-lie; success-failure; good-evil; guilty-innocent; health-sickness; right-wrong; pleasure-pain; prosperity-poverty, etc. Struggle, conflict, possible indecision, duplicity, dividing up. Concerns of the physical world. Symbolized by the two-faced Roman god, Janus, who was able to simultaneously look backward into the past and forward into the future; in other words, he stood inside the narrow line of the Present (i.e., the field of time) between two aspects of eternity Pythagoras regarded Two as the "number of strife," according to the Roman writer, Plutarch.[10]

Two warns that struggle is upon us; that we must either take it up or avoid it.

Three ---The Hindu trinity of Brahma, Vishnu and Siva personify, respectively, Sat, or Being; Cit, Consciousness, and Ananda, Love --- the components of godhood which cyclically creates, maintains and destroys the universe. The Celts worshiped their deities in groups of three, and identified them with three heads or faces. Among the Greeks, Fates, Furies and Graces came in threes. There were more than one hundred twenty triads in Greek myth and ritual.

Garden statue of Janus.

Close resemblance between the Egyptian trinity of Isis, Osiris and Horus has often been compared to the Christian trinity of the Father, Son and Holy Ghost. Three is associated with god-power through the phallic trident symbolizing the male genitalia, and wielded as the scepter of Poseidon or Neptune. It is not unlike the three-pronged wand held by the Hindu "Master of Creation", Siva, signifying, simultaneously his omniscient Third Eye, which reappears in the triangular pyramid with its Eye of God at the apex. The three-pronged weapon of the Roman *retiarius* (gladiator), with his net of interdependent

27

relationship in which all things are ensnared, made him the sacred impersonator of Uranus, the universal sky-god.

The Egypto-Greek *Hermes trismegistos*, later the divine personification of medieval alchemists, was "Thrice-Greatest Hermes."

The Vision of Hermes trismegistos
by Johfra Bosschart

In Latin, one who was *ter felix* was happiest of all. Three is the supreme number of wholeness or completeness, as found in the three Norns, or Norse

Fates personifying the stages of time: Wyrd, Verdandi and Skuld --- Past, Present and Future --- just as height, breadth and length comprise the dimensions of space, or the stages of matter proceed from the solid and liquid to gaseous states. West defines Three as "the principle of relationship, a reconciling principle, a Third Force. A sculptor and a block of wood will not produce a statue --- he must have an idea; a man and woman are not enough to produce a child --- there must be love, or at least desire."[11]

Nothing results from a single line, and two lines can only cross each other in conflict (Two as the Numeral of Struggle). But three lines joined to form a tree-pointed figure create the first contained space. Hence, the triangle or pyramid with a single all-seeing eye (the Egyptian iaret, "rearing cobra", better remembered as the Greek *uraeus*) near the apex as the symbol of God.

The appearance of Three in one's life suggests either a spiritual path that should be followed, or the need to resuscitate diminished spiritual powers.

Four --- Harmony; balancing the struggling pairs of opposites; equilibrium; signified by the four seasons, the four winds, the four divisions of life (plant, animal, stone and metal), the four virtues (justice, temperance, prudence and fortitude), etc.; Earth, or the field of physical action, symbolized in the four cardinal directions by the square, cube or cross. When these images or the Number Four emerge as elements in meaningful coincidence, they imply that balance is being achieved, or needs to be restored. The Pythagoreans regarded Four as their most revered number, because it represented the line, straight and true, over which they swore their sacred oaths.

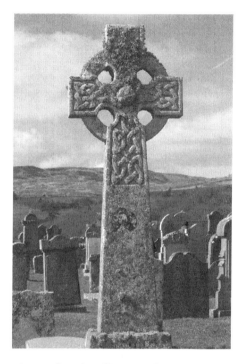

The four points of Ireland's pre-Christian Celtic Cross --- this example in Kilbrannan Chapel Graveyard, Skipness --- signified the Navel of the World, the sacred center of spiritual illumination attained in epiphanic moments, before the figure was appropriated by Dark Age churchmen.

Four means that we are either experiencing harmony in our lives, or we lack harmony.

Five --- Man; mankind; signified by the five senses, five fingers to a hand: manual dexterity; solar, male energy; light and enlightenment; Father Sky; Mars, the god of war; conscious action; acquisition; material achievement; technology; scientific inquiry; civilization; society; conquest; justice; honor; duty; "hard facts"; self-control; discernment; outward-going; sometimes the sacred center symbolized by a circle enclosing a cross or a single point at the center, where the imperceptible is perceived (i.e., manifests).

Male energy, thus characterized, occurs in both men and women. Five indicates its proper incorporation into one's life, or its degeneration into greed, theft, materialism at the expense of nature, aggression and tyranny. During his profoundly altered states of consciousness, Edgar Cayce stated that Five "represents man in his physical form, and the attributes to which he may become conscious from the elemental or spiritual to the physical consciousness, as the senses, as the sensing of the various forces that bring to man the activities in the sphere in which he finds himself."[12]

Five urges us to either use our male energies to materialize some concrete result, or to withdraw them before they do damage, according to our present situation.

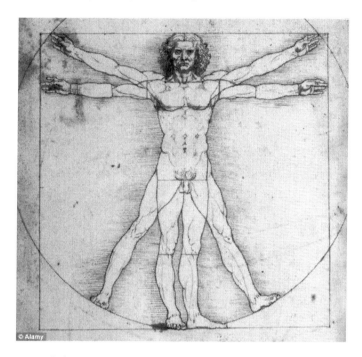

Leonardo's *Vitruvian Man* based on the work of the ancient Roman architect, Marcus Vitruvius Pollio.

Six --- Woman; lunar, female energy; intuition; Mother Earth; nature; nurturing; inward-going; artistry; emotion; fecundity; acceptance; tolerance; liberty (always represented by a woman); instinct; premonition; darkness and mystery; creativity; Venus, goddess of peace; fairness; acceptance, forgiveness; symbolized by the *hexalpha*, two triangles (of fire and water) intersecting, used originally by the Sumerians in Mesopotamia's Fertile Crescent between the Tigris and Euphrates Rivers, where wooden or straw six-pointed stars were planted among their crops to promote fertility.

These originally positive qualities may decay into foolishness, self-centeredness, pettiness, gossip, ignorant obstinacy, stubborn unreasonableness, dullness, self-indulgence, luxury, emotional instability, effeminacy, tolerance of the intolerable, injustice through unwarranted forgiveness, fashion-domination, or just domination, triviality, shallowness.

The renowned Romanian mythologist, Mircea Eliade, writes that Six "is the number of mother-love ... It is an even number, which means it is female and passive ... the number of marriage from the female point of view ... Six is essentially the number of the wife and mother."[13] These metaphysical implications appear in the *hexagram*, a six-pointed star formed by two intersecting triangles. It exemplifies the *hieros gamos*, the "sacred marriage" between Father Sky and Mother Earth --- the holy union of fertilizing force from above with innate potentiality below operating in the well-known principle of "as Above, so Below". The *hexagram* combines the spiritual with the material, or, as A.E. Abbot has it in his *Encyclopedia of Numbers*, "the external and the transitory."[14]

The sixth Tarot trump is known as "The Lovers". Eliade cites an anonymous numerologist, who observed that marriage license bureaus in the United States are forced to either work over-time or multiply their staffs to accommodate increased numbers of applicants during six-year periods.

The feminine aspect of Six was demonstrated by Mrs. James Maxwell of Torrance, California, when she gave birth to a baby girl on the sixth day of the sixth month in 1966 at 6:06 a.m. The infant weighted six pounds, six ounces.[15]

Six informs us that we must either use our female energies for nurturing, possibly healing, or recognize their present inappropriateness.

Seven --- The Completion of Cycles: the seven chakras, the seven days of the week, the seven colors of the rainbow, the musical scale of seven notes; the Seven Sages who escaped to Egypt after the Great Flood that brought the cycle of a former world to a close; the seven years Parsifal passed after his first, unsuccessful attempt to win the Holy Grail, and the next seven years he served as the Grail King; the so-called "Seventh Heaven" synonymous for perfect bliss, because it is supposed to be the highest level of the Afterlife, probably from Sanskrit lore, which mentioned seven levels of existence; the Seven Ages of Man enumerated by Pythagoras and restated so poignantly in Shakespeare's *Twelfth Night*.

In Tibetan Buddhism, forty-nine days separate a man's birth from his re-conception: $49 = 7 \times 7$, here signifying a double passage through the seven chakras, from the root, or base physicality, up to the crown of spirituality, then back down to the root chakra, associated with human re-birth into the material world. As West observes, "The folklore of innumerable peoples and the traditions of all the great civilizations are rife with seven: the seven Pleiades, the seven-headed dragons, the seven-branched candelabra, the seven strings of Orpheus' lyre, the seven Sirens of the seven spheres."[16]

The esoteric tradition of pre-Christian Hawaiians was the *huna*, "that which is hidden", based on seven fundamental principles --- *Pono* (truth), *Mana* (spiritual power), *Aloha* (love), *Manawa* (time), *Makia* (energy), *Kala* (limitlessness) , and *Ike* (reality).

The completion of cycles associated with Seven appears rooted in the cyclical patterns of Nature itself. Sailors have long known that, in high seas, the seventh wave in a regular sequence of breakers is the highest, leaving a deeper, wider trough before repeating another set of waves. Seven is traditionally linked to the moon (7 X 4 = 28 days of the month); i.e., lunar, female energy: "Lady Luck"; the cyclical meaning of Seven may go back to the Paleolithic, or "Old Stone Age", when human beings first observed that the moon's four phases lasted seven days each.

Living examples exemplifying Seven as the Completion of Cycles abound. For example, Alfred Marlow was a seven months baby born on 10 August 1897. When he was seventeen years old, he married on 17 October 1914 to a seventeen-year-old woman, whose birthday on 27 August 1897 made her seventeen days older than her husband. Their baby girl was born in her seventh month of pregnancy in July, the seventh month of the year. The infant lived only seven days. When Alfred had been married seven years, his wife died on 7 January 1924. He remarried on 27 July 1937, fathering seven children and had seventeen grandchildren. Alfred Marlow died on 7 August 1967. He was buried on his seventieth birthday.[17]

Clarence Seaton of Vestaburg, Michigan, was born the seventh of eleven children, seven of them boys. "When I grew up," he explained, "I met and married a girl who was the seventh in a family of seven children, and she's seven months younger than I am, and we were married in the seventh month of the year." Clarence Seaton fathered seven children, and had seven grandchildren and seven great-grandchildren.[18]

In an intriguing commonality, the human body, our DNA, and cells are seventy percent water, the same percentage of water on Earth, implying a relationship between mankind and the planet more fundamental than we may suspect.

According to Frederic Lionel, a British investigator of esoteric traditions, "The number seven symbolizes the movement of life in space and time. The seven days of the week, the seven colors of the spectrum and the seven notes of the scale remind us that birth and death bear witness to eternal life in an eternal becoming."[19]

Seven announces that a cycle is coming to an end, or should, in any case, be terminated.

Eight --- Death; the dissolution of forms; eliminating something that has completed its cycle (the previous Seven) to give place for something new: the eight hours of sleep necessary to function properly in a new day; the eight legs of the spider, which constantly kills, but out of its own body produces the beautiful engineering marvel of its web (i.e., life from death).

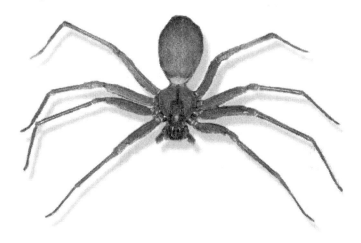

A Brown Recluse Spider

At sea, the traditional signal to "abandon ship" is produced by seven short blasts of ship's whistle, followed by a long, eighth blast --- the Death number preceded by the Completion of Cycles.

The king of Minoan Civilization in Ancient Crete was ritually killed at the beginning of the eighth year of his reign, as signaled by the cycle of the Planet Venus. In the Norse Day of the Wolf, the end of time, eight hundred warriors will destroy the universe. In both ancient Egyptian and Aztec belief systems, the human soul passed through death to the Afterlife in eight stages.

The renowned Irish poet, W.B. Yeats, developed an allegorical lunar calendar equating the eighth night of the moon with the death of childhood as a precondition for the birth of adolescence.

Eight's appearance in meaningful coincidence does not necessarily signify physical death, but more often implies a needful passing for something new to be given its chance. For example, Upczak tells of a woman who just moved into an address at 8th Street and Little Orphan Alley, when her father suddenly took sick and died after the daughter nursed him during his last days. His death left her a "little orphan" living on 8th Street.

Encounters with Eight signify that something or someone is going to die or should die.

Nine --- The Goddess. Three (godhood) + Six (woman) = Nine, or female energy raised to high spiritual levels: the nine months of pregnancy, which the Romans referred to as the sacred *nundunum* ("Nine Days"), similarly known by the Celts as the *noinden* ("the Nine Nights"). The same name belongs to a Hindu festival, the *Nava-ratri*, for the confession of sins to the goddess, Kali. It begins on the tenth day of the lunar month, *Ashvayuga*, when the moon approaches fullness. An image of the moon-goddess is worshiped for nine days, then thrown into a river, lake or the ocean. Her nine precious stones --- diamond, pearl, ruby, sapphire, coral, emerald, lapis lazuli, topaz and cow's eye --- were known as the *Navaratna.* Odin, to achieve Earth Mother wisdom, hung himself for nine days on the Yggdrasil Tree of Life, and Jesus hung on the cross for nine hours. Nine witches from Caer Lloyw --- Glouchester in the medieval epic, *Peredur* --- educated the hero in his quest for the Holy Grail. Heimdall, the divine guardian of the *bifrost* rainbow-bridge that led to Asgaard, the abode of the Norse gods, was nurtured in the sea by nine giantesses. The Norse heaven itself was divided into nine levels.

The *Ennead*, or "Company of the Gods", comprised the nine primary deities of ancient Egypt: Atum (the creator), Shu (the divine inventor of astronomy/astrology), Tefnut (goddess of destruction), Geb (Earth-god), Nut (sky-goddess), Isis (cosmic order), Set (god of evil), Nebthet (death-goddess), Thaut (god of wisdom), and Horus (the sun-god). The nine muses in Greek myth encompassed all the arts --- Calliope (poetry), Clio (history), Melpomene (tragedy), Euterpe (music), Erato (inspiration), Terpsichore (dance), Urania (astronomy), Thalia (comedy), and Polyhymnia (eloquence). The Etruscans worshiped nine primary female deities.

In the Catholic heaven, there are nine choirs of angles (Seraphim, Cherubim, Thrones, Dominations, Powers, Virtues, Principalities, Archangels and Angels), and the nine angels (Metatron, Ophaniel, Zaphkiel, Zadkiel, Camael, Raphael, Haniel, Michael, and Gabriel) rule heaven itself. The types of persons defined as "blessed" in the Sermon on the Mount (Matthew, Chapter 5) fall into nine categories. In Western theurgic tradition, the magic circle is nine feet across, just as cats are said to possess nine lives --- a carry-over from Ancient Egyptian times, when the animal personified Bast, the immortal goddess of pleasure.

Nine is always the result if it is multiplied by itself or any other single numeral, and the two numerals produced are added together. For example, 9 x 9 = 81 (8 + 1 = 9); 7 x 9 = 63 (6 + 3 = 9); 3 x 9 = 27 (2 + 7 = 9), etc. The result of any sequential number subtracted by its reverse invariably results in nine: 54 - 45 = 9; 65 - 56 = 9; 82 - 28 = 9; etc. These uniquely peculiar qualities underscore Nine's female creativity, which perpetually reproduces itself through innumerable "couplings". It is, therefore, the number of reproduction, renewal and rebirth.

Seeing Nine in synchronous circumstances heralds a return or urges one.

Ten --- Kingship; male energy elevated to power over the material world; a ruling family or dynasty; Plato's ten kings of Atlantis; the ten patriarchs instituted by the Hindu god, Manu; the original ten patriarchs in the biblical Genesis; the Babylonians' ten world-rulers before the Flood, etc.; the Earth's return to unity and good order; leadership; wise counsel; worldly perfection; conquest; dominion; civilization; political organization. As such, Ten likewise embodies humanity, as the dominant or kingly species of the planet, dominated by humankind.

When Ten manifests itself in meaningful coincidence, we are told that kingly energies are at stake for high purposes of either use or abuse.

Eleven --- This is really a more hazardous number than the better-known misfortunes commonly associated with Thirteen. Eleven signifies excessiveness, incontinence, lack of self-restraint, violence, destructive transition, danger, instability. These traits are generated by the removal of One from the cosmic order, as personified in Twelve, and the imbalance created when One is added to the equipollent relationship of the patriarchal Ten. Hence, Eleven is often associated with political instability and violence --- the upset of social order, as so graphically illustrated by contemporary events.

No better example of Eleven's negative aspects is more clearly dramatized than in a series of numerical synchronicities integral to the destruction of New York City's World Trade Center. The terror attack took place on September 11th --- (the 9th month) 9 + 1 + 1= 11. That date is also expressed 9/11/01 --- the same sequence of telephone numbers used to report serious emergencies. September 11th is the 254th day of the year: 2 + 5 + 4 = 11. After September 11th, 111 days were left to the end of the year. The Twin Towers, standing side by side, resembled the Number Eleven. The first jetliner to collide with the them was Flight 11. On board Flight 11 were 92 passengers --- 9 + 2 = 11. The other suicide aircraft, Flight 77, carried 65 passengers: 6 + 5 = 11. "Afghanistan," "The Pentagon," "George W. Bush," and "New York City" each comprise eleven letters. The name of Ramzi Yousef, the man convicted of orchestrating the first attack on the World Trade Center in 1993, is composed of eleven letters. The combined windows in the Twin Towers number 21,800, or 2+1+8=11. New York was the 11th state admitted to the Union.

When President Bush visited the ruins of the World Trade Center, he was photographed beside a fireman wearing a helmet emblazoned with the number, 164; 1+6+4=11.

At 1:11 on the morning of September 11, 2001, Geminorum-13, one of forty-eight stars in the constellation of Gemini, appeared inside the crescent moon. Gemini signifies the Twins, while the crescent moon is the emblem of Islam.

Among the sacred numerals of the Hebrew Quaballah, a mystical interpretation of the Old Testament, 911 stands for Eshim, or "flames"; Bar Shachath, "arsonists", "the Pit of Destruction," "the Fifth Hell," "the Sphere of Mars," Pachad, "fear," and Din, 'justice".

Just before their destruction, New York's Twin Towers exemplified the numeral 11.

Mohammed's birthday is celebrated throughout the Islamic World on the eleventh day of the ninth month.

Thirty years before the suicide attacks on the towers, numerologist Mary Valla wrote prophetically that persons associated with Eleven "can destroy anything that it touches, including self. You will conquer others, but in so doing, destroy yourself."20 Historical associations with the eleventh numeral abound. Another case in point was the conclusion of World War One on Armistice Day. Its occurrence at the eleventh hour on the eleventh day of the eleventh month ushered in an epoch of social chaos not witnessed in Europe since the Hundred Years War.

On 1 February 2003, the space shuttle, *Columbia*, blew up at 8:11 a.m. The timing was perfect, since these numbers --- Eight for Death and Eleven for Chaos --- combine to signify violent extinction. Nor was that the only synchronicity involved in the crash. Its remains were largely spread across Texas, George Bush's home state, a disastrous omen for the President, then on the verge of ordering American invasion forces against Iraq. It would seem the outer space disaster foreshadowed a worse calamity on Earth. On board was NASA's first Israeli passenger, ironically enough, because Columbia's debris field began at the Texas town of Palestine, the same name as that land forcibly occupied by Israel, and the flashpoint of strife in the Near East.

But the 11th Numeral does not only characterize major calamities. Synchronicity investigator Robert H. Hopcke tells of a couple whose troubled relationship was permeated by the number. As soon as they began dating, their attention was continuously called to the repetition of eleven in numerous forms. "I always look at the clock at 11:11," she said.[21] Only later did her boyfriend recall that he lent her his favorite sport shirt emblazoned with the number eleven. He remembers arriving home one evening after a date, and glancing at his VCR which was recording a program. It displayed 11:11 P.M. on Channel 11, and the recording time was 11:11:11. Their affair broke up on the eleventh day of the eleventh month (November). Before separating, they had been together for eleven months. After their relationship ended, the woman claimed that all synchronous appearances of number eleven stopped.

Upczak writes how "Eleven is the number of a cycle of new beginnings. In numerology, eleven is known to have the power to change environments, to create new conditions ... It represents the hidden Knower", and refers to "a new dawn of awareness."[22] Perhaps this is what the notorious 20th Century British occultist, Aleister Crowley, meant when he identified Eleven as the number of magical changes, sometimes through great violence.

The troubling nature of Eleven was introduced in the West after the Greek geometrician, Pythagoras, studied the mystical significance of numbers at the ancient Egyptian mystery school of Heliopolis, "City of the Sun." Could the early astronomers there have known about our star's eleven-year sun-spot cycle, the basis for Eleven's association with chaos? Sun-spots are cooler regions on the surface which seriously disrupt electronic communications and, some investigators believe, interfere with normal human thought processes. During the early 14th Century A.D., the inexplicable disappearance of sun-spots was coincidental with and, according to climatologists, somehow responsible for a relatively brief worldwide drought referred to as the Little Ice Age. They also suspect that the eleven-year sun-spot cycle was linked to the advance and retreat of glaciation over the last half-million years. The catastrophic scope of this number is cosmic.

Our Sun also changes its magnetic polarity every eleven years, interfacing with Earth's own magnetic field to cause worldwide break-downs in all forms of electronic communication. But disruption is not confined to radio and television. From the mid-20th Century, parapsychologists have traced a correlation between the solar flips and upsurges of emotional disturbances in human behavior. Other mammals, even fish, appear to be effected. Researchers speculate that the bio-electric field of many creatures is directly influenced by the Sun's eleven-year cycle. If so, modern science and ancient mysticism begin to complement each other.

In Pythagorean numerology, Eleven signified chaos because it was a cardinal number separating humanity or civilization, associated with Ten, from the cosmic order embodied in Twelve. The 12th Century scholar, Hugh of Saint Victor, categorized Eleven as "transgressive out of measure ... It goes dangerously beyond normal limits".[23] Mircea Eliade believed "the number is also more dangerous in a physical sense, because it means martyrdom, the death in the world that brings entry to the higher life of the next" --- an interpretation the Islamic fundamentalists who crashed their sky-jacked airliners into the Pentagon and World Trade Towers would have doubtless found appropriate.[24]

On a less cataclysmic scale, Eleven merely means opposition, an enemy's attempt at causing frustration, the appearance of serious obstacles. In any case, its occurrence bodes the onset of dangerous energies. However, these, too, are sometimes needful and even in the long run, of the utmost necessity. Although in every case, Eleven should be regarded as a warning, its proper interpretation must be gauged within the context of one's own particular circumstances at the time of its appearance.

Twelve --- The Cosmic Order: the Twelve Houses of the Zodiac, the twelve hours of the day, the Twelve Months of the Solar Year, the twelve Olympian gods, the twelve Norse gods (the Aesir), the Etruscans' League of Twelve Sacred Cities, the Twelve Apostles of Jesus Christ, the human body's twelve pairs of ribs and thoracic vertebrae in the human spine, etc. The first Roman code of law was written on twelve tablets.

In the closing chapters of the Book of Revelation, the celestial city of divine perfection has twelve gates, each guarded by twelve angels and inscribed with the names of the twelve tribes of Israel. Twelve foundation stones bearing the names of the twelve apostles and encrusted with twelve jewels support the walls. They surround the Tree of Life with its twelve kinds of fruit. The city itself is a cube, twelve thousand stadia high, broad and long. When traveling through the wilderness toward the Promised Land with the Ark of the Covenant, the Israelites formed their camp to represent the celestial city.

In Exodus (chapter 28), the "breast-plate of judgment" worn by the Old Testament high priest was set with twelve stones: carnelian, topaz, carbuncle, emerald, sapphire, diamond, jacinth, agate, amethyst, beryl, onyx, and jasper.

Twelve is the number of the structure of the universe. As such, its manifestation in meaningful coincidence implies that the experiencer is either in harmony with the cosmic order, or is in need to embrace that order.

Thirteen --- The World Out of Order; the most infamous number, associated with deception, destruction, loss, untimely death, murder, suicide and misfortune; often symbolized as a human skeleton armed with a scythe (the crescent moon), mowing down images of prosperity (i.e., a kingly crown, etc.). On the thirteenth night after its first crescent, the moon becomes full, a moment when irrational, even criminal behavior increases among human beings. It is from the full moon that the term, "lunacy," derives; hence, Thirteen's lunar association with misfortune. More fundamentally, Thirteen exceeds the proper limits of natural law by going beyond the celestial cycles and defying the cosmic order expressed in Twelve, causing the orderly rhythm to become lop-sided and self-destructive.

The belief that ill luck befell thirteen persons who sat down together at the same table did not originate with Jesus and his twelve apostles at the Last Supper. The Romans considered it a bad omen if thirteen people were in a room together, as did the earlier Hindus. In Norse mythology, the gods' favorite deity of resurrection, Baldur, was killed when their dinner party of twelve immortals was joined by the mischief-maker, Loki. He committed murder on Freya's Day (from which the modern "Friday" derives), equated during the Viking Age with the Number Thirteen. The Baldur-like Jesus was likewise supposedly crucified on a Friday, amplifying perhaps Thirteen's bad reputation in Christian tradition.

The Greeks similarly represented the number unfavorably in their myth of the twelve Olympians who threw a party, but refused to invite Eris, the goddess of discord. She gate-crashed the affair by rolling into their midst a golden apple inscribed, "For the Fairest". In squabbling over this prize, the Olympians started the Trojan War.

The Mayas of pre-Columbian America also held Thirteen as unlucky, associating it with winter and the death of their crops. Their cultural descendants, the Aztecs, included thirteen, known as Tlalpilli, in their ritual calendar. It was associated with Tezcatlipocha, or "Smoking Mirror," wicked counterpart of Quetzalcoatl, the virtuous "Feathered Serpent." Their relationship as twin brothers signified the eternal conflict between good and evil as personified in Thirteen.

The Hebrews alone of all peoples in the world regarded the numeral as fortunate. To them it signified Ziv, i.e., prosperity, glory, splendor. The prominent scholar of Hebrew mysticism, Isidore Kozminsky, quotes the old Quaballah masters as having said, "he who understands the number Thirteen has the keys of power and dominion."[25] They meant that advantage could be taken of heathens in their dread of Thirteen. During times of prevailing anti-Semitism, anything perceived as "unlucky" by the superstitious Gentiles was conversely fortunate for the Jews.

14th Century mask of Tezcatlipocha made with obsidian, jade and human teeth.

The image of a skeleton mowing a field of human heads with a scythe represents Death as the Tarot trump numbered thirteen. The number's lethal connotation likewise appears in necromancy, bringing the deceased back to life, which is identified with Number Thirteen. Greco-Egyptian magical texts of the first centuries A.D., describing procedures for re-animating a corpse, call in part for thirteen needles to be driven into a doll left on a grave.

The thirteen pastries found in today's "baker's dozen" is a corruption of Boucca's dozen, from a pre-Christian agricultural spirit, subsequently demonized as the "Devil's dozen" by Church zealots in the Dark Ages, when Thirteen became the traditional number of a coven of witches.

Of the hundreds of characters in Shakespeare's plays, thirteen commit suicide.

The negative power of this number to influence human behavior continues into modern times. Many hotels and even office buildings around the world do not list a thirteenth floor, and local jurisdictions do not designate the number for a street-address. In 1965, when Britain's Queen Elizabeth visited Germany, railway officials at the Duisburg station from which her train was scheduled to depart, changed the platform number from its original "13" to "12". Some persons have a pathological fear of Thirteen, diagnosed as triskaidekaphobia. Synchronicities involving thirteen are perhaps the most common of all. Gioacchino Rossini, the famous Italian operatic composer, dreaded Fridays and the Number Thirteen, not without reason: He died on Friday, 13 November 1868.

All his life, the composer, Arnold Schoenberg, was afraid he would die in his seventy-sixth year, because, added together, the digits total thirteen. He dreaded the arrival of the thirteenth of each month following his seventy sixth birthday, but survived one after the other until July 1951. That thirteenth fell on a Friday, increasing his perceived chances of passing away, so he stayed in bed all day, even though there was nothing wrong with him. Yet, at precisely thirteen minutes before midnight, he breathed his last word, "Harmony," --- ironically enough, because Schoenberg had done so much in life to undermine harmony with his "atonal" modernism.

A similar premonition occurred to another famous artist of the 19th Century, the British painter, Sir John Everett Millais. He told his friend, the renowned poet, Robert Browning, that an enigmatic series of "phantom numbers" --- 13, 1, 8, 9, 6 --- flickered across the surfaces of his unfinished canvasses. They seemed utterly inexplicable, until Millais died on August 13, 1896.[26]

In Minot, North Dakota, a three-car accident occurred at 1313 13th Street, on Friday the 13th, February 1976. At the same time, on the other side of the world, in the Philippines, several dozen patrons were injured as they fled a Manila theater during a strong earthquake. The movie they had been watching was the Hollywood film, Earthquake.[27]

In 1975, on February 13th, an elevator carrying thirteen passengers got stuck at the thirteenth floor of the Exxon Building, in New York City.[28]

Melanie Bracci described her boyfriend's encounter with a series of thirteens. "For weeks, Todd had been telling me that the bad luck number had been tormenting him. Whenever he made a purchase, either the bill had the number '13' on it, or the change did. When he took measurements for his carpentry work, more often than not they would involve thirteen inches, thirteen feet or thirteen yards.

"I'm not a superstitious person," he insisted, "but the number thirteen keeps cropping up. And let's face it, my luck has been pretty bad." That was certainly true. Neither of us realized it in the beginning, but Todd's bad luck spell began with the number thirteen. On 13 November 1982, he had a misunderstanding with his boss and was fired from a job he'd held for four years. When the local job market promised no hope, he decided to look for employment in California. After a hopeless search in San Francisco, we booked a flight back to New Hampshire on 13 December. On our way to the San Francisco airport, we had to stop to return our rented car.

"We were running late and an argument with the man at the leasing company over a $13.25 gasoline bill resulted in our arriving at the airport only minutes before our plane was scheduled to depart. We checked our luggage through and made it to the gate in time to see the plane (with our suitcases on board) taxiing toward the runway. When we went to the desk to change our flight, our tickets were gone --- and that's when we learned how serious lost tickets can be.

"We were told that we would have to purchase new tickets and wait as long as ninety days for reimbursement. So, there we were --- stuck in San Francisco with less than $20.00 and not a single change of clothes. Luckily, we had friends in San Francisco with whom we could stay. We were stranded for five days until my parents wired us money for air fare. There must have been some sort of misunderstanding, however, because, when the money arrived, it was $13.00 less than we needed. We borrowed that amount from our friends and finally flew home --- where the number thirteen popped up more than ever. On the night of January 26, 1983, we returned from visiting relatives, and as Todd reached to open the door to our house, I asked the time. It was 10:13; we both began to laugh. Our good humor did not last long, however. As we stepped inside, we immediately realized that our house had been burglarized. Only Todd's possessions had been taken. Because we had no telephone, Todd went out to a store to call the police." While he was waiting to use the pay phone, he looked inside the store window: the number 13 appeared in oversized letters on a white sheet of paper.[29]

Police and military forces, which routinely deal with numbers and dramatic life experiences, often encounter difficulties with the jinxed number. Badge Number 13 was retired from the Muskegon, Michigan police department and Officer Donald Bedwell was assigned a new number. While wearing Number 13, he had been beaten by a gang of teenagers, injured in an auto accident, and suffered a sprained ankle falling on the ice. Police chief Bob Adams of Hutchinson, Kansas, ordered a new number for police car number 13. In one year, it was involved in three accidents. [30]

In an example of applied reverse bad luck, on Friday the Thirteenth, June 1969, the United States Navy commissioned its latest nuclear attack submarine, the *Bergsall*, after a World War Two submarine of that same name. Over a two-year period, the first U.S.S. *Bergsall* sank thirteen enemy vessels, torpedoing a battleship on February 13, 1945. At any rate, the Second World War the *Bergsall*'s run of Thirteen certainly meant bad luck for the Japanese Navy.[31]

Although Thirteen is usually unfortunate, it may sometimes play a neutral, if no less intriguing role in synchronicity, as Eric Tiedt's experience demonstrates: "On a Sunday in 1978, my brother, Curtis, gave me thirteen boxwoods to plant in my front yard. The next day, I left my home in Tallahassee, Florida on Wednesday, 13 September. While driving north on I-95, in North Carolina, I noticed a sign that indicated the next turn-off would lead me to the best route to New Jersey, New York and New England. I took it, and I found I was on Route 13. In Virginia, I bought gas. It cost $13.00 to fill the tank. In Delaware, I stopped at a motel, and the room rate was $13.00. The next morning, a tire was flat on my truck. It was repaired by the Highway 13 Garage at a cost of $13.00. On arriving in New Jersey, I checked into a motel and decided to spend the evening in New York City. I took Exist Number 13, and went through a toll booth numbered 13 to get to the city. No one can convince me that such a run of thirteens is mere coincidence."[32]

Experiencing Thirteen means less that one is doomed to bad luck, than that misfortune may be avoided if he or she recognizes the causes --- more likely internal than external --- for adverse chance.

Fourteen --- Another difficult numeral, it signifies the wide-spread fracture of established forms at the hands of a great power or potent evil. In Egyptian mythology, Ausar (known to the Greeks as Osiris) was killed by his wicked brother, Set, who then dismembered the corpse into fourteen pieces. Like Osiris, the moon appears to progressively dissolve into its fourteenth phase. His murder foreshadowed major world break-ups like World War One, which began in 1914, and shattered the long-established old kingdoms of Europe into numerous national states.

Fourteen is the number of phalanges in the human hand and foot; also, the number of bones in the human skull. This anatomical comparison implies separateness, but, in the broader scheme of the human body's organization and cooperation of parts, its apparent disunity is, in the cosmic sense, a necessary function of the universe.

The emergence of fourteen in synchronous events warns of impending dissolution, or suggests that such thorough fragmentation or separateness is fundamentally required in order for the greater scheme of things to function properly --- even though this bigger picture is usually so immense, we lack the objectivity to see, much less comprehend it.

Fifteen --- An erotic number associated during the European Middle Ages with Germany's pre-Christian *Walpurgis Nacht*, or the English "Witches' Sabbath". This was an annual fertility celebration (April 30, or May Eve), which was accompanied by orgiastic festivities at the onset of springtime. The following day, phallic May poles were erected and universally celebrated. Beginning in the 6th Century, scandalized Christian officials tried to "de-paganize" the holiday by claiming it for a non-existent saint by the same name; the original Walpurga was the May Queen, divine patroness of sexual freedom as the generative force of life itself.

Walpurgis night bonfires.

In 1945, Adolf Hitler died on Walpurgis, April 30th. Thirty years later, to the day, American forces evacuated Saigon, ending the long conflict in Viet Nam. Both dates define war's end and the flowering of peace, just as the Walpurgis signified the conclusion of winter and the onset of spring. So too, in the Hebrew Quaballah, Fifteen is synonymous with Aviv, or "spring."

The appearance of Fifteen in synchronicity means we must somehow confront an erotic situation or circumstances, possibly threatening, related to the Liebestod, or "love-death" inherent in physical attraction. The male Black Widow spider is driven by a powerful instinct to mate with its female counterpart, but is lucky to escape the encounter without being devoured for all his overwhelming passion. So too, potent instinctual behavior we experience, like all powerful energies, can become easily self-destructive, without the strength and/or skill to master them.

Other numerals are generally less frequently encountered in synchronicity, but when they do emerge, their appearance can be no less significant. For example, his whole life long, Russian Czar Nicholas II regarded Seventeen as unfortunate. He often noted in his diary how that number always seemed to accompany some close tragedy, usually the death of a royal relative, sometimes by assassination. Of course, Nicholas was dethroned in 1917.

Czar Nicholas II in Bolshevik custody. Perhaps his last photograph.

Nearly two thousand years earlier, another statesman, the Roman heir to the imperial throne, Germanicus, brother of Emperor Claudius, had a life-long dread of the Number Seventeen. It was said to have mysteriously appeared in a series of meaningful coincidences immediately prior to his death, as he succumbed to his final illness.

The turning-point in the War for Independence occurred at Saratoga on the 17th day of October 1777, when forces under General John Burgoyne laid down their arms, signifying the fall of British imperialism in North America.

These historic events would not have surprised the ancient Egyptians, who believed Seventeen belonged to a particular kind of bad luck that characterized the downfall of rulers, because Osiris was killed on the seventeenth day of the moon. So too, the Pythagoreans, who first learned of the numerical mystical significance, associated Seventeen with opposition, obstruction, evil and the day the Devil triumphed over God. Seventeen is the value of the Hebrew word for "sin," and represents the natural order of things violently severed from all its spiritual connections.

Seventeen's mortal significance is the result of Four plus Thirteen (or, Established Harmony undone by Misfortune), and Seven plus Ten (the Completion or End of a Dynasty).

Seeing Seventeen in synchronicity warns of some powerful institution, personality, family, or group in danger of collapse.

According to Kozminsky, Nineteen is the "Angel of Unwinding Destinies," a characterization exemplified in the life of Azelea Davis McKinney.[33] She was born on 19 October 1899, and married her husband, Charles, on 19 October 1919. Their second child was born on 19 October 1924, and two of their sons were murdered on 19 February 1960. Their son-in-law died on 19 January 1963. Mr. Charles McKinney passed away on 19 February 1966. Azelea died on 19 October 1966. [34]

The occurrence of Nineteen in meaningful coincidence is related to the patterns of our personal destiny.

The ancient Egyptians believed that the human soul, or *ba*, once released from the physical body by death, was escorted to the Hall of Judgment, where the spirit of the deceased underwent an ordeal known as the Negative Confession. It consisted of standing before one judge after another to deny that the soul, in life, had committed a specific sin: "I have not robbed with violence", "I have murdered neither man nor woman", "I have not uttered falsehood", etc., etc. Before the *ba* could be admitted to heaven, it had to have spoken truthfully before each of the forty-two judges. This figure is double twenty-one, which, according to Kozminsky, is "the number of absolute Truth, and the smallest particle of truth is never gained without a very big sacrifice (death) ... Twenty-one is symbolized as 'The Universe'... In the *Sepher Yetzirah*, the Twenty-First Path is the Path of Conciliation."[35] These qualities are reflected in the Negative Confession's forty two judges.

The appearance of Twenty-One in synchronous circumstances involves matters of powerful truths, discoveries or revelations sometimes of life-and-death importance.

In the Hebrew *Quaballah*, the twenty-third path is synonymous for stability, which seems reflected in the human biorhythms' twenty three-day cycle and the twenty-three seconds needed for blood to make a complete circuit through the adult human body while at rest. The *Sepher Yetzirah* likewise associates Twenty-Three with the Royal Star of Leo, defining the transition from matter to spirit. The ancient Egyptian New Year's Day was 23 July, when *Sopdit*, better known now as *Sirius*, appeared on the horizon just at dawn.

When Twenty-Three calls attention to itself through meaningful coincidence, we are prevailed upon to examine the condition of our own stability, in whatever form it is at present an issue --- psychological, medical, financial, spiritual, etc.

Kozminsky's "Table of Interpretation" associates the number Thirty with marriage, a relationship demonstrated by the mother and father of Alice Gosnell, in Sykesville, Maryland. They met on 30 May 1920, and were married the next year on 30 May. Alice was born the following year on 30 May. Twenty-three years later, Alice married on 30 May 1930; in another twenty-three years, her father died on 30 May.[36]

Thirty's appearance in synchronicity involves questions of matrimony, before and after the fact.

In Kozminsky's "*Quaballah* of Pythagoras," thirty-three is associated with "purity and grace," suggested by the same number of years King David reigned in Jerusalem.[37] He founded it as a holy city and residence for that paramount object of spiritual purity, the Ark of the Covenant. The Old Testament likewise specifies that a mother "must wait thirty-three days to be purified from her bleeding" before she is allowed to "touch anything sacred or go to the sanctuary until her days of purification are over" (Leviticus, Chapter 12).

Dante Alighieri divided his *Divine Comedy* into three sets of thirty-three cantos each, with one additional *canto* for the introduction. The deepest pit of Hell, where souls are "purified," is described in the Inferno's thirty-third *canto*.

A full sequence of human DNA is completed at thirty-three turns, and the human foot comprises thirty-three muscles. DNA is the most basic or "pure" manifestation of organic existence, while the foot is commonly associated with grace.

Long-playing records, noted for their pure sound reproduction, were standardized at thirty-three-and-one-third revolutions per minute.

Questions of purity are found in meaningful coincidences involving the thirty-third numeral.

A number signifying fundamental revolutionary change is Fifty-Seven. It is, in one historical example, intimately characteristic of the American War of Independence, as investigator Arthur Finnessey abundantly demonstrates in his well-researched book, *History Computed*.[38] Among the outstanding examples he sites is the last time the Liberty Bell rang, in tribute to George Washington, before it cracked on 22 February 1846 --- fifty-seven years after his fifty-seventh birthday. Together with his titles and signature, the closing paragraph of the U.S. Constitution, following its original seven articles, makes up fifty-seven words. It was ratified by fifty-seven yes-votes from New Hampshire, and every Constitutional law begins with the Constitution's fifty-seventh word --- that word being, "All."

Washington's only two victories over British Commander Cornwallis were fifty-seven days apart. So too, fifty-seven days separated the other decisive battles of the war, at Cowpens and the Guilford Courthouse. The final anniversary of Lexington and Concord celebrated during the Revolutionary War was precisely fifty-seven months, fifty-seven weeks and fifty-seven days after they were fought. In South Carolina's most famous assault at "Fort Ninety-Six," fifty-seven Americans fell.

The American Revolution's fifty-seventh month concluded on 19 January 1780; the Redcoats took Charleston exactly twice times fifty-seven (one hundred fourteen) days later. Twelve (the cosmic order) times fifty-seven (six hundred eighty-four) days before, the decisive Battle of Monmouth was fought.

In numerical symbolism, fifty-seven is the combination of two numerals, Five and Seven. Five is associated with male energy (i.e., war), while Seven signifies the completion of cycles. Together they form a symbolic concept perfectly reflecting the completion of major military cycles running like inter-linking themes throughout the history of the Revolutionary War. Kozminsky refers to any number from fifty-five to sixty-four as "the Sword," associated with military victory (fifty-one).[39]

These ancient interpretations of fifty-seven make its frequent recurrence throughout the War of Independence extraordinarily appropriate. Yet, we stand in awe of its historical significance: Was it somehow an out-growth or expression of America's violent struggle for freedom, or did it from the beginning (from before the beginning) determine historical events? In any case, it joins with all other numerals as the expression of a compassionate consciousness that makes itself known in human synchronicity.

Whenever Fifty-Seven appears in meaningful coincidence it signifies radical change to be dealt with or implemented.

Previous to a global cataclysm, the world was dominated by seventy-two solar dynasties, according to Persian myth. An Old Kingdom Egyptian Tale of the Shipwrecked Sailor tells of a distant island ruled by seventy-two serpent-kings before it was destroyed by "a fire from heaven" and sank into the ocean. In the better-known Egyptian myth of Osiris, the mortal king who achieved resurrection and eternal life, he was murdered by seventy-two conspirators. The total number of angels in arcane Hebrew tradition (the *Quaballah*) is seventy-two. These and similar traditions suggest that the numeral signifies divine authority, with emphasis on its ancient lineage. Hence, its occurrence in synchronicity suggests a great background, legacy or inheritance somehow associated with equally great struggle or sacrifice.

David Ovason, in his thorough investigation of the arcane symbolism that went into designing the dollar bill, points out that the truncated pyramid depicted in a circle contains seventy-two stones. Interestingly, in many mystical systems around the world, God's name is pronounced and written in seventy-two different ways. The number was particularly significant in ancient Egyptian mortuary practices, because a corpse, after being mummified, could only be buried seventy-two days after the deceased passed away. The number is associated with the Sun's apparent movement across the sky, especially when it seems to fall back against the stars. The rate at which this occurs, one degree in every seventy-two years, is known as precession. Ra, the Egyptians' supreme deity, was a solar god, the divine personification of immortality.

Hence, the recurrence of Seventy-Two in one's life signifies something vocal involving especially potent godly energies, perhaps powerful prayer or religious music. It could also appertain to sacred nomenclature of some kind.

According to Quaballah encyclopaedist, David Godwin, eighty-seven was associated with the "Angel of Picses."[40] It is the last sign in the Zodiac, closely bound up with the symbolism of water, particularly the dissolution of forms, or, as the renowned Spanish mythologist, Juan Cirlot, writes, "the resurgence of cosmic energy". It "denotes the final moment which ... contains within itself the beginning of the new cycle. ... when transposed by analogy to the existential and psychic plane, denotes defeat and failure, exile of seclusion, and also mysticism and the denial of the self and its passions. The dual aspect of this symbol is well expressed by the zodiacal sign itself, composed of two fishes arranged parallel to one another but facing in different directions: the left-hand fish indicates the direction of involution, or the beginning of a new cycle in a world of manifestation, while the fish that faces right points to the direction of evolution, the way out of the cycle."[41]

Cirlot's explanation of Pisces perfectly fits into eighty-seven symbolism: eight (signifying the end of something) plus seven (the completion or recurrence of cycles. This interpretation is in turn underscored by the *Quaballah*, which associates eighty-seven with the moon (*Levanah*), which, unlike the constant sun, continually goes though cycles in which it waxes and wanes, appearing to grow, die and grow again. In short, encountering eighty-seven in your life suggests something is coming or about to come to an end, so that a new cycle may begin; i.e., eight (ending) followed by seven (new beginning).

Eighty-eight is encountered by persons either experiencing a great flow of harmony in their lives, or are either denying or missing it in some way. It is not an extension of the deadly Eight, but related to and a magnification of the harmony embodied in Four, just as there are eighty-eight keys in a grand piano.

For Aleister Crowley, ninety-three was of supreme importance, because it epitomized the kernel of his philosophy, *agapa*. The divine personification of this Nietzschean-like will-to-spiritual power was *Thelama*. Separately, both her name and *agapa* expressed the Numeral 93: The central tenet of Crowley's *Book of the Law*, "What thou wilt will be the law," was codified in ninety-three.[42]

Of the three U.S. airliners sky-jacked on 11 September 2001, only the passengers and crew aboard Flight 93 demonstrated the will to fight the terrorists to the death. After the aircraft was destroyed, the F.B.I. investigator in charge at the crash scene was an Inspector Crowley. Some of the aspects of this drama are echoed in the *Quaballah*, where ninety-three signifies *Magan*, "defense" and *Tzava*, "army."

Totaling the catalog value for used copies of the one-cent and ten-cent United States postage stamps commemorating Columbus' late 15th Century discovery of America (Scott Nos. 230-37) produces a sum of $1,492 .[43] But the significance of higher numerals such as these is less often apparent unless a self-evident break-through occurs, as demonstrated in the obvious connection here between the total catalog value of the American stamps and the year in which Columbus discovered the New World.

Kozminsky observed that the perfectly-timed appearance of meaningful numbers in appropriate coincidence is beyond "that which we are too fond of contemptuously relegating to chance."[44] Such coincidences are most powerfully dramatized in the great disasters of history, and especially by the early 21st Century's most infamous example.

Chapter 3
Tragic Synchronicity

"Man did not weave the web of life. He is merely a strand in it. Whatever he does to the web, he does to himself."
—Chief Seattle, 1848 [1]

Synchronicity is the acausal bond linking two or more apparently unconnected events, which combine to create a meaningful coincidence. They are components of something greater than themselves, pieces belonging to a puzzle that may only become comprehensible when fitted together as separate parts of a broader whole. It is in the nature of this definition that synchronicity appears to transgress time, or, at any rate, the inviolable boundaries dividing past, present and future, as delineated by conventional understanding. The mechanism or engines driving this phenomenon, as described in *Synchronicity and You*, are passion, emotion or involvement. Tragedy is not only the consequence of living in the physical world --- with its inevitable cycles of life, decline and death, plus all their attendant suffering. It is also the intensification of emotion that sometimes triggers meaningful coincidence.

Modern instances of synchronous events that symbolically presaged greater tragedies following soon after were preludes to both the First and Second World Wars. The latter conflict was thematically foreshadowed by three years with the destruction of the *Hindenburg,* as it attempted to dock at Lakehurst, New Jersey, in 1937. As the largest man-made flying machine ever flown, the eight hundred-foot-long dirigible embodied the Third Reich's economic and technological coming of age more than any other, single object. With its huge, swastika-emblazoned tail bursting into flames, the *Hindenburg's* fate was a microcosm of the fiery doom that would soon overwhelm Hitler's Germany.

So too, the earlier global conflict was preceded by another eerily prescient accident. The sinking of R.M.S. *Titanic* two years before the outbreak of World War One has often been regarded by parapsychologists as an archetype that was intuited on a subliminal level of mass-consciousness as a metaphor for the British Empire specifically and Western Civilization generally. In 1912, both were at the zenith of military, economic and cultural might. No one imagined that the fratricidal war about to erupt would initiate the demise of English imperialism and Oswald Spengler's "Decline of the West." All this was prophetically symbolized in the loss of R.M.S *Titanic.* Hardly any other single occurrence during the 20th Century generated such a large collection of meaningful coincidences that implied the macrocosmic catastrophe to come. So many, in fact, they embraced virtually every category of synchronicity.

The disaster was foretold by more than fifty recorded premonitions, making it among the most uniquely documented incidents of its kind. The significance of particular numerals also played its part during the Titanic sinking --- namely, that classic bad-luck number, Thirteen. That this traditionally unfortunate numeral was factually associated with the most infamous of unlucky ocean liners should come as no surprise. Two separate examples serve to illustrate. Originally from Youngstown, Ohio. George Wick had been traveling with his family through Europe for several months and booked homeward voyage on Titanic. While in transit to Cherbourg, where the ship would make final docking before attempting her transatlantic crossing, he stopped at Paris. There he purchased a Grand Prix sweepstakes ticket, deliberately choosing Number 13, just to prove to his friends that he was not superstitious. "Watch and see what it does for me!" he exclaimed.[2] Several days later, Wick went down with the vessel.

A fellow passenger who lightheartedly challenged the deadly number was British journalist, William Thomas Stead. He demonstrated his contempt for superstition by deliberately concluding a story with which he had been amusing friends on 13 April 1912. His narration described the discovery of an ancient Egyptian sarcophagus and the curse of violent death alleged to overtake anyone who verbally translated its inscription. The next day, R.M.S. Titanic met the disaster in which Stead perished.

He appears to have had a fateful, synchronistic relationship with the doomed liner long before her death at sea. As far back as January 1897, a palmist, Robert Machray, who examined Mr. Stead, was so impressed with what he saw he published a photograph of the journalist's hand in the January issue of Pearson's Magazine. Machray commented that the so-called "life-line" clearly indicated death at sixty-three, Stead's precise age when he, in fact, died aboard Titanic. Around the turn of the century, and long before the super-liner was even envisioned, he published a prophetic story in his own periodical, Review of Reviews. Although from the Old World to the New was written as fiction, it told of a huge passenger ship of the White Star line, commanded by a Captain Smith. More than a decade after the story appeared, R.M.S. Titanic sailed under the White Star line, commanded by Captain Smith. Stead described the hazard of icebergs, writing with unconscious foreboding, "The ocean bed beneath the run of the liners is strewn with the whitening bones of thousands who have taken their passages as we have done, but who never saw their destination." He might have been writing of himself in the distant future.

But Stead did not take his own precognitive fiction seriously. In the year prior to boarding the doomed vessel, he was cautioned that "travel would be dangerous in the month of April 1912", and that he would find himself "in the midst of a catastrophe on water," where several thousand persons would perish.[3] A clergyman was so overcome with premonitions for tragedy when Titanic was being built, he informed Stead that the ship would never complete her crossing to New York. None of this phased Stead, who expressed his excited sense of anticipation for the voyage to Shaw Desmond, another writer. For no apparent reason, Desmond was suddenly overcome with a dark certainty that his friend would soon be dead.

***Titanic* casts off on her last voyage.**

Warnings and irrational premonitions of disaster proliferated around *Titanic* prior to her fateful voyage. A White Star insignia crumbled to pieces in the hands of Mrs. Arthur Lewis while she was pinning it to her husband's cap. He was just about to board the *Titanic*, where he was a steward. At the time, she regarded the incident as a "bad omen," although he dismissed her expressed anxiety as foolishness, until the ship foundered a few days later. Fortunately, Mr. Lewis survived.

In another *Titanic*-related warning, Colonel John Weir, a mining engineer with a worldwide reputation, almost canceled his first class ticket because of distressful feelings about the voyage. Staying at London's prestigious Waldorf Astoria, he awoke on the morning of April 10th to find that the water pitcher atop his dresser had unaccountably shattered, soaking his clothes. He seriously expressed his premonitory feelings to the hotel manager, who allayed the Colonel's "superstitions" enough for him to reluctantly board the "unsinkable" ocean liner. While at sea, Weir told his secretary about the significantly burst water pitcher, could not shake his sense of foreboding, and said he must get off *Titanic* at the next opportunity, when it docked in Queenstown, Ireland. Again dissuaded, he remained aboard, only to go down with the ship he intuited was doomed.

As some measure of the magnitude of synchronous phenomena associated with the disaster, no less than eight hundred ninety-nine persons who initially booked passage for *Titanic*'s maiden voyage eventually refused to board her because of warnings they experienced in the form of various omens, premonitions, dreams and precognitive events. An additional four thousand, sixty-six would-be passengers either missed the sailing or canceled their reservations, usually under apparently normal circumstances, but sometimes through unusual coincidences that prevented them from sailing.

Blanche Marshall suffered a hysterical outbreak on 10 April 1912, as she and her family watched *Titanic* steam past the Isle of Wight from the roof of their home overlooking the River Solent. In a virtual panic, she claimed the liner would sink before it reached New York, and railed against her husband, daughters and servants for being blind to her vision of masses of people drowning in the freezing waters of the North Atlantic. While neither Mrs. Marshall nor anyone she knew sailed aboard *Titanic*, she was prevented from boarding another fated vessel just three years later by similar precognition. In 1915, her husband had booked tickets for their return trip to England from America aboard the Lusitania. She thought nothing of it until she saw the May 1st date on the tickets. Convinced the ship would be torpedoed and sunk on that passage, Blanche convinced her husband to change their booking. Interestingly, she felt safe traveling aboard *Lusitania* at any other time. It was only the prospect of a May 1st crossing that alarmed her. True to her strong sense of foreboding, the vessel was torpedoed and sunk with heavy loss of life on the same voyage she refused to take.

While steaming out of harbor at Southampton, *Titanic*'s enormous wake caused another vessel tied up at moorings to snap her lines and uncontrollably swing out, threatening to crash into the new super-liner. Collision was avoided by a mere four feet. Many passengers regarded the incident as a bad omen, particularly because the ship they narrowly missed hitting bore the same name as their final destination: New York. A day later, at sea, *Titanic*'s Chief Warrant Officer Wilde wired his sister back in England, "I still don't like this ship. I have a queer feeling about it."[4] Previous to the fatal collision, Eva Hart's mother stayed awake all night, because she felt certain a terrible accident was about to happen.

The premonitions related by Wilde and Hart were typical of apparently hundreds of such paranormal forebodings experienced by *Titanic*'s crew and passengers. In the rational world, such forewarnings were exceptionally remarkable, because they were obviously more groundless where *Titanic* was concerned, than any other ship afloat. She was, after all, the most seaworthy vessel of her time, a state-of-the art luxury-liner manned by superbly trained, dedicated and skilled professionals. Indeed, Captain Smith was one of the highest paid and widely respected sailors in Britain. Nothing in physical reality implied the slightest hint that *Titanic* would or could encounter trouble of any kind. Everything about her suggested confidence, pleasure and safety. But in spite of all indications to the contrary, many of her victims and survivors saw through the veil of appearances to what lay on the other side of the allegedly "impossible."

As *Titanic* was being readied for her maiden voyage, the May issue of *Popular Magazine* was coming off the presses with a "fictional" story about the Admiral, an envisioned eight hundred-foot-long ocean liner crossing the North Atlantic through calm seas at twenty-two, one-half knots. She strikes an iceberg and sinks, leaving the survivors among her thousand passengers to be rescued by a steamer. Similarities to the real-life tragedy convinced readers that the story had to have been based on *Titanic*'s real-life details. But author Mayn Clew Garnett claimed he received most of the specifics for his novelette in a dream he had while sailing on the *Titanic*'s sister ship, *Olympic*. Although he may have been influenced by physical parallels noticed during his passage aboard the virtually look-a-like vessel, Garnett's selection of forty-three north latitude for the imaginary Admiral's collision with the iceberg was virtually the same position at which *Titanic* met her identical fate.

The *Olympic* went on to further participation in *Titanic*'s fatal synchronicity. The latter's maiden voyage was originally planned for March 20, but needed to be postponed another twenty days for repairs following a minor collision with her sister-ship. The delay made it possible for *Titanic* to keep her date with death in the mid-Atlantic. Had she left England on her scheduled sailing date, she would have missed the same killer iceberg that sank her.

Violette Jessup was a stewardess on board *Titanic* and one of its survivors. Later, she survived another serious accident at sea, when, serving aboard *Olympic*, it collided with R.M.S. *Hawke*. Miss Jessup's next survival experience was aboard the *Titanic*'s other sister-ship, *Britannic*, which sank in the

Mediterranean Sea after striking a mine during World War One.

Literature is not alone among the arts that figured into the *Titanic*'s synchronous events. More in black humor than in any conscious precognition, a crewman and his wife made recordings for each other, the husband singing "Only To See Her Face Again" to her "True Til Death," on 7 April 1912, prior to his service on the world's greatest ocean liner. Three days later, he sailed on the *Titanic*, never to return.

Nor was animal coincidence missing from the fate of R.M.S. *Titanic*. The age-old sailor's belief that rats leave ships long before any apparent danger of sinking was exemplified aboard the ill-omened ocean liner, when two crewmen in a forward boiler room saw panic-stricken rodents scampering aft, away from the starboard bow, for no discernible cause. The deadly iceberg struck that very spot from which the rats fled twenty-four hours earlier. Both men escaped with their lives, because the rats' sudden appearance had made them uneasy enough to station themselves, as often as possible, in the immediate vicinity of the lifeboats. Another incident of animal synchronicity associated with *Titanic* concerns Bess, a thoroughbred horse belonging to Isadore Strauss, the co-founder of Macy's Department Store. The same night he and his wife were killed in the sinking, six-year-old Bess suddenly died of causes the veterinarian was unable to determine.

"Sinking of the *Titanic*", by German artist, Willy Stöwer, 1912.

One day after Titanic sank, May deWitt Hopkins strangely detected the fragrance of roses in her London home. Although word of the disaster had spread to England by that time, names of those on board were not yet published. But with the flowery scent filling her room from no apparent source, Hopkins suddenly felt that someone she knew was trying to make her aware of his or her death. She later learned that a friend, who was, unbeknownst to her, a passenger aboard the ship, had indeed perished when it went down. Interestingly, her own mother, during the late 19th Century, had been similarly alerted to the death of a loved one by a mysterious, flowery odor.

Inanimate objects, like the White Star insignia that fatefully disintegrated in the hands of Mrs. Lewis, comprise a wide-ranging group of synchronous experiences associated with the *Titanic* disaster. The Managing Director of the White Star Line, Joseph Bruce Ismay, survived the sinking, but thereafter resigned his post, because he was publicly, although unfairly, blamed for the tragedy. He spent the next twenty-five years of his life in virtual seclusion, dying on 17 October 1937. That same Sunday afternoon, a framed, oval mirror that hung in Ismay's office during his tenure at the White Star Line suddenly crashed from its hook, scattering broken pieces across the floor. As mentioned in Chapter 11, the Number Seventeen is associated with the downfall and death of prominent authorities.

Two weeks after *Titanic* was lost, a large wooden crate left unclaimed at Pier 61, in New York harbor, was opened by port authorities. They were surprised to see that it contained a meticulously detailed model of the sunken vessel. It had been originally sent to the United States for promotional purposes on behalf of the White Star Line, and was supposed to be returned to the London offices on the ill-starred ship's return voyage. But the thirty-foot-long representation was accurate in more particulars than anyone could explain. Although it presented a full compliment of twenty davits, there were only a dozen miniature lifeboats, just as on board the actual vessel at the moment of tragedy. Moreover, the model's bow was partially ruined, and a long crack appeared from the keel toward the upper deck, mimicking the actual damage sustained by *Titanic* in its collision with the iceberg.

Dreams, like those of the novelist who wrote of the *Titanic* sinking before it happened, figure importantly into meaningful coincidence. For example, while traveling in Europe during the spring of 1912, a New York lawyer, Isaac C. Frauenthal, dreamt of being aboard a large ship that collided with some floating object and began to sink. His was a long, vivid nightmare, in which he clearly recalled the sights and sounds of calamity. Several nights later, the identical psycho-drama repeated itself, and he told his brother and sister-in-law that it must be a warning against their up-coming voyage on R.M.S. *Titanic*. But they laughed at his dream, and convinced him to go through with their return trip to America aboard the magnificent White Star liner. Happily, all three survived the sinking foretold in Isaac's recurring nightmare.

A story that originally appeared in the *Toronto Sun* reported that the Rev. Charles Morgan, minister of Rosedale Methodist Church in Winnipeg, Manitoba, arrived early at his church one Sunday morning to prepare for the evening service. Before going into his study, he posted the choirmaster's choice of hymns, as he had always done. When his other preparations were completed, there was still considerable time until the service, so Morgan took a short nap, during which he experienced a vivid dream. In it he saw only surging darkness, but distinctly heard an old hymn, one he only very rarely used. He had not thought of it in years, but now his dream was filled with the music accompanied by a sound of rushing waters. The minister awakened with the old hymn still ringing in his ears. He glanced at his watch, but found he still had a long time before services would begin, so he dozed off once more.

As before, he dreamed of the same hymn, now sung by a disembodied chorus, and again there was the sound of crashing waters. This time he awoke with a start. The dream had alarmed him, although for no reason he could understand. Groggy but with the melody still fresh in his memory, he looked up the old tune and half-consciously posted it on the hymn board. Later, during the service, it was the first number sung by the congregation, even though "Hear, Father, while we pray to Thee, for those in peril on the sea" seemed out of place thousands of miles inland. During the singing, Rev. Morgan was surprised and embarrassed to find his eyes filling with tears. Only later did he learn that the *Titanic* was sinking at the same moment his congregation was singing the hymn from his dream.[5]

Perhaps the most inexplicable aspects of synchronicity are those more infrequent instances of parallel lives, as in the case of Lucien P. Smith, who narrowly escaped death during a terrible fire aboard *Viking Princess*, in 1966. It was his second major disaster at sea. A survivor of the *Titanic*, he was in his mother's womb when that ship sank, just as Mrs. Astor, aboard the same stricken vessel, was pregnant with her son, John Jacob. Both children were born eight months after the sinking, in which their fathers perished. And their mothers died in the same year, 1940.

The destinies of individual lives and major conflicts are events sometimes so powerful they echo beyond their own time and appear to replay themselves in the future. Such an extraordinary case of parallel history began to unfold when William C. Reeves went aboard the tramp steamer, *Titanian*, as an ordinary seaman, departing Scotland for New York in April 1935 on traditionally its most unfortunate day, the thirteenth. Ten days later, at twenty-three hundred hours, he was ordered into the foc's'le head to stand watch.

Although the sea was calm, the night was moonless and impenetrable. Reeves began to feel increasingly uneasy, not only because of the very poor visibility conditions he now faced as ship's look-out. He thought, too, of the premonitory novel he had been reading in his cabin, Morgan Robertson's *The Wreck of the Titan*, or *Futility*. Like Stead's *From the Old World to the New*, this remarkably prescient novel foretold the *Titanic* disaster in uncanny detail. Published in 1898, fourteen years before the actual disaster, Robertson's "fictional" account described a super-liner sunk during her maiden voyage from England to New York after striking an iceberg. Of Robertson's novel, Tony Allen states in *Prophecies, Four Thousand Years of Prophets, Visionaries and Predictions*, "it remains one of history's most extraordinary examples of accurate prevision."[6]

Reeves was unable to keep his mind from drifting back to that dramatic moment in the book, when *Titan*'s look-out missed seeing the iceberg in time to avoid disaster. Also, he could not help but notice the ironic similarity of his ship's name, *Titanian*, and Robertson's *Titan* with *Titanic*. As his sense of irony deepened into anxiety, he realized that the time was now twenty-three thirty five, just five minutes before the hour *Titanic* struck the iceberg. Reeves knew that penalties were severe for raising a false alarm, the darkness ahead showed no sign of danger, and for some moments he hesitated to act. But at last his feelings of imminent collision overwhelmed him and he ordered the bridge to stop engines, "Iceberg ahead!"

No sooner had the ship's speed dropped off and the vessel rapidly slowed, than she smashed into several large fragments of ice, which twisted her bow and disabled her propeller. Coming to a full stop, *Titanian*'s crew-members were astonished to behold an enormous iceberg looming directly ahead out of the darkness. The floating mountain appeared at 23:40, the same hour of *Titanic*'s collision. Doubtless, had the *Titanian* not stopped in time, she would have followed her predecessor to the bottom. An SOS sent to Cape Race, Newfoundland, brought rescue to the stranded crew.

The multiple synchronicities of this parallel event --- the similar ships' names, Reeves' powerful premonition, his reading of Robertson's book, precisely the same hour for meeting with a deadly iceberg --- far out-strip all considerations on behalf of mere chance. Instead, they clearly define the operative principle of meaningful coincidence as a legitimate phenomenon.

While the *Titanic* disaster drew to itself an extraordinary volume of meaningful coincidence, it was not the only event at sea touched by synchronicity. Another famous, doomed ocean liner, the *Lusitania*, sank three years after *Titanic* went down. On the last night of his final voyage, *Lusitania*'s captain, William Turner, saved himself by making a long, hard swim through cold waters to the Irish coast, off Old Head of Kinsale. Exactly fifty years before, on the first night of his maiden voyage, he made precisely the same swim to Ireland's Old Head when the merchant vessel on which he served as a cabin boy was wrecked.

Lusitania **by Norman Wilkinson for** *The Illustrated London News*, **1915.**

The *Lusitania* was a civilian victim of World War One, unlike the *Cap Trafalgar*. In summer 1914, with the outbreak of hostilities, the German steamship was converted into a special kind of auxiliary cruiser disguised as an Allied ocean liner. "Q-ships," as they were designated by the British Admiralty, were operated by both the Royal Navy and the *Kaiserliche Marine*. Their purpose was to lure enemy vessels within shooting range under false colors, sending up their real flag only after the victim had been fooled and ordered to surrender. *Cap Trafalgar* had been thus transformed into the duplicate of an obscure liner, the *Carmania*, to resemble the enemy vessel in every detail. But beneath her decks lurked eight 5.9-inch guns concealed by wooden flaps that could be raised in seconds to point their muzzles seaward. On 14 September, the masquerading German warship confronted its first target off the coast of Trinidad. But as the two vessels drew closer together, their crews were astounded to see that both were absolutely identical in appearance, even to the name on their sterns.

The Cap Trafalgar had stumbled upon the very ship she impersonated, the Carmania. But the British original had herself undergone transformation into a Q-ship, and blasted the German counterfeit with a superior firepower that sank her.

There was an additional component of high strangeness to their synchronous encounter. The Cap Trafalgar had been redesigned to pass for the Carmania, even down to the dismantling of a funnel. At the same time, the Carmania had likewise undergone refitting, during which a dummy funnel was added, so that when the enemy ships met, they were mirror images of each other.

Sinking Cap Trafalgar by **Charles Dixon**

Precognitive dreams envisioning disaster are likewise commonly associated with tragedies at sea. The Greek Poseidon was as much a god of the subconscious as of the ocean. The surface of the sea, which reflects light and images, hides a world of dynamic, living energies in its dark depths. So too, the mind in its waking state needs light to function, while the subconscious realm of night is alive with powerful forces underpinning the basis of our identity. Accordingly, *Titanic* was infamous for the many visionary nightmares surrounding its fate. In a typical example, an American businessman was one of numerous booked passengers saved by this phenomenon. According to Allen, he was about to board the liner, when a cable arrived from his wife in

Nebraska. She implored him to cancel his reservations, because a dream had vividly revealed an iceberg that would sink the vessel in the dead of night with terrible loss of life.

Such synchronistic dreams are part of what a U.S. mathematician, William Cox, characterized as "accident avoidance," subconscious awareness of dangerous future events. During the 1960s, he compared the number of passengers killed or injured in train accidents with those who rode on days without mishap. To his astonishment, he observed that far fewer persons were usually aboard when accidents took place than during normal operations minus incidents. Cox cited as typical the collision of the *Georgian*, carrying just nine passengers when it crashed on 15 June 1952. During the preceding month, the same Chicago train averaged nearly fifty passengers per trip.

But the "accident avoidance" mechanism postulated by Cox cannot explain what must amount to a whole sub-category of synchronicity, wherein airline disasters are accurately envisioned in dreams. Among the most cogent of such cases involved the deadliest accident in U.S. aviation history. Late one night in early May 1979, David Booth was startled awake by a terrible dream, unlike any he had ever experienced. In it, the twenty-three-year-old Cincinnati, Ohio office manager witnessed a jumbo jet take off from Chicago's O'Hare International Airport, rapidly gain altitude, then rolled over on its back, out of control, as an engine fell off. The airliner then plummeted nose-first into the ground, erupting into a colossal fire-ball from which no one could have survived. Although shaken by his extraordinarily vivid nightmare, Booth discussed it with no one and even forgot about it. But his peace of mind would be disturbed by the same dream for almost the rest of the month. By mid-May, he was a nervous wreck. Anticipation of the recurring nightmare combined with sleep-depravation to induce profound dread and anxiety interrupted by fits of uncontrolled weeping. Fearing for his own sanity, but reluctant to consult a psychiatrist, he took a leave of absence from work. Still the dream continued to plague his rest.

Finally putting aside his life-long distaste for any kind of paranormal "superstition", Booth telephoned Chicago's International O'Hare Airport. "I know you'll think I'm crazy," he began apologetically, but he forged ahead, describing what he felt could have been a warning of some kind. To his surprise and relief, the voice on the other end of the line was considerate and helpful. "What you have dreamt might be a real premonition," said the airport security officer. "But you haven't given me enough detailed information to do anything about it. There are dozens of DC-10 flights arriving and departing O'Hare everyday. If you knew the exact date and hour of the accident --- even the airline or runway --- it might be preventable. Next time you have the dream, try to see and remember the plane's N-number. That's the big numeral on the tail. We could identify the flight from that. In any case, call me back anytime."[7]

Booth was sincerely grateful for the officer's sympathetic assistance, but did not realize he had recorded their conversation and traced Booth's telephone number. Twice more the dream returned, and even though Booth made an effort to pre-program himself, he did not awake with any additional information, and felt no need to call O'Hare ever again.

On 25 May, still home on a leave of absence from work, he was watching the Friday evening news. The lead story described American Airlines Flight 191 bound for Los Angeles. At 3:02, it had been cleared for take off. Half-way down runway 32-R, the DC-10 nosed upward at full power, rapidly gaining altitude, as the port engine suddenly tore loose, pivoted up and over the leading edge and top of the wing, then shot away from the aircraft at high speed. Meanwhile, the 379,000-pound jumbo-jet continued to climb, until it rolled 112 degrees to port at about three hundred feet. It nose-dived into the earth, erupting on impact into an enormous, mushroom-shaped conflagration forty-six hundred feet beyond the landing strip, not far from the Touhy Mobile Home Park, in suburban Des Plaines. All passengers and crew, plus two persons on the ground, were incinerated, resulting in a death toll of two hundred seventy-three victims, the worst airline disaster in U.S. history.

Artist rendition of American Airlines Flight 191's last moments.

Upon seeing the news coverage of his recurrent nightmare, Booth suffered a complete nervous breakdown. While recuperating in the hospital, he was visited by a pair of agents from the Federal Bureau of Investigation alerted by the security officer, who turned over his taped telephone conversation to the government men. After extensive examination and background checks revealed no relationship between the distraught Iowa systems analyst and the destruction of the DC-10, the F.B.I. concluded that any apparent connections were entirely coincidental. Booth did not agree. He knew his repeated visions had been correct. However, to his dying day, thirty-five years later, he never understood why he had been "given" the ability to foresee the disaster he was powerless to prevent. "How can you make sense of something like that?" he asked. "There's no explanation for it. No meaning. No conclusion. It just doesn't make sense."[8]

Nineteen years after the loss of American Airlines Flight 191, a British investigative reporter researching the Chicago crash came across a brief article about David Booth in *Mystics, Visionaries, and Prophets*, by Shawn Madigan, Professor of Theology and Christian Spirituality at the College of St. Catherine, St. Paul, Minnesota. Using the Internet to locate any similar incidents of precognition, he was shocked to discover no less than twenty-six other newspaper accounts of men and women around the world who claimed to have experienced the identical, vivid dream night after night before the 25 May 1979 disaster. "I'm sure many more persons who experienced the same nightmare," Reginald Steward wrote in his feature for the *London Daily Herald*, "but they didn't get reported. Just how many more, I cannot guess. But even these twenty-seven documented cases of precognitive dreaming amount to persuasive evidence tending to confirm the authenticity of this phenomenon. [9]

Inspired by Steward's article in early 2003, I learned as much as possible about David Booth, and interviewed six others of the more than two-dozen individuals, who envisioned the O'Hare crash in their nightmares. I learned that while no two were identical, they were all similar enough to convince me each precognitive dreamer had witnessed the event in advance from different perspectives. Searching for some commonalities they might have shared, I found that all of them were deeply frustrated by their inability to have saved a single life, and could not explain why they had received so disturbingly accurate visions of the catastrophe. Probing further into their lives, I uncovered what may have been a metaphysical cause behind their tragic synchronicity.

Prior to their prophetic nightmares, each of the dreamers might have been described as not particularly compassionate persons. Fellow human beings did not figure very high in their regard, and they were generally indifferent to the feelings or sufferings of others. The loss of Flight 191 had changed them. And while no one ran off to spend the rest of his or her life in a monastery or convent, something had nonetheless been broken open. Their shriveled-up seed of compassion suddenly blossomed somewhere deep inside. If so, then their revealing dreams had nothing whatsoever to do with saving lives for preventing a terrible accident from taking place.

The fate of Flight 191 was unalterable, because it had already happened in the Eternal Now that is the real nature of time. Past, present and future are only human conventions enabling our narrow understanding of the incomprehensibly vast cosmos as a practical means of getting through life in this small corner of the universe. Related coincidences did, after all, underscore something strangely fixed or predetermined about the disaster. Among the victims was a business manager and executive producer for popular musical groups, Leonard Stogel, whose mother and father were lost seventeen years earlier aboard another American Airlines passenger plane --- Flight 1 --- on 1 March 1962. The First Numeral prominently links his fate to theirs. As mentioned in the previous chapter, the negative side of this number indicates that "we are in danger of losing a sense of completeness," which was shattered with the loss of his parents.

Another Flight 191 casualty was author Judith Wax, outward bound to Los Angeles for the promotion of her latest book. In it, she described her instinctual dread of flying: "When the job required travel, I developed such a fear of airplanes, my head trembled from take-off to landing." These words appear in *Starting In The Middle*, on page 191, the same number of her fatal flight.[10]

The horrific crash was not a senseless catastrophe, however, but announced in the dreams of individuals who needed the experience to demolish the high walls they erected against their innate sense of fellow feeling. The Compassionate Intelligence that oversees all creation used a synchronous event to break through to the frozen well-springs of their own humanity.

Similarly unlocking a dammed spiritual instinct was discussed in the early 20th Century by Isodore

Kozminsky's *Numbers, Their Meaning and Magic*, released in 1912, the same year *Titanic* was lost. He pointed out that the liner's name totaled (not in letters, but their corresponding mystical significance) Eighteen, "an evil number," known in various traditions as "The Blood-Stained Path," and associated with bad judgment.[11] But the real mystery posed by the disaster and others of similar traumatic magnitude is this: Because they attract exceptionally high frequencies of meaningful coincidence, particularly precognitive and premonitory synchronicities, are such events predetermined and beyond prevention?

The question may not be altogether proper, because it has less to do with debates about free will than a traditional concept of time. But this perspective is without doubt narrowly subjective and useful only for getting us through the challenges of our daily, earthly existence. In a more broadly correct, cosmic sense, time expands immeasurably beyond human restrictions into an Eternal Now. Through their mystical power, episodes such as the Titanic disaster cause brief rifts in our myopic definition of time, melding the transitory with the eternal. They suck events into an unknown Otherworld, like light into a "black hole." Tragedies of such scope seem to create a rift in the fabric of time, into which synchronicities of many kinds are sucked, as into a powerful vortex we may recognize but perhaps never fully understand.

Chapter 4

Parallel Lives and a Presidential Curse

" ... the universe, as a whole, the planet Earth, and our own, individual lives are all parts of one, gigantic, evolutionary continuum."

——Tim Wallace-Murphy and Marilyn Hopkins [1]

In August 1994, a man walked into a department store in the United States, and tried to cash a check. "I know Doug McFadden," the suspicious clerk said, upon seeing the name on the check, "and you're not him." But the man pulled out his identification papers. Sure enough, he was Dave McFadden, of Henderson, Kentucky. The Dave McFadden who was familiar to the store clerk was a local fire-fighter. So, the second Dave McFadden walked over to the nearby fire station, and shook hands with Dave McFadden of Michigan.

The two men compared notes. Both were career fire-fighters. Both were born in August. Both collected model fire trucks. Both liked guns, and preferred Smith & Wesson (a well-known American manufacturer of firearms). Both were also into fire prevention. Both worked at fire stations designated "Number 2." Both were emergency medical technicians. Both bit their fingernails. Both had blond wives. But, wait. There's more. Another firefighter by the name of Dave McFadden from Appleton, Wisconsin, surfaced. The Wisconsin Dave has three daughters, and the Michigan Dave has three boys. If the three Dave McFaddens represented the only such instance of synchronicity, then we could dismiss it as merely the result of statistical probability, however extreme.

In fact, however, it belongs to a whole sub-category of meaningful coincidence known as "Parallel Lives". They represent the most enigmatic aspect of the entire subject. When two or more unrelated persons, often separated in space and/or time, nonetheless share numerous similar events and personal traits in common, they are said to have led parallel lives, as the following examples illustrate.

"When new neighbors moved into the house next door to my parents' home in Aberdeen, South Dakota," wrote Carole Nelson in January 1978, "both families were struck by the woman's resemblance to my mother. Both women were small and dark-haired and almost the same age. However, most unusual was the coincidence of names. My mother's rather uncommon name is Theresa Philomena Weiss, and the new neighbor's name is Philomena Theresa Schumacher." [2]

"Robert E. Fraser of Warwick, Rhode Island, and John M. Fraser, Jr., of Cranston, are not related and never met until a Rotary Club luncheon in September 1972. Both were born in May, although Jack is four years older than Bob. Each has three children. Both grew up in the Elmwood section of Providence and later attended Hope High School. Each attended junior high school with the other's wife. More striking were their political careers. At the time of their meeting, both were running for the city council in their respective cities. Both were seeking to replace a republican councilman from the second ward who was retiring after twenty years in office. The two wards abut along the Pawtuxet River. The men finally met because both are active in Rotary."[3]

"In November 1975, two new employees of a major food chain arrived to have their identification pictures taken. When the photographer called Tom Murphy, two voices echoed in response. The photographer then asked for Thomas J. Murphy, and once again both men responded. In both cases, the 'J' stood for Joseph. The next logical separation was by occupation. 'Will the Tom Murphy with the CPA background please come forward?' Both men came forward. The perplexed photographer asked if they were playing some kind of joke. The Murphys shrugged and insisted both were assigned to the controller's department. Finally, the photographer established that one Murphy was starting as a senior accounting specialist and the other as a senior auditor. Figuring the two were in for real trouble if the only way people could tell them apart was by their jobs, the photographer asked their nicknames. 'T.J.', came the response from Number 1. 'Ditto', from Tom Murphy Number 2, 'but at one time my friends called me "Murf".' This smoothed out the situation.

"For the rest of the picture-taking session, he was known as 'Murf', and the other Tom was called 'T.J.'

Later, Murf was asked about his hobbies. 'Skiing, reading and international travel,' came his reply. What about T.J.? You wouldn't believe it."[4]

There may be something magical in "Murphy", as another parallel synchronicity of two more men with that name demonstrates: "Charles F. Murphy lives at 1950 Madison Road in Cincinnati. Another Charles F. Murphy lives at 1949 Madison Road in the same city. They just happen to be neighbors --- but there's more. Both are 'the Rev. Charles F. Murphy'. One is a Catholic priest; the other, a United Methodist minister."[5]

"A new resident of Marshalltown, Iowa, Kenneth L. Koehler, may have to move unless he and another Kenneth L. Koehler, a long-time resident, can exist peacefully in a state of confusion. Both men's middle name is Leroy. Each has four children. Their fathers are named Fred, and both men have uncles named John. Both have families who settled in the Galena, Illinois area years ago, but so far they can find no records to show they are related."[6]

Robert Hopcke describes three American women named Deborah who met by accident in the 1960s. They never knew about each other before. The first two Deborahs shared the same birthday, were the same height, build, hair color, eye color and complexion. Although unrelated, they so resembled each other, strangers assumed they were sisters. Both had married at age twenty, gave birth at the same age, and moved to the state of South Dakota, again at the same age. They happened to settle only three miles from each other.

Before they met, the daughter of one Deborah was named "Missy," the same name given by the other Deborah to her dog. The husband of one Deborah and the favorite horse of the other were named "Skip." Another Deborah, sharing numerous traits and life-events in common with the other two, appeared six months later. This third Deborah was particularly close to one of women. Both had been married twice. The marital difficulties they simultaneously experienced caused them to move to the same city at the same time. When one Deborah was sixteen years old, another sixteen-year-old girl, not a relative, moved into her home, dying that same year of leukemia. The other Deborah, at sixteen years of age, lived in the home of a sixteen-year-old girlfriend who also died of leukemia within the year. When the three finally went their separate ways, they were astonished to learn that they had all resettled exactly sixty miles from each other.

Such remarkable parallel lives seem beyond rational comprehension. But that is the nature of the mystical experience, an exercise of the soul, not the mind. However, the numerical symbolism of their connection is obvious. Variants of the Number Six highlight the many meaningful coincidences binding the three women together in a mystical relationship. They met in the 1960s, shared an important meaningful coincidence at sixteen years of age, moved sixty miles away from each other, etc. As discussed in our Chapter, "The Synchronicity of Numbers," Six is the numeral of female energy, Mother Earth, darkness and mystery.

When two women named Edna, strangers to one another and unrelated, met by chance in a Hackensack, New Jersey hospital for the first time, they learned that their lives were mirror images of each other. Sharing the same birthday, these "time twins", as West refers to them, each gave birth in the same hour. Both babies were named Patricia Edna before they were delivered. Their husbands had the same name (Harold), were born on the same day, had the same occupation, and drove the same make, model and color of car. Both Ednas belonged to the same religious faith, and had an identical number of brothers and sisters. Both owned dogs named "Spot."

Teresa Turner and Teresa Turner had more in common than a name. Besides living in the same town (Titusville, Florida), and each having a three-year-old daughter, they both delivered sons in the same hospital on the same day.[7] William E. Lynch, of Havana, Illinois, and William E. Lynch, of Peoria, Illinois, found themselves in the same hospital room, recovering from the same type of surgery, performed by the same doctor. The men, who are not related and never met before, both are 81.[8]

Mr. and Mrs. Roger Call of Barboursville, West Virginia, were born on the same day, June 19, 1943, were graduated from elementary school, junior high school and high school on the same dates in May, and from Marshall College on 13 May 1965. They were married 5 September 1964, and both entered the teaching profession after graduation. Mr. Call's paternal grandmother and Mrs. Call's maternal grandmother died on the same day, 8 August 1979, and were buried two days later.[9]

The parallel lives of twins seems to defy the presumed logic of mere biological relatedness, suggesting instead that both individuals are more than physical look-a-likes, and share a common psychic bond. For example, Marshal Bedol and his twin, Alan, were both in an army ski patrol during World War Two. When Alan was wounded during battle in Italy, Marshal, a few hundred yards away, fell to the ground. "In a hail of gunfire, we got separated," said Marshal. "Then I suddenly had a burning pain in my thigh. I fell over, but there wasn't any blood. The pain, though, was intense. Suddenly, the truth dawned on me. I wasn't wounded at all. It must have been Alan." It was. A piece of shrapnel had hit Alan in the thigh at the precise moment Marshal felt the pain.[10]

The special relationship between twins often exceeds even the psychic links that connect them. Although sometimes separated by great stretches of distance and time, their destinies are no less identical than their common physical traits, indicating a shared soul stamped from the same spiritual pattern. A pair of twins born in 1924, were separated after birth and put up for adoption. One grew up in Toronto; the other in Vancouver. Neither knew of each other's existence. "Although these young women (Mrs. Margaret Judson and Mrs. Marion Smith) did not meet until they were twenty-one," Tocoma's *Washington's News Tribune* reported on 12 January 1959, "amazing parallels exist in their lives. In their teens, both had been expert roller-skaters and considered becoming professional. Both had taken piano lessons, sung alto in church choirs, and had their tonsils removed in the same year. Both married sailors the same age, size, weight and build, who had been in the service four years, and were making the navy their careers. Perhaps oddest of all, the day after their first meeting in brown suits in the Toronto store, both women turned up for their second meeting wearing identical plaid skirts and similar heart-shaped lockets which had been gifts from their foster mothers on their twenty-first birthdays."

The *Helsinki Herald* on 9 March 2002 reported that a pair of seventy-year-old brothers from Raahe, just north of the Finnish capital, was riding their bicycles on the same day, when they were killed during a snowstorm in separate but remarkably similar accidents. According to constable Pauli Ketonen, both died a little more than two hours apart when each was hit by a different truck on the same highway.

Margaret Gaddis reported for *Fate* magazine that, "in Bellafonte, Pennsylvania, nineteen-year-old identical twins Donald and Dale Henry went deer-hunting --- separately. At the end of the day, each of them returned with an eight-point buck. Each used three shots!" In the same article, she tells of a pair of

106

Chicago twins separated at birth during the 1930s, one of the brothers relocating to Topeka, Kansas. Meeting by chance forty years later, "he was flabbergasted to learn that they both worked for the Bell Telephone System, had received very similar educations in similar homes, had married girls of the same general type in the same year, each had a four-year-old son, and each of them had a fox terrier named Trixie."[11]

Another writer for *Fate* observed how "the strangest aspects of twin togetherness are the numerous cases of twins who die at the same time. A London cab driver named Jonathan Meeres, fifty-eight years old, died of a heart attack with no previous illness, on 18 April 1961. A few days later, a letter came to his address stating that his identical twin, Arthur, had died on 18 April, in Freetown, Sierra Leone, Africa. The brothers had been separated for thirty-four years" In 1966, Washington, D.C. brothers, Francis and Joseph Marcellino, married sisters. Their wives gave birth within the same hour to sons, each of which weighed six pounds."[12]

In "The Phenomenon of Identical Twins," Shirley M. Cunningham recalled how "on June 25, 1954, I gave birth to a set of twin boys, Ronald and Donald, in Marion General Hospital, Marion, Ohio. In 1953, also on June 25, I gave birth to a set of twin girls, Bonnie and Connie, in the same hospital and in the same delivery room. Newspaper and television sources stated that this event had a chance of happening about once in a billion times. Both sets were identical twins, which added to the phenomenon, for only one out of every four sets of twins born are identical twins."[13]

This incredible account of twin destinies appeared in *Fate* magazine: "Jack Clatworthy thought the chap in the next bed looked familiar as he awakened in the Taunton, England hospital from a concussion in March 1974. He was right, reports United Press International: The man in the next bed was his identical twin brother Frank Clatworthy, also recovering from a concussion. The twenty-year-old twins had been involved in separate automobile accidents on the Taunton-to-Minehead road. Frank's car had overturned as he was on his way home from work. Within an hour, his brother Jack's car crashed through a hedge. The brothers first learned of the coincidence on finding themselves in adjacent hospital beds."[14]

A fascinating inflection of the Parallel Lives phenomenon comprises common birthdays and dates of death, or, more often, the deaths of influential individuals on the anniversary of some event that epitomized their lives. These meaningful coincidences occur especially for men and women who made some unique impact on history. As Shakespeare has Cassius say in the last act of *Julius Caesar*, "Where I did begin, there I end." Cassius was referring to the suicide he was about to commit on his own birthday, after having been defeated by the forces of Mark Antony. In the late First Century, B.C.

Shakespeare himself died on 23 April 1616, his own fifty-second birthday.

Mark Anthony's daughter, the Queen of North Africa's Mauretania, Cleopatra Selene, or "Cleopatra of the Moon", died during the lunar eclipse of 3 March 6 A.D. America's own "Jazz Age Cleopatra", Josephine Baker, died on 12 April 1975, fifty years to the day of her Paris debut. Germany's great 19th Century composer, Richard Wagner, was the dominant influence in the life of his 20th Century counterpart, Hans Pfitzner, who died in1949, on 22 May, Wagner's birthday. Thomas Jefferson and John Adams, the framers of the U.S. Declaration of Independence, died on Independence Day, July 4, 1826 precisely fifty years after both men signed the Declaration of Independence.

During 1892, American author, Ignatius Donnelly, wrote *Caesar's Column*, an internationally acclaimed futuristic novel, in which he predicted events occurring during the 20th Century with sometimes astounding accuracy. He died on the morning of 1 January 1901, just as New Year's bells were ringing in the new century he was so perspicacious in anticipating.

As mentioned earlier, Adolf Hitler died among the flames of Berlin, in 1945, on 30 April. For millennia before, this day had been commemorated throughout Western Europe and Germany in particular as May Eve, or *Walpurgisnacht.* It is an ancient, pagan festival, during which a man impersonating Baldur, the god of death and resurrection, is chosen by lot (by fate) to leap through ritual fires, still known as "Baldur bale-fires" in rural Scandinavia. Encyclopedist Barbara Walker observes, "Clearly, these were customs dating back to real burning of the man who represented the god in his love-death (*Liebestod*)."[15] Walpurga is the Teutonic goddess of seasonal and spiritual transformations experienced by shamans or "witches." May Eve signified a pivotal moment between the end of winter (the apparent death of Nature) and the beginning of spring (the rebirth of life); the dissolution of an old world before the coming of a new one.

Of course, Parallel Lives are more commonly recognized among famous persons, because their biographies are widely known. Nonetheless, most cases seem to involve individuals involved in statecraft. For example, England's George III was born on 4 June 1738, the same day Samuel Hemming, a London businessman, came into the world. King George ascended the throne on the same day Hemmings opened his iron-monger factory. Both men were wed on the same day, and fathered an identical number of children belonging to the same sex. The monarch and the iron-monger experienced ill health and personal accidents at the same time, and both passed away suffering similar ailments on 29 January 1820.[16]

The most famous series of Parallel Live comparisons, again involving politicians, occurred in the relationship between U.S. presidents Abraham

Lincoln and John Fitzgerald Kennedy. In my first study of this mystery, *Synchronicity and You*, I pointed out a dozen points of uncanny comparison between the lives of both men. Since its first publication in 1999, I investigated their similarities, and was astounded by their number, far too many to be recorded here. But some of the particularly outstanding parallels serve to illustrate the validity of this phenomenon, especially as it pertains to Synchronicity. For example, "Kennedy" and "Lincoln" each comprise seven letters, just as the names of their respective Vice Presidents, Andrew Johnson and Lyndon Johnson, were made up of thirteen. Seven, as we learned in Chapter 2, is the Number of the Completion of Cycles, while Thirteen's unfortunate associations were likewise defined. More to the point, Lincoln was skipper of the *Talisman*, a Mississippi River boat, while Kennedy was skipper of PT 109. Both suffered from so-called "lazy-eye muscles," which occasionally caused one eyeball to loll about in its socket. Lincoln was a second child, and so was Kennedy.

Eight, as pointed out in Chapter 2, is the Number of Extinction, and during the year of his death, Lincoln received over eighty letters. In the year of his death, Kennedy received over eight hundred letters. Both presidents were killed on the Friday just before a major holiday. Lincoln was murdered on Good Friday (symbolic of resurrection), while Kennedy was assassinated on the Friday immediately prior to Thanksgiving. Lincoln sat in Box 7 at Ford's Theatre. Kennedy rode in Car 7 for the fateful Dallas motorcade --- again, the fateful Number of Cyclical Completion. Both presidents passed away in a place with the initials "P" and "H". Lincoln died in the Peterson House, while JFK died in Parkland Hospital. Lincoln was sitting in Ford's Theater, and Kennedy was sitting in a *Lincoln Town Car* made by Ford Motor Company. Joseph Burroughs operated the concession at Ford's Theatre the night Lincoln was shot, and Butch Burroughs was the concession stand operator at the Texas Theatre when Kennedy was assassinated.

Poignant, even prophetic synchronicity occurred in Lincoln's own family. The President's grandfather, likewise named Abraham, was also shot from behind, murdered by an assassin's bullet in Washington (Washington County, Kentucky). Both Abrahams had sons named Thomas, and married women named Mary. Abraham, the President, was declared legally dead after a severe accident, from which he miraculously recovered, when he was ten years old. His own son died at ten years of age.

Numerous extraordinary synchronicities constellated around the Kennedy assassination itself. A federal mint in Dallas issued a dollar bill just two weeks before J.F.K. was killed in that Texas city. The dollar in question has since come to be known as the "Kennedy Assassination Bill." Because Dallas is the location for the eleventh of twelve Federal Reserve Bank Districts, "K", the eleventh letter of the alphabet, was printed on the bill's face. Moreover, the Number 11 appears in each of the four corners. The serial number of this bill begins with "K" and ends with "A", suggesting "Kennedy Assassination". He was murdered on the eleventh month of the year. Adding the two "elevens" on either side of the bill makes 22 --- the date of the shooting. The series number is 1963, the year Kennedy died. An additional synchronicity theme appearing among these coincidences is the evil reputation of Numeral Eleven for violence and terror, as described in our Chapter about numerical significance.

Lincoln-Kennedy synchronicity extended beyond these two men to impact the key players in their mirrored lives. Shortly after Lincoln was assassinated, his wife, brother and son, Robert T., relocated to a home at 3014 N Street, N.W., in Georgetown. Shortly after his father was assassinated, John F. Kennedy, Jr. was taken by his mother to a home located at 3017 N Street, N.W., in Georgetown. Mary Todd Lincoln and Jackie Kennedy, both twenty-four years old when they married their presidential husbands, suffered the deaths of their children while living in the White House. Both lost a son during their husband's terms. When they were shot, Lincoln and Kennedy were seated beside their wives. Both families had four children; two of them passed away before reaching adolescence.

A mystical bond with the respective Vice Presidents of Lincoln and Kennedy has already been cited, but it went further than numerical commonality. Both Andrew Johnson and Lyndon Johnson were opposed for re-election by men whose names began with "G", namely, Ulysses S. Grant and Barry Goldwater. Both Johnsons were plagued by urethral stones, and were the only men to suffer from this shared ailment while serving as the nation's Chief Executive. Neither Johnson chose to run for reelection in 1868 or 1968. Even both presidential assassins shared a macabre series of meaningful coincidences. In 1864, then General U.S. Grant sent an official War Department letter of thanks to Edwin Booth for saving the life of Lincoln's only surviving son, Robert, during a mishap aboard a crowded train in Jersey City, New Jersey. The next year, Booth's brother, John Wilkes, murdered the President.

Booth and Oswald were alike privates in the military; the former served with the Virginia militia; JFK's assassin was a Marine Corps private. Born, respectively, in 1839 and 1939, both were Southerners, who preferred to use their three names. Either was born a second child, and each had two brothers whose careers they envied. Edwin and Junius Booth achieved far greater renown in the legitimate theater, while Oswald coveted his brothers' higher military standing. A Lewis Paine helped Booth escape from Washington, D.C.; a Mrs. Ruth Paine got Oswald his job at the school-book depository, from which he escaped after shooting President Kennedy. Booth was eventually trapped inside a barn by cavalry leader, Lt. Luther B. Baker. So too, Oswald was briefly detained on the second floor of the school-book depository by a Dallas motorcycle patrolman named Marion L. Baker. Booth and Oswald were shot to death without trial, before they could give their version of the presidential assassination, and both were killed by a single round from a Colt revolver. Both died in blazing illumination: Booth in a barn fire and Oswald was nearly blinded by banks of television camera lights.

When, as a young student Booth attended a Quaker boarding school in Cockeysville, Maryland, a gypsy living in the woods nearby read his palm. "Ah, you've a bad hand," she exclaimed, "the lines all cris-cras! It's full enough of sorrow. Full of trouble. Trouble in plenty, everywhere I look. You'll break hearts, they'll be nothing to you. You'll die young ... You're born under an unlucky star. You've got in your hand a thundering crowd of enemies - not one friend - you'll make a bad end ... Now, young sir, I've never seen a worse hand, and I wish I hadn't seen it, but every word I've told is true by the signs. You'd best turn a missionary or a priest and try to escape it."[17]

Synchronicity connected the Kennedy assassination with individuals otherwise utterly removed from the event. Mr. and Mrs. Edwin A. Bergman, prominent Chicago art collectors, were lunching with the sculptress, "Marisol", on 22 November 1963, when news reached them that JFK had been shot. They went to view her "Kennedy Family", something she had sculpted in wood two years before. It had just been shipped back from a west coast exhibition, where a fellow artist had, for a joke, drilled a bullet hole in Kennedy's chest.[18]

"On Friday, 22 November 1963, I was a witness to an amazing forecast of the event that was to shock and sadden the nation. At about 11:30 a.m. that day (E.S.T.), my wife, Mary, and I were preparing to sit down to lunch with my cousin, Mrs. Frank Creser, and her children in Bridgeport, Connecticut. My cousin's oldest son, Frank, Jr., aged eleven, was out in the back yard, playing with some friends. When he came inside upon being called, we sat down to lunch. While we were eating, Frank, Jr., suddenly said, 'Mommy, President Kennedy got shot!' Imagine our astonishment. 'What!' I exclaimed, 'Why do you say that?' 'I don't know,' the boy answered. 'It just came out.' He seemed even more surprised than I. We dismissed the incident as a childish prank. Thinking no more about what he had said, I finished my lunch. About 2:00 that afternoon, we heard the news of the assassination while watching tv Recalling the remark that Frank, Jr. had made at the lunch table, I was dumfounded. In some strange way, an eleven-year-old boy had possessed knowledge of the tragedy some two hours before it occurred."[19]

A calendar for 1963, printed the year before, "mistakenly" indicated 22 November, the day President Kennedy was killed, as a legal holiday. The name of the St. Louis, Missouri firm that produced the precognitive calendar was Skinner and Kennedy Company.[20]

The famous comedian, Red Skelton, emerged from sleep on the first day of November, 1963, to scribble on a piece of paper, "President Kennedy will die on

November 22nd." Five years earlier, American clairvoyant, Jean Dixon, was quoted by *Parade* magazine as having said that in the 1960 presidential race a democrat would win, but die in office, the victim of assassination.

Meaningful coincidences seem to gather around the power and death of American presidents, not only Lincoln and Kennedy. The most cogent examples are found in the so-called "Zero-Year Curse". This was supposedly uttered by a Shawnee Indian chief, in 1811 (again, the dreaded Eleven!). In that year, Tecumseh led several tribes out of the reservations set aside for them, in an effort to return to their traditional way of life. In Ohio, his followers gathered at Utopia Town, a village he established near Tippecanoe Creek. Later, his brother was killed in a skirmish with U.S. Army troops led by General William Henry Harrison. In revenge, Tecumseh rounded up about two thousand warriors to serve as allies of the British during the War of 1812.

Defeated again, and for the last time, he pronounced a curse on Harrison, who was campaigning for the presidency. "He will not finish his term," predicted Tecumseh. "He will die in office. And when he dies, you will remember my brother. You think that I have lost my powers --- I, who caused the sun to darken and Red Men to give up fire-water. But I tell you, Harrison will die. And after him, every Great Chief chosen every twenty years thereafter will die. And when each one dies, let everyone remember the death of our people."[21] Harrison was in power just a month, when he became ill and passed away on 4 April 1841, the first U.S. president to die in office.

Portrait of Tecumseh by George Catlin

Ever since, presidents have been expiring according to "The Zero-Year Curse:" Abraham Lincoln, elected in 1860, assassinated five years later; James Garfield, assumed the presidency in 1880, shot to death the following year; William McKinley during his second term of 1890 was murdered in New York; Warren Harding, elected in 1920, died of a heart attack three years later; Franklin Roosevelt, having won an unprecedented third term in 1940, succumbed to a massive cerebral hemorrhage, in 1945; John Kennedy, became president in 1960, but was murdered three years later. Ronald Reagan was elected in1980, and narrowly escaped death the following year when an assailant's bullet just missed his heart.

Some investigators believe that Tecumseh's "curse" was broken by Reagan's near-miss. It is nonetheless intriguing that he was the victim of an attempt on his life that came within inches of succeeding. According to American astrologer, Mark Dodich, the series of presidential deaths is actually a "cosmic coincidence" caused by the alignment of Jupiter and Saturn, whose orbital alignments occur every twenty years. He points out that the one failure in the pattern --- Reagan's escape --- took place under an "air sign," signifying survival, whereas the other presidents perished under "Earth signs," which signify death. Was Tecumseh's "Zero-Year Curse" a malediction that spanned centuries, or a series of unrelated coincidences?

While modern skeptics may dismiss Tecumseh's malediction as so much coincidental superstition, they may nevertheless be interested to learn that it was not his only such pronouncement to gain attention. In late September 1811, he addressed an annual council of the Creek Confederacy at the tribal village of Tuckhabatchee, Alabama, for the purpose of uniting various Native American "nations." His impassioned plea fell on deaf ears, however, and his fellow Indians refused to risk war against the whites.

Just before he left the meeting, he declared angrily, "You do not believe the Great Spirit has sent me. You shall know. I leave Tuckhabatchee directly and shall go straight to Detroit. When I arrive there, I will stamp my foot on the ground, and shake down every house in Tuckhabatchee."

According to historian Jay Feldman, "Early on the morning of December 16, the day of his calculated arrival, Tecumseh's prophecy was fulfilled. The earth began to tremble violently. The Creek village was destroyed." With an estimated 8.1 magnitude on the Richter Scale, the Missouri-centered New Madrid Earthquake was the most powerful geologic upheaval in North American history.[22]

Tecumseh's was not the only Indian curse that has come to pass, thereby validating the fundamental principle of synchronicity; namely, the connection of two or more otherwise unrelated incidents that assume significance from the standing-point of a particular viewer. Official city records of Kaskaskia, the first capital of Illinois between the years 1818 and 1819, contain the story of a curse placed on the town by an Algonquin Indian. At the time, Kaskaskia was a small colonial settlement on the Kaskaskia River, a short distance from its confluence with the Mississippi. Infuriated by his failure to win the hand of a French maiden who lived there, the Indian shouted at the villagers, "May the filthy spot on which your church stands be destroyed, may your homes and farms be ruined, may your dead be torn from their graves, and may your land be a feeding place for fishes!"

In 1881, the rampaging Mississippi River did wipe out most of the town of Kaskaskia. It destroyed the Church of the Immaculate Conception, buried the crops of the French settlers and unearthed the dead from their cemetery. Most of the houses disappeared in the angry flood, slipping one by one into the turbulent muddy waters. The Mississippi created a new channel as well as an island, leaving the original town of Kaskaskia in the middle of the stream --- "a feeding place for fishes" --- as the wrathful Algonquin had prophesied.[23]

A case for Dodich's astrology and the verity of parallel lives may be ascertained in a simple, if tedious experiment anyone can perform. Open the first volume of any general encyclopedia, and read the biographies of persons who were born on your birthday. If you go through all the volumes of the encyclopedia, collecting biographical information about individuals sharing the same birth-date, you are certain to observe an abundance of close comparisons between your own life and the lives of the persons described. To underscore their similarities, read the biographies of others not born on your birthday; they will not match your personality or destiny. While the results of such an informal experiment may or may not have anything to do with astrology, they do tend to confirm that everyone has a parallel life somewhere in time, and that the phenomenon is real.

Parallel lives, whether discovered in the remarkable correspondences between twins or among persons sharing the same birthday, suggest that the observable patterns of nature such as revealed in the reproduction of animal species or recurrence of leaf designs, are no less applicable to human affairs. In other words, both Lincoln and Kennedy belonged to a pattern that repeats itself through time, just as we find our own doubles in the biographies of others born on the same day we came into the world. If acknowledgement of these patterns begins to provide some recognizable basis for the conclusions of astrologers, who likewise perceive designs in human behavior and fate, synchronicity of this kind also implies a mechanism for reincarnation.

A case in point is the extraordinary set of coincidences in the life and death of Carl Edon, as reported in *The Middlesbrough Evening Gazette* and *Daily Mirror* (respectively, 15 and 16 January 2002). Born in 1973, in Middlesbrough, England, when just three years old he began telling his incredulous family about his previous life as a German airman killed when his bomber was shot down in 1942. Throughout his childhood, Edon drew numerous and surprisingly accurate illustrations of Luftwaffe aircraft and instrument panels without the aid of published references. He insisted that he had died in the crash that severed his right leg, and continued to tell the same story after he reached adulthood, although no corresponding historical details of his memory could be validated. In 1995, while on the job as a railway employee, Carl was in Skinningdrove to collect box-cars, when he was violently murdered.

Two years later, the wreckage of a World War Two aircraft was accidentally discovered by water board workers just a few hundred yards from the same spot were Edon met his death. Examination of surviving serial numbers revealed that the light bomber was a Dornier Do. 217E-4, shot down by ground-fire on 15 January 1942. One of the crew members who perished in the crash was *Oberfeldwebel* (staff sergeant) Heinrich Richter, a gunner, whose Dornier had bombed Skinningdrove, the same place visited by the railway man at the time he was killed fifty-three years later. During their excavation of the bomber, investigators found Richter's boot with his leg, which had been severed during the crash, still inside, just as Carl Edon had described. His recollection of having lived as the German airman appears to have been remarkably confirmed by the synchronicity of Richter's death, in the same immediate vicinity of Carl's murder.

Parallel lives --- whether inflected through common destinies, the extra-biological relationship of identical twins, or even possible reincarnation --- represent a variation of synchronicity. The core experience of meaningful coincidence, whatever the category in which it occurs, is the thrill of genuine mysticism, that deeply personal sense of connection with divinity. A final example serves to illustrate. Some months before writing this book, I was standing on a bluff above the Mississippi River, near my home in Minnesota. Below me was a springtime carpet of wild flowers and dense vegetation. In the distance, I noticed a single flower growing all alone in the shadows. Its sight filled me with melancholy, and seemed symbolic of the inherent loneliness of every living creature and the sad vanity of existence. Some men, like the German 19th Century "Philosopher of Pessimism," Arthur Schopenhauer, believe that "life was something that should never have been."[24]

A German Air Force bomber of the type crewed by Heinrich Richter, 1942, who reincarnated thirty-one years later as British-born Carl Edon.

In a like frame of mind, I thought, "No one will ever appreciate the beauty of that solitary flower. Its loveliness will wither and die without any other creature paying it the least attention."

This gloomy conclusion had no sooner entered my mind, when a magnificent hummingbird swooped in from out of nowhere, and inserted its graceful bill into the lonely flower to take a long drink of nectar.

124

Chapter 5

The Fate of Synchronicity

"This thing has more fortitude than fortitude itself, because it will overcome every subtle thing and penetrate every solid thing. By it the world was formed."
—Emerald Tablet of Hermes Trismegistos[1]

The popular American magazine, *Fate, True Accounts of the Strange and Unusual*, has been in continuous publication since 1948. During all that time, its reputation as the premier metaphysical periodical in the United States still stands unchallenged. *Fate*'s nearly seven hundred issues form a unique library of paranormal lore, in which intriguing evidence for the perennial subject of synchronicity is not neglected. Culling this treasure trove of anecdotal material, I have selected those specimens which best serve to illustrate the categories of mystical experience described in previous chapters. They not only contribute significantly to a clearer understanding of the phenomenon, but put a human face on it, thereby rendering meaningful coincidence more approachable.

"My father, Robbie Robinson, had a triple-whammy: In addition to an aortic aneurysm, he also suffered from a stroke and a heart attack. He was completely paralyzed on his right side, barely able to move his left side, and completely unable to talk. His lack of motor ability was so extreme that they had to put him on a ventilator. He was unconscious most of the time, and when he would wake briefly, he just barely mumbled, incoherently. The doctor told me on the third day that if they didn't see any improvement within three and a half days, he would probably remain in a persistent vegetative state, kept alive only by machines. I got the distinct impression that the doctors added the extra half day for my benefit, because we had already passed the three-day mark. Since my Dad had signed a 'Code Blue' arrangement prior to the operation, they were specifically instructed by him, in the case of such an eventuality, not to resuscitate for use any heroic measures to save him. So, it didn't look good.

"About ten hours later, I returned by myself to the hospital with my old dog-eared copy of the *Bardo Thodol*---the so-called 'Tibetan Book of the Dead'. I had read it years ago, but never fully understood it, nor did I even know why I read it. Now, suddenly, it all hit me like the clear light of reality. If only to console myself, and maybe to head off the Jesus freaks they always send in to administer the last rites (Dad wasn't into that stuff), I thought a little Tibetan Buddhism might be in order.

"So, there I was, sitting next to my father's deathbed, reading aloud to him: 'Oh, nobly born, when thy body and mind were separating, thou must have experienced a glimpse of pure truth, subtle, sparkling, bright, dazzling, glorious, and radiantly awesome, like a mirage moving across a landscape in springtime, in one, continuous stream of vibrations.

Be not daunted thereby, nor terrified, nor awed. That is the radiance of thy own, true nature. Recognize it!'

"I looked over at him. He still seemed unconscious, and his breathing was very shallow. I continued: 'From the midst of that radiance, the natural sound of reality, reverberating like a thousand thunders simultaneously resounding, will come. That is the sound of thine own real self. Be not daunted!'

"I read on for a while, randomly picking out verses, all of which were not only beautiful, yet somehow seemed to fit the present situation perfectly. But something stopped me dead in my tracks when I read the following verse: 'O, nobly born, thou hast been in a swoon during the last three and one-half days. As soon as thou art recovered from this swoon, thou wilt have thought, "What hath happened?"

"'Three and one-half days, huh?', I thought to myself. 'That's strange.' I looked up at the clock. It was less than an hour away from that deadline. I was getting really tired, not having slept much throughout this ordeal. I found another, empty room down the hall, sat down on a couch, and, before I knew it, dozed off.

"Suddenly, I awoke, almost an hour later. I ran back to my dad's room in the intensive care ward. To my utter amazement, he was sitting up, no longer on a ventilator, looking around the room, fiddling with all the wires and tubes hooked up to him. His eyes were tracking perfectly, as he turned his gaze my way. He grinned at me. Now, I don't know if it was due to paralysis on one side of his face, or what, but then he winked and said, 'What happened?'" [2]

Greek air force pilot, Ioannis Kalaras, promised his mother he'd make several passes over her village while on a training flight. Trying to do so, he flew too low and struck some power lines. His aircraft crashed into a cemetery where he died, fifteen feet away from his father's grave. [3]

While walking through the tranquil ski country of Labelle County, just north of Montreal, Susan Paine and her friend were enjoying the lovely surroundings. "Through this tranquility," she wrote, "an enormous crow swooped, shrieking, so close to me that its wing tip brushed my temple. We identify crows by their raucous cawing, but this crow screamed. My friend said gently, 'That crow was speaking to you. The name crow comes from the Greek *cronin*, meaning 'Crier of Death'. I hope you haven't lost someone you love!' I glanced at my watch nervously. It was 4:33.

"We continued our walk home quietly, unable to dispel the ominous pall imparted by the crow. It was the last day of my visit. I was expected home the following day, on May 15. During the long drive, the word *cronin* circled like a bird inside my head.

"The ringing telephone greeted me as I opened the door to my house in Lansdowne, Ontario. My father's voice answered my hello. 'I've been trying to reach you all day,' he said. 'I'm afraid I have some sad news.

Your Uncle Alan (Ross) died of a heart attack yesterday afternoon'

"'What time?' I asked numbly.

"'About 4:30,' my father replied. 'Why do you ask?'"[4]

In Riverside, Illinois, a thief stole a blank payroll check, and looked through the phone book for a suitable name. He randomly picked the unusual name "Miles F. Huml", and went to the Riverside National Bank to cash the check. The cashier promptly called the police; she was Mrs. Miles F. Huml.[5]

During a matinee performance of the Broadway musical hit, *Sweeney Todd*, stars Angela Lansbury and Len Cariou barely escaped injury when a heavy bridge fell on the Uris Theater stage, missing them by inches. Lansbury was singing the song, "Nothing Can Harm You", at that very moment.[6]

Virgil Puckett of Alliance, Ohio, was walking through a cemetery some three hundred fifty miles from his home, when an old headstone toppled over on his leg, pinning him down. After someone finally pried the headstone off his leg, Puckett was shocked to read on it the name, "Virgil Puckett."[7]

American novelist, Stanley Loomis, was famous for his books on the French revolution, especially Paris in the Terror and The Fatal Friendship, dealing with Marie Antoinette and her lover. Reviewers and readers always commented on how graphically Mr. Loomis portrayed the victims of the guillotine, making the reader feel as if he were witnessing the scene.

Angela Lansbury in 2014.

While visiting Paris in December 1972, Loomis, forty-nine, was killed in an automobile accident on the Place de la Concorde, at the exact site of the guillotine that took the lives of Marie Antoinette and the other characters from Loomis' books.[8]

Two turn-of-the-20th Century Arab prophecies foretold the future of their land. One held that domination by the Turks would end when "the waters of the Nile flow into Palestine". The other predicted greatness for the city of Jerusalem when a "prophet of God from the west" would enter the city on foot. During World War One, in 1917, Sir Archibold Murray's British Army engineers laid a pipeline across the desert from the Suez Canal to Al Arish. Then, on 9 December, a British commander entered Jerusalem through the Jaffa gate to claim the city from the Turks. Out of respect for the religious center holy to Moslems, Christians and Jews, he entered on foot. In Arabic, "prophet of God" is Allah Nebi; the British commander was General Edmund Allenby.[9]

General Allenby enters Jerusalem.

During 1944, a woman, V.S., was living about three miles from Burton, in British Columbia. She was awakened early in the morning of 2 July by "the loudest noise I ever heard." Out of bed in an instant, she ran to see if an accident had occurred on the highway. She found nothing in view that could explain the magnitude of the explosion. She puzzled about it for a few days, but finally dismissed it as "one of those things."

Two weeks later, she received a letter from her sister-in-law saying that her brother had been killed in Trafalgar Square in London by a German V-2 rocket. The date of his death was 2 July 1944. V.S. immediately recalled the explosion that had wakened her and compared the London and Canadian times, adjusting for the difference. They were close enough to convince her the explosions occurred almost simultaneously --- one in England and the other in Canada. But how could she know whether the sound she heard tallied with the blast made by the V-2?

When she described what she had heard to veterans returning from London, she received the final confirmation. It was the loudest sound they had ever heard.[10]

One afternoon, alone and with nothing to do, Kandie Sanford happened to think of a cemetery she had passed on a Toledo, Ohio street. She remembered that each time she passed the place, she had a strong urge to enter. This particular afternoon, having time on her hands, she decided to walk through the cemetery. "I don't like cemeteries," Kandie said. "They're spooky. But something pulled me into that one. I walked around among the tombstones, half-wondering what I was doing there.

"At first, I just wandered aimlessly, but suddenly I felt a strong impulse to sit down and rest. I saw an overturned stone that seemed a good seat, and sat down. At that moment, I felt a terrible loneliness. I happened to glance at the name on the tombstone right beside me. Seeing the name Franklin Joseph Stanford gave me a real start, because that's my father's name. When I recovered from my sense of shock, I read the rest of the wording and learned this was my grandfather's grave! He was the first Franklin Joseph Stanford. My father is the second."[11]

Not long after the Whitney Museum of American Art opened in its new $6 million building in New York City, a slate sculpture by Japanese-born artist, Noguchi, toppled from its pedestal and shattered. The title of the sculpture, which must have tempted the fates, was "Humpty Dumpty."[12]

Ashton Miller of Nassau, Bahamas, never won anything, so he decided to buy a raffle ticket in the name of his dog, Benji. Sure enough, that ticket was drawn, and Miller won a twenty thousand-dollar car. The raffle sponsor was the Humane Society.[13]

Mrs. Gordon Hittenmark of Joplin, Missouri, jokingly scolded her dog for being such a big eater and not paying for his keep. That evening, he ran after something fluttering in the breeze, grabbed it and brought it home. It was a dollar bill.[14]

Early in 1973, an eighty-foot barge ran into a reef near Key Largo, Florida, spilling its cargo of twenty three hundred tons of molasses. Appropriately enough, the barge had grounded on Molasses Reef. [15]

A passing motorist reported to police that a car appeared to have torn through the fence around the Canton Town Cemetery in July 1973. Police found that the car driven by Glenora Fletcher of nearby Dorchester, Massachusetts, had careened out of control, slammed through the chain-link fence around the cemetery, slid down a one hundred-foot embankment and flipped over on its roof, breaking Mrs. Fletcher's neck and killing her. The woman's car finally had been stopped by a headstone on which the name "Fletcher" was engraved.[16]

A few months after Mrs. Sharon Bradshaw of Oakridge, Oregon, adopted a baby girl, a small mole appeared on the infant's leg. Mrs. Bradshaw has a mole the same size and shape at the same place on her own leg.[17]

In 1974, Vicky Hearst created what she imagined was an original stained-glass design for her school art class: a hooded cobra identical to the soon-to-be-infamous emblem of a self-styled terrorist group, the "Symbionese Liberation Front," whose members kidnapped her famous sister, Patricia Hearst, two months later.[18]

Mr. and Mrs. Gay Breneman of Clayton, Illinois, were married at 2:00 p.m. on 25 June. Twenty-five years later, Mrs. Breneman died at 2:00 p.m. on June 25.[19]

Mrs. Victor Sprangler of Chattanooga, Tennessee, heard her car sputter, and knew she was out of gas. As she steered her dying car to the side of a street, her car radio announced that her automobile license number had won a traffic contest. The prize --- ten gallons of gasoline. [20]

In Grand Rapids, Michigan, two brothers, Marcell Venden Heubel, fifty-one, and Clarence Heubel, fifty nine, were injured when the car Marcell was driving went out of control and crashed into Mt. Cavalry Cemetery. It ricocheted from marker to marker, finally stopping on a big headstone bearing the name: Vanden Heubel. [21]

Chapter 6

We are the Children
of Meaningful Coincidence

"Matter is but a thin, transparent film situated between Man and God."
—George Berkeley [1]

While teaching a class in synchronicity at Minnesota's Open U, in Minneapolis, my students sometimes wondered how they could encourage the frequency of this common, albeit mystical phenomenon in their lives. They wanted to experience more synchronous events, because the greater the number, the more recognizable the patterns in their lives became.

I told them about a simple, two-part exercise that seemed to work for me. All they had to do was sit quietly and focus on counting their breaths by sevens --- breathing normally from one to seven, then returning progressively to one; from one to fourteen, back again to one, and so forth, as high as a forty second cycle, if they desired. The objective here was nothing more than temporarily clearing the mind of all distractions we normally accumulate during the course of our daily lives. This is achieved by gradually decreasing our heart rate through conscious respiration. In other words, just quietly paying attention to our breathing will naturally slow one's cardiovascular system, thereby pumping less blood to the brain, resulting in a mildly altered state of awareness and inner calm. The procedure takes from twenty to forty minutes to complete, depending on how many breaths were counted.

Thus calmly prepared, our consciousness felt centered and ready for the second half of the meditation. This was a visualization of the seven major *chakras*, an Asian Indian word for "wheels," first described three thousand years ago as energy centers connecting the physical and spiritual sides in every man and woman. Shiva, the god of "body wisdom" (the subconscious), gave them to Vishnu as weapons with which to defend himself against all the hazards of physical life on Earth. Vishnu is a compassionate spirit that occasionally manifests himself in human form, appearing as Buddha, the Dalai Lama, et al. In any case, the chakras correspond to the fundamental aspects revealed in modern human psychology, beginning at the base of the spine with the root chakra. It is concerned with our regard for basic survival. Moving up along the spine to the top of the head, the six other *chakras* are concerned with pleasure (at the sacral), self-control (navel), love (heart), self-expression (throat), foresight (brow), and spiritual feeling (crown).

The second part of our mediation was aimed at setting these "wheels" in motion, because only after they begin to turn can they create vortexes linking body and mind. And the faster we can get them to whirl, the greater our sensitivity on all levels of awareness. I compared the human chakras to pistons in the engine of a car. If one or more pistons do not operate in sync with the rest, performance falls off. In order for the engine to run at its maximum potential, all pistons must fire at their designated time. If their timing is off, the automobile does not function as intended.

The same is true if one or more of our *chakra*s are not sufficiently activated, they drag down the power of the others, we fail to perform at our best, and our personality suffers. To get them all turning properly was the goal of the mediation I described for my students. By thereby putting themselves in accord with their inner and other selves, they were supposed to open themselves to greater possibilities for synchronicity, which is itself the meaningful harmony of events.

The *chakra*s are activated by simply visualizing each one turning with increasing velocity, until they less resemble rotating wheels than swirling whirlpools, such as occur in water draining from a bath-tub. Each chakra has its own colored light, too: red for the root chakra; orange for the sacral; yellow for the navel; green for the heart; sky-blue for the throat; indigo for the brow; and purple for the crown. As each *chakra* turns faster, its appropriate color is visualized as a light streaming from the vortex. Toward the end of the meditation, an imaginary rainbow emanates from the length of the spine, as all the *chakra*s become illuminated. The session concluded by taking three deep breathes, each one held for seven counts.

The benefits of the chakra meditation were immediately apparent after a few sessions. My students reported a sense of inner calm, but also vitality. Often acute anxieties and even aggression were muted, with a proportionate rise in mental clarity, objectivity, and self-assurance. Even days after the meditation, some individuals said they still had feelings of centeredness, serenity, well-being, and connectedness to all sentient beings. They experienced a kind of low-key, but lingering euphoria that produced a discernible decrease in stress.

Noticeable increases in the frequency of synchronicity did take place. More commonly, however, the students found that they were better able to understand the significance of otherwise inscrutable coincidences they felt were meaningful somehow, but could not until then explain. Still other meditators claimed to have experienced flashes of fresh insight that put them on new paths of thought. These personal events might be classified as "visions" --- sudden recognition of some truth with the power to transform previously held views of our world.

Like some of my students, I too experienced something of an insight during a *chakra* meditation while teaching. The session just concluded, when the concept for this book suddenly enfolded itself fully developed before me. In that moment, I recognized at once how the seven major chakras not only make up our constituent psychological parts as individuals, but I saw that the chakras themselves represent seven personality types that comprise the whole human race.

In other words, there are men and women who may be described as "Root Chakra Persons," or "Heart Chakra Persons", "Brow Chakra Persons", etc. To be sure, all people are blends of all these vortexes. But their leading character traits seem gathered into one that predominates. They are not, however, prisoners of the chakra that most defines their thoughts and actions. They may change from one to another, although how they think and behave at any given time indicates the chakra that most typifies them. No chakra is better or more necessary than any other. And all chakra personalities have their positive and negative qualities.

Recognizing the dominant chakra, both in ourselves and others, must lead to a heightened sense of identity and even compassion. We begin to discern a fundamental inter-connectedness of all human beings on a common spiritual level. Such recognition could also help us avoid those persons, often so deceptively charming, with potential for harm. No less importantly, being able to distinguish the seven human types can lead us to individuals capable of doing the most good for us.

The following chapters describe these fundamental types and inform readers how to distinguish them for improved relationships. My purpose has not been to categorize anyone on account of their particular personality, but to rather illuminate who and what they and we are in the context of their own and our leading chakra. In so doing, the thrust of this investigation into human character is to put mundane associations among our fellow men and women in touch with their spiritual common ground. This may be achieved by combining understanding of the chakras (those energy centers uniting body with soul) with the like phenomenon of synchronicity --- that modern-day mystical experience whose basis is inter-connectedness.

In examining these Seven Human Types, we look at ourselves and our fellow man in a different way. What people say and why they act as they do become less baffling. And our own motivations, which often mystify and even distress ourselves, grow clear. We are sometimes as much a stranger to ourselves as persons we meet. Yet, we may discover just who we and they are among the kinds of personalities expressed in our own chakras. The following seven chapters illuminate various types found everywhere throughout all humankind. These recognizable categories universally persist, regardless of cultural differences, because they are personifications of the chakras carried by every man and woman.

Together, the chakras comprise the full range of human potential. Their totality comprises the human soul. Descriptions of each one are divided into its positive and negative qualities. Both are then represented by a pair of personality types. These are further exemplified by well-known celebrities. In identifying others according to these fundamental types, we may grasp the motives and desires, strengths and weaknesses, of our fellow men and women.

Archetypical figures symbolic of specific *chakras* are cited to elucidate their particular personality through enduring oral folk tradition. As the great American scholar, Joseph Campbell, often pointed out, the function of myth is to dramatize truths otherwise beyond normal expression. Myth is a metaphor pointing beyond its own image to a more distant mystery. Its heroic or divine characters form a discourse between human consciousness and cosmic subconscious. Myths are symbolic of unseen, universal powers personified as gods or goddesses, themselves associated with various *chakras*. These divinities are personifications of energies that operate inside and around us. As such, they are collections of metaphors for the spirit, not historical or material facts. They embody understanding beyond obvious, physical evidence for the intangible, invisible, yet influential energies of the universe. In this regard, myth describes knowledge we intuit or sense, but cannot rationally explain. To demonstrate the universality of these spiritual metaphors, examples of immortals from the Hellenic West and the Japanese East are cited to parallel the qualities of each *chakra* personality.

The Japanese deities are especially cogent to our discussion, because a set of them known as the *Shichi Fukujin* exactly parallels the seven major human energy-centers. These seven Beings of Happiness are still evoked by pious travelers prior to undertaking an important journey. While divine examples demonstrate the psychological depths to which *chakra* imagery may probe, synchronicity takes place when the human microcosm and the cosmic macrocosm intersect at a special point in time to become one for an immeasurable instant.

At the opposite extreme of comparisons is the animal that most typifies each of the *chakras*. We instinctually respond to our fellow creatures as universal symbols, because their imagery haunts what Carl Jung called "the collective subconscious." Thus, the features of each *chakra* personality telescopes into humankind's deepest psychological plateaus through the perennial agencies of myth and symbol. They enable synchronicities, those little miracles through which a universal awareness communicates with us. We may speak to the gods in prayer, but meaningful coincidence is the medium whereby they speak to us.

So too, the intimate relationship between our spiritual and physical identities has been traced to a particular gland associated with each of the *chakra* personalities. The specific energy of each personality type impacts a corresponding area of the body. For example, the root chakra, with its emphasis on self-defense and physical dynamism, logically effects the adrenal gland, while the spiritually oriented crown chakra activates the pituitary, which secretes hormones associated with growth of both the body and soul.

Certain gemstones identified with the *chakras* may be used in meditation and/or as physical representations of the energy to be called upon or strengthened. Just as silicon, a form of quartz, is the most important mineral facilitator for the modern computer industry, select stones have likewise been found to interact on an energy level with particular psychological conditions and states of varying intensity. Traditionally, these equivalent gemstones are believed to magnify or amplify the powers associated with the chakras in question.

Metals mostly lack the augmentative qualities attributed to certain stones. While the heart chakra's copper or the crown chakra's gold are excellent conductors of energies in the human bio-electrical field, the root chakra's lead is little more than an insulator. But the tactile sense metals may engender when held in the hand by someone meditating on a corresponding energy vortex can at least assist in centering concentration. Proper incense is another physical contact we may establish with our chakras. It has a calming effect, thereby fostering our receptivity during meditation.

Use of an appropriate color is a visual stimulus that can combine with the olfactory and sensual aides of gemstones, metals and incense to evoke subtle potentialities. Human beings instinctively react to the same colors signified by their chakras. Red is generally regarded as an exciting color, orange is sensual, and yellow, commanding. Green is universally associated with growth, light-blue with clear water, azure with the sky, and purple with majesty. As Cirlot observes, "the seven colors are severally analogous to the seven faculties of the soul, to the seven virtues, to the seven vices, to the geometric forms, the days of the week..."[2] In Chapter 2, the mystical qualities of seven were described, as they particularly apply to our major energy centers. Seven is the Number of the Chakras, as established by the universality of its significance, and everywhere it is regarded as the Numeral of Completion.

A particular image or "icon" associated with each of the *chakra*s helps to identify them and codify their import. All these elements are keys we may use to unlock various secret compartments of each vortex personality. The chakra energy system, no less than the human skeleton, is hot-wired into every man and woman on Earth. Knowledge is always power. And understanding the fundamental workings of persons with whom we interact, we are better able to cooperate with them for mutual benefit, or, if need be, successfully defend ourselves against their negative aspects.

We may look among the seven major vortexes to find our own personality reflected there. Since they all combine to make up just who we are, we seem to be different *chakra*s at different times. But one energy center always predominates, and the more we know about it, the better we understand ourselves --- how to combat its less positive qualities which retard our success, while nurturing its merits to increase our power.

We are the Children of Meaningful Coincidence

Finding one's own chakra personality can be a form of self-discovery, wherein we trace those subtle themes and drives that mold our behavior and shape our personal destiny. An increased awareness of identity establishes a sense of purpose in the world, or, at least, reconciles ourselves to it.

Beyond these undeniably salubrious effects, appreciation of our place among the chakras begins to put us in accord with the invisible rhythms of life. Establishing a rapport with our own energy centers opens the door upon a broader dimension of spiritual order, the realm of synchronicity. This is where the true mystical experience of the 21st Century is to be found. The mystery cults of the past, with their ritual enactments of myth, took their secrets with them to the grave of history. Institutionalized religion replaced the mystical experience with dogma, while science rendered generations of skeptics and cynics. Establishing a genuine relationship between modern man's soul and the universal compassion that organizes all existence occurs in that connecting flash of meaningful coincidence.

Synchronizing the unseen but deeply felt vortexes which unite our own mind, body and spirit with that cosmic consciousness is to harmonize with it. The resulting spiritual bond is expressed in a modern mystical experience known as "meaningful coincidence." Over and above its benefits in terms of guidance or surety in the existence of a divine intelligence, an appreciation of synchronicity can instill a profound centeredness, an inner conviction that one's individual existence does have meaning and purpose after all, because we, together with every particle in the universe, comprise the sum total of God's identity. Each one of us is an inflection of the eternal spirit of creation moving through time. Activating our chakras begins to put us in touch with that pervasive force to expand and transform our lives as nothing else can.

Chapter 7
The Root Chakra Person

Located at the base of our spine, the root chakra is our first such vortex, because it is the foundation for our physical existence. Without it, we could not exist in the real world. All our natural instincts for self-preservation, survival and self-defense are focused in the root chakra. If its energy is extended beyond itself to connect with fellow human beings, we become loyal friends, supportive family members and good citizens. If its emphasis is upon itself, however, we degenerate into selfish misers and narrow-minded egotists. Humans are children of the planet, and the root chakra is our spiritual-physical connection to the mother of us all --- the Earth. This is more than some fatuous generalization: Our very bodies are made of iron, magnesium, potassium, copper, salt, and so forth --- all the minerals of the world in which we are born. Without them, we cease to be. Our very biological existence is physically chained to the Earth itself. Lightning flashing across the sky is the same electricity generated by our brain, heart and other muscles.

We maintain a fundamental relationship with our planetary parent through the root chakra, as does every living thing inhabiting its biosphere. These bio-spiritual energies are the consciousness of the Earth, and they connect with us through the root chakra. Only from this lowest level may they arise and intertwine with our own consciousness and arise, serpent-like, to empower the rest of our vortexes. Persons who acknowledge the root chakra as a basis upon which to stand for the attainment of their higher energy centers become fully-fledged men and women engaged in the development of all their human potential. For them, this chakra is not an end in itself, but a means for activating the complete set of their energy centers.

Other persons who choose to stay at the root chakra level are no better than the lowliest beasts, unable to conceive of life beyond a heartless struggle for survival and primal existence. For good or ill, the root chakra grounds us to the physicality of the world in which we live. But it also makes possible the realization of our hopes and dreams. In the spirit world, we are only thought-forms, ghosts, conscious, but unable to materialize anything. That is why we are on the Earth plain: To concretize our will. The root chakra allows us the manifestation of our creative ideas.

Some scholars extol the crown chakra for its ultimate spirituality at the expense of the lowly root chakra, on the opposite end of our spinal column. But without roots, all trees, even the Tree of Life, must perish. Without being grounded to Mother Earth through our root chakra, no subsequent spiritual development is possible. The highest leaves of all trees survive and draw their nourishment from the roots, far below. Similarly, all healing energies enter our psycho-physical system through the root chakra.

It is the well-spring of regeneration for the body, mind and soul. The root chakra is that primeval link between material and spiritual realities. After all, the Kundalini power lies coiled there, waiting to be aroused like a serpent from its hiding place summoned by a snake-charmer. This "coiled power" is an indwelling, instinctive or libidinal energy capable of putting us in accord with the Compassionate Intelligence that creates and oversees the universe and communicates with us through the symbolic language of synchronicity.

Root Chakra Character

"Survival" is the most important word in the root chakra person's vocabulary. His or her chief interest is in all things pertaining to their physical well-being. They work hard to secure the necessities of life for themselves and their families. They are practical persons, whose aim is to achieve material security. They prefer tangible reality and proven or established facts over speculation and theory. Sensible and practical, their first order of business is to secure an earthly existence for themselves. Self-respect is the degree of their success in either making a living as a wage-earner or someone simply trying to stay alive in a life-and-death situation. They are physical achievers who will do anything to obtain a sense of security.

Root Chakra Personalities are acutely aware of themselves. Their devotion to loyalties are passionate and local. In other words, they feel strong emotional ties to their immediate family, tribe, gang, club or restricted clan of some kind. The myth or world-view of the group to which they are viscerally affiliated is their own, personal outlook by which they live. Root chakra persons have a heightened sense of identity, because they see themselves as direct extensions of the group from which they spring or are connected. They are very defensive of these loyalties, while maintaining a monolithic belief system that gives meaning to their lives. To them, situations, problems and other people are cut and dried in black and white, good or bad, desirable or repulsive, with no middle ground. Such persons are firm of purpose, resolute and self-confident. They have very specific views and opinions, and equate criticism or alternate ideas with the subversion of their world-outlook, which is based on personal feelings of security.

The root chakra person regards life as a "to-be-or-not-to-be" proposition. He or she has alternative potential for either selfless devotion to their own group, or self-worship and greed. They may view life from the very narrow perspective of their own struggle for existence, to which everything and everyone are incidental. As an example of how individuals may change the chakra emphasis of their lives, someone dedicated primarily to spiritual matters may at least temporarily exchange their crown chakra personality for a root chakra if their physical existence is threatened. Conversely, a Root Chakra Personality may be transformed by an act of compassion that breaks through his or her selfishness into the broader love of the heart chakra.

Preservation is the overall concern of root chakra persons. If they are spiritually well-balanced, they are practical and frugal. They are sometimes idealistic, becoming conservationists or ecologists who work to save our planet's natural environment from the ravages of industrialization. The root chakra person often recognizes the historical foundations on which his or her people stand, and strives to preserve the national understructure of their past greatness and continued existence. They are not dreamers, but grasp the essential importance of most situations. They are no-nonsense individuals, more serious than whimsical, less interested in dubious speculation than physical reality.

Their souls are grounded in everyday life. To be "grounded" means that all their material means of support are very deliberately controlled. Everything for maintaining their survival --- financial savings, health insurance, solid shelter, employment security, enough food and clothing --- are paramount. While everyone living in modern society must deal with these concerns, they are commonly the central focus of the root chakra personality, to whom all other issues are subordinate. Such persons are traditionalists. They enjoy all the "classics" in art, music, literature and architecture, and heartily dislike anything avant-garde. They are uncomfortable with modern fads or passing fashions, opting instead for established forms. They prefer law and order to social protest, unless revolution promises to re-assert fundamental principles perceived as endangered. They often become historians, because they have a superior sense of the past, although they may be inferior office workers if called upon to learn innovative methods of production. The excellent root chakra historian who matured before the advent of computers may not be able to successfully operate a PC. For example, America's outstanding novelist from the mid-20th to early 21st Centuries, Gore Vidal, churned out his manuscripts on a manual typewriter.

But a disproportionate level of root chakra energy warps the personality. Politically, the root chakra man or woman may become ultra-conservative, resistant on principle to all change, even the most universally beneficial, because he or she regards any alteration in the status quo as a personal affront to their physical well-being. The negative side of the root chakra is selfishness, stiff-necked stubbornness, heartless avarice and naked greed. The pointless acquisition of wealth for its own sake springs from deep-seated feelings of insecurity, an unresolved lack of self-esteem, and unjustified fear of poverty. For such persons, the worth of every human being, starting with themselves, is reckoned exclusively by their bank balance. Money alone becomes the sole standard by which all values are determined.

The root chakra's dark side is implicit in the old Law of the Jungle: "Trust no one!" But the base instinct apparent in this dehumanizing judgment of one's fellow creatures are engendered by even deeper, more primeval impulses. They are the resonating echoes of our ancient savagery, not only as early humans, but of our animal nature. Our first energy center swirls with genetic memories carried down into our present phobias and hatreds over thousands and millions of years of evolution, even from our pre-human origins. Those were the days, unthinkably long ago, when we fought and were sometimes killed by monsters against which we had as much defense as a mouse from a cat. The trauma of those events that molded the long course of our development from proto-hominid to homo-sapiens has never left us. They still impact our present-day character. The beast within dwells at the root chakra level. All our innate capacity for violence and cruelty lies there. Whenever its dark potential emerges, the world experiences satanic phenomena, like the Aum Shinrikyo's gas attacks on Japanese subways or Tootzie genocide in Ruanda. Every man and woman carries this potential for barbarism like a boil of poison in their root chakra. All of us at some time or other experience the irrational thoughts or urges it sends into our unconscious mind as nightmares, or attempts to manifest in our waking lives, especially under periods of emotional stress. We do not sin in possessing such destructive impulses, because they are part of the human condition.

Our root chakra still resonates to the demonic drives left over from our ancestral struggle to survive against a prehistoric world of monsters. We may feel ashamed to even acknowledge they exist, but we are guiltless until we follow them. Yet, they must be recognized, else we inadvertently give them power. A devil is any negative force we have empowered by trying to suppress or ignore it. Such forces are like little, spoiled children who scream louder the more they are ignored. Better to recognize such wicked impulses as a legacy all human beings share, like it or not, and find safe, even useful places for them in our lives. "The strength of the vampire," Professor Van Helsing explains in Bram Stoker's *Dracula*, "is that people do not believe in him." [1]

When Buddha overcame devils and monsters, he did not kill them. Instead, he put them to work, usually as temple guardians. In following his example, we understand that our demons are not destructible, because they are part of our own nature. Buddha-like, we should find similarly gainful employment for them, making them work for, not against us, by diverting their dynamic energies into the cause of our higher self. In short, we master the root chakra; it does not master us.

Root Chakra Celebrity-A:
Hiru Onoda

During 1944, Hiru Onoda was a foot-soldier in the Army of Imperial Japan. Like millions of his fellow infantrymen, he was dedicated to honorably serving his country. In the course of military operations on one of the many islands of the Philippines, Onoda and a handful of other men from his unit became separated from the main body of troops and lost contact with their command. The last orders they received instructed them to hold their secluded position in the mountains.

Hiru Onoda gives the Japanese Imperial Army salute

Hordes of enemy forces eventually moved around and beyond the small group of hidden soldiers. Days, then weeks went by without further radio communication from their superior officers. Even the sounds of fighting and military maneuvers were no longer heard from the jungles below. In time, it became obvious that Onoda and his comrades had been left behind when Japanese forces evacuated the island. Surrender was not an option, because they received no orders to disband. Their objectives now were to continue monitoring the enemy whenever possible, while trying to survive. After their meager rations ran out, they hunted monkeys and rats for food, or skirmished for eatable fruits. Weeks stretched into months. Sickness ravaged the few soldiers, and they began to die.

In late 1945, the war was over, but they could not have known what had taken place outside of the Philippines. Eventually, all the marooned infantrymen died, save for Onoda. The decade came to an end. But he continued to live, true to his oath of allegiance. All through the 1950s, he survived alone in a cave on little more than whatever the jungle could provide him. He made clothes from plants, and reckoned time by observing the sun, moon and stars. Occasionally, he stealthily raided a Philippine village, down below, for a few supplies small enough he could carry back to his place of concealed refuge.

Onoda continued to live unknown but successfully in his mountain vastness. Only in the early 1960s did one of his former superior officers find the solitary figure and convince him that World War Two had ended nearly twenty years before. When he was returned to Japan, doctors examining him were surprised by the forty-year-old man's robust physical condition and mental acuity. Emotionally too, he was not trapped in memories of the past, but adjusted rapidly to modern society, which he critically and insightfully contrasted to the world left behind in 1944.

Hiru Onoda idealized the will-to-survive explicit in the root chakra personality. The loner's solitary existence depended upon an intense devotion to his national community, as epitomized in the Army. While his life had narrowed to issues primarily concerned with food and shelter, he flourished in a state of honor, transforming him from a common soldier, one among millions, into a hero admired around the world for his unbroken loyalty and extreme survival ability.

Root Chakra Personality-B:
Mikhail Khodorkovsky gives the Communist "clenched-fist" salute.

From the collapse of the Soviet Union arose another tyranny run by financial oligarchs. These were a handful of money-barons who amassed phenomenal fortunes by buying up the country's natural resources and institutional wealth at drastically reduced prices during rigged auctions in the last decade of the 20th Century. Foremost among them was Mikhail Khodorkovsky. Like his fellow members of the super-rich man's club, he piled up a vast economic empire on the backs of average Russians, who could never profit from his gigantic corporate acquisitions. Instead, they were forced to labor overtime at starvation wages.

Although now a self-proclaimed entrepreneur, immediately prior to the USSR's demise, Khodorkovsky belonged to the Young Communist League. But illimitable greed, not ideology, was his sole motivation. He rose to political prominence because it gave him entree into circles that made possible his state property deals. The first of such moves was a take-over of the Menatep Bank, through which he snatched up massive amounts of shares in companies that had been privatized at bargain prices. With this expanded wealth, he seized the Yukos oil conglomerate for a knocked-down $350 million. After firing all but the most essential staff to maintain its bare operation, the up-and-coming oligarch parlayed Yukos into a private annual income of one billion dollars over the next eight years.

Meanwhile, growing millions of Russians found making a subsistence living barely possible, save for the most menial jobs, whenever infrequently available. Khodorkovsky's mountainous assets were heaped up by armies of workers suffering under appalling, dangerous conditions for puny wages that kept them forever indebted to his financial imperium. But in 2003, the oligarch went too far. He was arrested for failure to appear in court on a warrant accusing him with fraud, forgery, and embezzlement on an unprecedented scale. The Grand Rabbi of Moscow, Vladimir Perlzweig, warned that Khodorkovsky endangered his fellow Jews with an anti-Semitic reaction, because of the abominable example he set. "It now appears," Perlzweig remarked sadly, "that Mr. Khodorkovsky's financial contributions to our various charities were expedient in buying him a good reputation. We, too, have been used."[2]

Every ruble of Khodorkovsky's enormous wealth was stained with bloody toil and sweated misery. He lived entirely out of his root chakra, like a crab in its shell, incessantly shoveling a super-abundance of substance into its mouth. For all his staggering fortune, he was an abject failure in human terms. He lost the love of his fellow human beings by horribly exploiting them, then made the mistake of cashing in his own spiritual insecurities for exchange securities.

Mikhail Khodorkovsky is a negative root chakra type going all the way back to the Greek legend of King Midas. Similar to his royal Phrygian predecessor, everything the billionaire touched turned into loveless gold. His ilk survives today, not only in the likes of other selfish manipulators like himself, but in the dark capacity of the root chakra possessed by each one of us.

Greek Root Chakra Deity:
Hades

He is the ruler of the underworld, the abode of the souls of the dead. They join him in his subterranean realm ill-lit by millions of precious jewels decorating his huge, gloomy palace. Despite his riches and power, Hades is a morose deity, because his gemstones are as cold as the ghosts that flit about his shadowy kingdom. Even so, he knows all the secrets of the world since it began, and his heart is happy at the return of his wife each autumn. He kidnapped Persephone long ago, then tried to bribe her with his great wealth. But she would not trade all his diamonds for one day in the sunlight. She did agree, however, to spend half of the year with him.

Persephone's compassion brought warmth in the Underworld for the first time, and ameliorated its darker aspects. Henceforth, Hades reigned as a kinder, though still somber monarch of the dead.

Japanese Root Chakra Deities:
Hani-yasu-bime-no-kami, Asuku-nyorai and Ebisu

Hani-yasu-bime-no-kami is an Earth deity, the goddess of industry, concerned with practical affairs and all things necessary for material existence. As "Hani-yasu Princess Deity", she is the patroness of commerce. Probably her earliest manifestation goes back many thousands of years, to the very beginnings of Japanese civilization in the First Jomon Epoch, about ten thousand years ago. "Jomon" derives from the sophisticated pottery which typified this early period, when Hani-yasu-bime-no-kami was known as the "Clay-Tempering Deity." It is a title by which she is still honored by potters. Root chakra imagery is clear in her myth, which describes Hani-yasu-bime-no-kami's power to transform the chaos of mud into the organized, up-lifting form of a finished vessel. So too, root chakra energy changes fundamental need into physical survival.

Hani-yasu-bime-no-kami's companion is Asuku-nyorai. Known today as "the Immovable Buddha," in pre-Buddhist times he was regarded as the living personification of the Earth. Like the Greek Hades, he possessed knowledge of the unseen world. His name signifies the power to manifest images or ideas. Ashuku-nyorai is the keeper of the pillars on which our planet stands. He holds them steady until humans neglect to pay him homage. If the abuse is allowed to continue, he grows angry and violently shakes his world-pillars, causing earthquakes.

Ebisu, one of the *Shichi Fukujin*, or seven Beings of Happiness, is associated with the root chakra, because he is the divine patron of honest labor, and often depicted as a fisherman with his catch.

A Root Chakra People:
The Americans

Global commercialism has Americanized civilization, shifting emphasis from spiritual goals to economic priorities, thereby relegating all other values to purely secondary status, if not discarding them altogether. At the core of this sovereign materialism is a persistent sense of insecurity. Many Americans endeavor to overcome it by becoming so-called "workaholics" --- laboring day and night, long after the necessities of life have been obtained. In this frenetic process, the means and ends of living become confused, until any semblance of significance in life is reduced to economic terms.

The "American Dream" formerly signified liberty. Today, it means simply wealth --- not of the mind, heart or spirit. As some indication of the shift from spiritual to materialist emphasis in the United States, the tallest buildings in American cities are no longer churches, but corporate headquarters. Americans nonetheless have an unrivaled heritage of freedom, in which a practical balance was more than two hundred years ago struck by the country's founding fathers between the material necessities of life and other, higher values. That balance has been terribly upset, but the potential for re-establishing its equilibrium still exists.

A primeval North American people are the Eskimo, masters of survival, and the only people able to survive in their Arctic homeland. It is difficult to conceive of a more physically challenging environment. Yet, generations of Eskimo continue to thrive near the top of the world after unknown thousands of years. They do not have much for material culture, but what artifacts they do possess are almost strictly utilitarian. Severe natural surroundings determine virtually every aspect of their lives. The rules of existence are clearly drawn for them everywhere they look. And they must strictly abide by those rules to survive.

Consequently, the Eskimo are known for great determination and strong family loyalty. A perpetual winter realm of ice has born in them ingenuity and perseverance. But it has also isolated them from the outside world. Their fixation on survival makes them oblivious to the rest of mankind, and limits their horizons of existence to a bleak domain of snow and sky that often merges into a colorless, single-dimensional whiteness.

A Root Chakra Animal:
The Snake

The serpent coils in its hole like Kundalini energy in the root chakra. The snake lives only to kill, consume and breed. Its dwelling is in darkness, within the bowels of the Earth. Yet, when it appears on the verge of death, it throws off its flaking scales, and puts on a bright, new skin, as though miraculously restored to life. Here lies the serpent-wisdom and danger of the root chakra.

A Root Chakra Profession:
The Military

A soldier performs his duties in life-and-death situations. "Kill or be killed" is the principle focus of all his training and expertise. Although schooled in self-defense, he is taught to think of himself as part of a team demanding his absolute loyalty. Soldiery is an ambivalent profession, just as the root chakra is a conflicted energy center. Warriors have the potential for the noblest human virtues, particularly self-sacrifice for others (so long as they belong to the appropriate group), individual courage, and purposeful action.

They may also possess limitless capacity for ruthlessness and cruelty to innocent persons outside their group, and are afflicted by simplistic, myopic views of the world around them.

The Root Chakra Gland:
The Adrenals

The adrenals are responsible for balancing salt and water in the body. They can trigger "fight-or-flight" response in emergency situations threatening personal survival. These are two, small, triangle-shaped endocrine glands that are almost identical. They secrete adrenaline, which increases heart-beat and blood-flow rate, putting the body in a stress mode for some extraordinary physical task. They are psychologically activated by a perceived challenge to one's well-being. This relationship between mind and body exemplifies the Chakra System itself, which functions as an intermediary connecting the physical and spiritual dimensions of our identity.

Persons experiencing lower back pain for no apparent medical reason are usually suffering from a malfunctioning root chakra blocked by intense feelings of insecurity.

Root Chakra Food:
Bread

The "staff of life," the gift of Mother Earth.

Root Chakra Gemstones:
Bloodstone, Hematite and Garnet

A green chalcedony flecked with red spots, bloodstone is associated with calming influences and the removal of discord. It preserves the general health of anyone who wears it, especially for sufferers of inflammatory illnesses. Bloodstone has long been credited with dispelling nightmares, which are often repressed impulses from our early evolution.

Garnet brings out the primeval energies of the root chakra, which, if given free reign, reveal its darker aspects. However, its power, when controlled, may be put to creative use.

Hematite is a red iron oxide. When abraded, it reveals a red streak responsible for its name, from the Greek word for "blood", *haima*. Soldiers in the ancient world rubbed their bodies with hematite before going into battle, because its color and iron content were associated with Ares, the god of war. The earliest known reference to the stone highlights its root chakra qualities. During the early 1st Century B.C., a Babylonian gemologist, Azchalias, taught that hematite softened the hearts of otherwise stern kings and judges.

Root Chakra Metal:
Lead

Lead signifies the individual human potential for transmutation from visible, dead weight to the invisible lightness of breath (spirit). This was the real goal of medieval European alchemists, who sought to change lead into gold; i.e., the base matter of materialism into spiritual enlightenment.

Root Chakra Incense:
Myrrh

Myrrh was a temple-maiden who gave birth to Adonis, the ancient Greek, Christ-like god of life and death. Even the early Christians referred to the mother of Jesus as "Myrrh." A particular incense burned during the mysteries of Adonis was given the name "Myrrh", associated with the relationship between life and death.

Root Chakra Icon:
A Life-Preserver

Root Chakra Color:
Blood red, or fire red.

Dr. Jolan Jacobi, in her study of Carl Jung, points out that his clients usually regarded red as "the color of the pulsing blood and fire of life, for the surging and tearing emotion."[2] In Pueblo Indian religious symbolism of the American southwest, red is associated with the south, the Direction of Becoming. The Tennessee Cherokee identify red with east, because that is the direction from which material success arrives.

Root Chakra Function:
Grounding

Root Chakra Issue:
Survival

Root Chakra Goal:
Stability

Lesson the Root Chakra Needs to Understand:
Everything material is transitory.

Negative Root Chakra Aspect:
Selfishness, dead-end materialism

Positive Root Chakra Aspect:
Manifesting creativity, physical security, well-being, prosperity

Chapter 8
The Sacral Chakra Person

The second human energy vortex is called the Sacral, because it is located in the area of the sacrum, Latin for "the sacred bone," similarly known to the earlier Greeks. They understood its transitional position separating the beast from the human, as the *hieron osteon*. The sacrum is a thick, triangular bone situated at the lower end of the spinal column, but above its base, where it joins both hip-bones to form the dorsal part of the pelvis. The sacral chakra corresponds to our genital organs, because it concerns our natural capacity for pleasure. Bare existence, as expressed in the root chakra, without enjoyment is mere survival, not life. An act of creation generates pleasure, so the sacral chakra is activated by every form of happiness we experience, from the act of sexual intercourse and every manifestation of physical exhilaration to intellectual fulfillment. Our appetites and sense of taste --- the things we find attractive --- arise from the sacral chakra.

If the first vortex embodies our survival instincts, the second is the seat of our physical drives. They are the inducements Nature uses to preserve and perpetuate our species. Food tastes good, so we eat and survive. Sex feels good, so we make love and our race is renewed. If we refrained from enjoying these inborn pleasures, we would starve to death and mankind would become extinct. Yet, some religious leaders claim the quest for physical happiness leads along the slippery slope of disaster. They urge renunciation and celibacy. To be sure, the risk of habituation lies in simple enjoyment. As metaphysical investigator, David Pond warns, "We tend to lose awareness during the pursuit of pleasure."[1]

There is nothing intrinsically wrong with wine; even Jesus Christ drank on occasion. However, over-indulgence leads to alcoholism. Every pleasure, no matter how innocent, bears within itself the potential for misconduct. But to simply deny our natural urges because they might lead to our downfall is sometimes a form of cowardice, a refusal to take responsibility for our behavior as mature adults. The sacral chakra says "yes!" to life. But, like its six counterparts, it is open to use or abuse.

It distinguishes the lowest creatures, which dwell on the base level of simple survival, from the first level of outward-facing consciousness. And it is here that synchronicity can begin to manifest, because the chief component of meaningful coincidence is passion. A root chakra life represents the Right-Hand Path of obedience to established authority, earning a living, going along with majority opinion, and generally doing everything expected of a well-kept citizen. Traveling the Left-Hand Path, as Joseph Campbell, termed it, is living "the authentic life," whether or not others approve of your course; to follow what is in your heart to do; to act upon your own truth.

As soon as a person steps from the Right-Hand to the Left-Hand Path in pursuit of that which means the most in his or her life, synchronicities begin to constellate as forms of guidance and reassurance. Passion, therefore, is the mainspring of meaningful coincidence, and the sacral chakra is its headquarters.

The Sacral Chakra Character

We have an instinct for joy. Happiness has always been and still is the common goal of humankind. Ultra-sound scans of expectant mothers reveal how unborn infants actually smile within the womb. Such an inherent delight in life bears out the veracity of the sacral chakra as our natural capacity for enjoyment. So, when Campbell admonished his students to "follow their bliss," he was telling them, in effect, to bring their lives in accord with their second chakra.

This powerful vortex is particularly exemplified in some persons more than others. They are usually high-energy men and women, sometimes engaging in the performing arts, a profession requiring often intense physical participation. Like the twin theatrical masks of comedy and tragedy, the sacral personality may be either very jovial or exceptionally sad; the former, as a direct expression of the chakra energy charging his or her life; the latter, if that energy is seriously blocked, either due to external circumstances, or arising from an imbalance within themselves. If the root chakra person is introverted, or self-absorbed, the sacral chakra person is outgoing and extroverted. Fear of loss motivates the root chakra, while the sacral chakra's need is physical pleasure.

The personalities of this energy vortex include the gourmet, epicure or connoisseur. Surely, one of the goals of our lives should be to enjoy the pleasures of the beautiful planet on which we live. Sacral chakra persons believe that going through life without thoroughly appreciating it is like rushing through an art gallery without giving its paintings more than a glance. To neglect our innate capacity for enjoyment is against Nature. We do, after all, live in a physical world of the senses which attract us to beauty in endless forms. The sacral personality is sensitive to comfort, and may develop into an artist or art-lover. His or her life can assume real value in recognizing beauty, both natural and man-made, and participating in its creation.

But excess makes the difference between healthy appreciation and destructive over-indulgence, although the border separating both is often indistinct. And making the pursuit of physical pleasure the goal of one's life must inevitably exhaust it. Our consciousness (or "soul"), with its yearning for spiritual truths, is confined inside a flesh-and-blood body lusting for the physical pleasures of the material world through which it walks. This is the basis of the conflict between our spiritual longing and physical needs. If we incline more to one at the expense of the other, we feel guilty or regretful.

The ancient Egyptians understood this fundamental conflict well, and explained it in simple terms. They believed that the human being is a kind of bubble composed of two, basic parts: the *ba* and the *ka*. The former represents everything in us that aspires to lofty ideas and feelings --- virtue, compassion, creativity, duty, honor, selflessness, and so forth. The *ka* --- literally, "shadow" --- is our need to survive in the real world --- to earn a living, defend ourselves, and reproduce our own kind. Neither half is better or worse than the other. Both are necessary for a proper buoyancy with which to float through life. If our *ba* dominates us with excessive concern for non-Earthly matters, we become too light, and our physical existence suffers, because our yearning is for the Next World. If the *ka* demands more than its share of material pleasures, we grow heavy, and our spirit is dragged down. In order for us to successfully pass through the real world, the *ba* and *ka* must be balanced, each given its proper recognition. At death, the Egyptians believed, the *ba* and *ka* were separated from their life-long connection. Bound as it was to all the physical things of our planet, the *ka* became a "shadow" of its now-lost, physical desires, while the living *ba* --- portrayed in temple art as a human-headed bird --- flew up to heaven.

The sacral character belongs to the *ka*. If mortals understand that they must balance their pleasures against the spiritual needs of the *ba*, then they may enjoy themselves successfully throughout life. Only when they accumulate too many pleasures for their spiritual side to compensate do they sink toward annihilation.

Foreigners sometimes wonder why so many women in the United States are grotesquely overweight. Indeed, U.S. government studies show that Americans in general and women in particular are averaging higher rates of chronic obesity than any other nation in the world. The answer is simple: they are mostly self-indulgent. Food has become the most important thing in their lives. They are pitiful examples of the sacral chakra personality gone horribly wrong. Aside from their increased chances for heart failure, bone deformation, muscle deterioration and a host of serious medical problems, to say nothing of early death, such persons typically push out of their lives all those higher qualities which define the soul from the body --- the human from the beast.

Men and women similarly addicted to smoking, narcotics, alcohol, sex, or any number of obsessions that exert an overpowering hold on their free will have over-indulged the sacral chakra's natural capacity to enjoy the pleasures of this world. They have weighted it against their other six energy centers, and begun a process that must inevitably destroy them all.

Sacral Chakra Celebrity-A:
Josephine Baker

She was the most photographed woman in the first half of the 20th Century. Remarkably, every photo taken of her in which she was surrounded by a crowd shows each person wearing an identical facial expression of bright joy. She seemed to literally radiate excited happiness to everyone in her vicinity, a radiance that energized them and they reflected back. It was not the result of anything she said or did, nor her appearance. She simply was Josephine Baker.

When she made her 1925 debut in Paris, she was utterly unknown --- a young Black-American performer the French came to see as a curiosity, more than a serious artist. But she took them completely by surprise. Josephine fairly exploded on the stage in a dance number of such unprecedented energy that her success was intense and instantaneous. For the next fifty years, she reigned as Europe's super-star, dancing, singing, recording, and acting in films. Everything she put her hand to became a huge success. Although a great dancer, she was not the best, and retired from that aspect of her career relatively early. Her first recordings reveal little vocal ability, but she eventually blossomed into a very fine singer, although, again, there were other female vocalists of superior talent. She was a fine actress, but not among the century's best. While certainly glamorous, she was less beautiful than many other famous women of her day. What, then, enabled Josephine Baker to rise so far above all her contemporary performers?

The question is complicated by a life that would appear to have absolutely forestalled any measure of public success. Born into the poverty of an East Saint Louis ghetto, in 1906, she was an irrepressibly happy little girl, oblivious to the squalor that surrounded her childhood. Her later life was filled with personal hardships, including a miscarriage, failed marriages, bankruptcy, eviction, and a prolonged, painful illness that almost killed her. In spite of these challenges, her exuberance was infectious. It imbued all her artistic talents with a unique energetic quality. She channeled the inherent potential of her sacral chakra into everything she did, allowing it to imbue her entire personality. Josephine's fully awakened vortex was the driving force of her life. It was the spiritual vigor that empowered her performance skills, and stamped them with her own, inimitable style. Her public appearances elicited almost hysterical ovations from audiences, whose own sacral chakras had been highly charged through the energized field of sympathetic resonance she generated.

A particular case in point demonstrated her sacral power to influence others was Josephine's 1930 performance in Vienna. A week before her arrival, the leaders of Austrian Catholicism undertook a public campaign of defamation against her, condemning her as "satanic," because of her "lewd" dances on the Paris stage. As she entered the city, all the cathedrals and churches tolled their funeral bells lamenting her arrival, and her car was assaulted by crowds if incensed people, convinced she was the devil incarnate. "They opposed me with true Christian hatred," she later recalled.[2] In the theater that evening, the audience was no less hostile, and the nervous management forbade her from appearing. She ignored them, and walked on stage alone before an enraged mob that screamed cat-calls and hurled rotten vegetables at her.

Dressed in a modest, full-length gown, she stood expressionless, unmoved and without a word throughout the torrent of abuse. It lasted for at least ten minutes, until the crowd, amazed at her brave self-control, began to settle down. When conditions had quieted, she signaled the cowering musicians to emerge from their hiding place in the orchestra pit, and they began to play the first number. It was a simple American lullaby, "Pretty Little Baby," which she sang in a small but firm voice through to the end without interruption. After several moments of tension-filled silence following its conclusion, the audience burst out into thunderous applause, as much for Josephine's lone courage, as for her singing. Having thus won over her violently antagonistic listeners, they stayed for the remainder of her performance, showering her at the end with loud acclaim and requests for encores.

From her Viennese victory, she went on to conquer the rest of Austria, despite endless anathema hurled at her from the Church. Josephine Baker understood the power of the sacral chakra. By calling upon its great capacity for joy and infusing its spirit throughout her life, she triumphed over opposition that would have overwhelmed others less empowered.

Sacral Chakra Celebrity-B:
Marilyn Monroe

Another famous entertainer named Norma Jean Baker, likewise used her second chakra as a spiritual engine to power her life and career. Under the stage-name of "Marilyn Monroe," she soared to the heights of fame as a mid-20th Century sex-goddess. While other women may have been more beautiful or talented, her sacral energy was stronger and less restricted by inhibitions. Consequently, her screen appearances emit an engaging potency unlike any other performer of her generation. The secondary chakra vitality she unleashed through her films stamped them as her own. That is why, half a century later, they continue to attract viewers, most of whom were born after her death, and will doubtless continue to allure audiences for the foreseeable future. Marilyn Monroe was the personification of a "classic" artist --- less for what she did, than for what she was. It was her sacral-powered character that made Marilyn great, not her questionable abilities as an actress. As an earlier American cinematic sex-goddess, Mae West, said of herself, "It's not what I say, but the way that I say it."[3]

Chakra energy is hazardous material, however, especially that found in the second vortex, with all its physically tempting pitfalls. It ran away with Marilyn Monroe. She exercised her sacral power on and off screen, a failure in discernment that blurred the distinction between art and reality. She did not control that pleasure-power by confining it to her performances. Instead, she used a kind of sexual bribery to drive her career toward higher levels of success. Along with her personal surrender to the second chakra came other, baser temptations in the form of narcotics and alcohol. But she was drunk on a much more potent intoxicant --- extra-artistic power. Through her, even the president of the United States betrayed his wife, the mother of his children, to become her lover. By that time, Marilyn Monroe was no longer in charge of her own life. She was dominated by perhaps the most self-destructive of all chakras, and died prematurely, still a young woman.

Greek Sacral Chakra Deity:
Aphrodite

A particularly dramatic statuary group from antiquity may be seen in Rome's Vatican Museum. It is the full-size sculpted marble of a beautiful woman representing the goddess of love with an armed soldier personifying Mars, the war-god. He is caught in the act of withdrawing his sword, an aggressive but uncertain expression on his face, as she gently restrains him. The extra-artistic associations implicit in this ancient sculpture are many, but at least one suggests the ameliorating effect of the sacral on the root chakra. The work infers a balance between peace and violence. In certain circumstances, one may be more preferable than the other, but the ideal, as intimated by the statuary, is a shared relationship. That is the same goal all chakra-workers strive to attain: the harmonization of their fully activated energy centers.

Of course, the love-goddess portrayed in stone is Aphrodite. Her deification of the sacral chakra is evident in her ability to grant beauty, grace --- poise or balance --- and elegance to the most deformed creatures (the deformed Hephaestus was her husband). In other words, sacral power makes even otherwise unattractive persons desirable in the eyes of their beloved. She excites love between men and women, and rekindles extinguished passions. Aphrodite shows that such feelings are not confined to human beings, but, on the contrary, they are bound to all other living things through the drive to reproduce themselves. She is also the divine patron of spring. The fourth month in the Western calendar, April, when life returns to the world, was named after her title, *Aphrilis*.

Because lovers feel they were somehow destined to meet, she may be considered a goddess of synchronicity. According to Zenon, a sage who headed an Aphrodite cult on Cyprus during Classical Times, she taught that "mankind and the universe were bound together in a system of fate".[4] The goal of human existence, Zenon taught, should be to live in harmony with the great mechanism of nature. In her dual personality, the goddess who personified her Cyprian cult was additionally called Aphrodite

Urania-Pandemos to epitomize her deification of the sacral chakra, with its diversity of pleasures. As Urania, she embodied spiritual love. In the guise of Pandemos, she was sexual pleasure. Both aspects were simultaneously celebrated by the Greeks during the *Aphrodisia*, festivals in her honor often observed throughout the ancient Mediterranean World.

Japanese Sacral Chakra Deities:
Uzume and Jurojin

Amaterasu was so angry with the extremely rude behavior of Susa-no-wo, the storm-god, she indignantly shut herself up in a cave, known as the Heavenly Rock Dwelling. Horribly insulted by her twin brother, she refused to ever show her face again. Now, her disappearance was a terrible calamity for the world, because she was the sun-goddess. The entire Earth was plunged into darkness. All the other eight hundred deities tried to entice her emergence, but she refused to even listen to them. They piled beautiful jewels in front of her cave, decorated its exterior with rare song-birds and placed before it a celestial mirror, all to no avail. In desperation, they enlisted the aid of Ame-no-Uzume. The goddess of mirth, whose name meant "Whirling," went before the mouth of the cave lit by torches. In their lurid glare she told risque stories, while executing a sexy dance, her beautiful body naked, except for an elaborate headdress of tinkling gold and silver flowers, a flimsy, moss sash around her slender waist, and a sprig of bamboo grass wielded in her right hand to chase away all unhappiness.

The other gods laughed and applauded the little goddess's energetic performance. Unable to restrain her curiosity, Amaterasu emerged from her subterranean hide-out to ask how they could laugh when the whole planet was enveloped in darkness. One of the divinities answered they were celebrating a deity who was not so peevish. Amaterasu's jealousy was piqued, but she paused to pick up the celestial mirror intended to distract her. It did just that, and, while she admired her radiant beauty, the lesser gods hurriedly stretched a "Rope of No-Return" across the front of the Heavenly Rock Dwelling, preventing her re-entry. Ever since, the sun shines all day long.

For her invaluable services, Ame-no-Uzume was hailed the "Magic Ancestress" of the Sarune. These were a clan of chieftains who venerated her as an archetype of the psychic medium able to conjure enlightenment even from the supreme light-giver herself. Uzume's effective performance is still danced by mortal artistes at commemorative Shinto festivals. In this, she suggests Inanna, with her own Dance of the Seven Veils, which restored her dead lover to the light of day. Both the Japanese and Sumerian goddesses infer that sacral energy is the primal force driving all seven chakras toward higher levels of life. Indeed, Uzume represents the tremendous power of the sacral chakra to move even the sun itself. Her myth presents the potential possessed by our second life-vortex to bring life out of the darkness, thereby illuminating the world.

Jurojin is one of the Shichi Fukujin, or Beings of Happiness, synonymous for the sacral chakra, because he is the divine patron of a long life, but only if it is joyful. He is usually portrayed as a kindly old man riding his white stag, accompanied by a tortoise --- symbolizing longevity --- and a crane for good luck in traveling.

A Sacral Chakra People:
The Italians

Famous for enjoying life, their foods are probably the most generally sought after on Earth, and their music is regarded as the extraordinarily cheerful and romantic. Love and wine are synonymous for Italy, while Venice would be impossible in any other land. The Italians are an energetic people, whose well-known vivacity and capacity for enjoyment is one of the great secrets of life, because existence without appreciation is merely pointless survival.

A Sacral Chakra Animal:
The Cat

Cats are born experts in determining the most comfortable spot in which to sit. They seem driven to enjoy each moment, to make the best of every situation or run from it to a better condition. Their chief concern is enjoyment and they refuse to concern themselves with anything else. Whereas the root chakra personality involves worry and serious concern, sacral energy, as personified in the cat, is joy-oriented.

The Sacral Chakra Age:
The Child, whose primary interest in life is to have fun.

A Sacral Chakra Profession:
Entertainment

The Sacral Chakra Gland:
The Gonads

These are the primary reproductive glands, the producers of gametes, or reproductive cells.

Sacral Chakra Food: Wine, associated with love and vivacity.

Sacral Chakra Gemstones: Coral, Quartz, Carnelian

Coral was traditionally believed to have a dampening effect on bewitchment, obsession and madness, and what madness is greater than physical passion? Cirlot calls coral "the aquatic tree," simultaneously symbolizing the World Axis (the human spinal column with its energy vortexes) and ocean (or subconscious).[5] Coral is often orange, the same color of the sacral chakra. The calcareous material is formed from colonies of skeletons belonging to tiny marine animals, and used by both Chinese and Hindus to adorn the images of their gods. Even today, dancers, especially in the ballet, wear coral for good luck.

Quartz is believed to enhance the sacral chakra's positive qualities. The stone's sexual aspect was acknowledged during pre-Christian times in Britain, particularly at the Shetland Islands, where quartz stones were believed to cure female sterility. Pebbles of the crystallized silicon dioxide were collected by women, then cast into a pool, where the same women bathed their feet.

Carnelian is said to have an adverse or overly powerful effect on the sacral chakra, and anyone who prefers it as an adornment may be too passionate for his own (and others') good. Jafar, a Moslem scholar of the Middle Ages, declared that the gemstone had the power to grant every desire a human being could imagine.[6] Interestingly, Napoleon carried about a carnelian seal, from Persia, incised with Arabic characters. His royal descendant, Napoleon III, wore the same piece on his watch-chain. A 17th Century Armenian writer reported that in India at the time carnelian, if powdered and taken in a potion, excited joyous emotions.[7] The stone was interred in the Iron Age burial mounds of ancient Japan, as a talisman for happiness in the next world.

Sacral Chakra Metal:
Tin

From pre-Classical times, tin has been associated with the Roman god, Jupiter, the god of "joviality."

Sacral Chakra Incense:
Saffron

Paralleling the color of the sacral chakra, saffron is the dried, orange-hued stigmas of the autumn crocus flower. For many thousands of years, going back to the beginnings of the Ancient World, saffron was prized for its flavor and fragrance. In the Old Testament *Song of Solomon* (iv, 14), it is described as highly valued by the Hebrew priests. Saffron was sprinkled as a joy-inducing scent in the theaters, courts and palaces of Greece, as a presumed aphrodisiac. In the Arabian Nights, saffron was powerful enough to make women swoon with carnal desire. The Arabs believe that the two things which corrupt the female sex are gold and saffron perfume. They introduced saffron into Europe during the Middle Ages, when the English herbalist, Gerard, wrote that it "quickens the senses, makes merry, and shakes off drowsiness." He warned, however, that too much of it effects the brain.[8] Saffron's sexual connotations were also recognized in England, where its flowers were known as "naked ladies."[9]

Sacral Chakra Icon:
A Silk Gown

Silk is associated with sensuality and tactile pleasure.

Sacral Chakra Color:
Orange

It corresponds to the second band in the rainbow, coral, and the sexually seductive saffron. Orange fruit is the symbol of erotic love. Buddhist monks wear orange robes to signify that they have exchanged the pleasures of this physical world for the greater joys of a spiritual life. Cirlot writes that the color is synonymous for fire and flames. The German mythologist, Oswald Wirth, agrees, adding that it also connotes ferocity and egotism. [11]

Sacral Chakra Function:
Emotions

The Sacral Chakra Issue:
Sex

The Sacral Chakra Goal:
Desire

A Lesson the Sacral Chakra Needs to Understand:
Eat to live; do not live to eat.

The Sacral Chakra's Negative Aspect:
Self-indulgence

The Sacral Chakra's Positive Aspect:
Joy

Chapter 9
The Navel Chakra Person

The third major human energy center is our seat of personal power. Properly corresponding to broad belts worn by wrestlers or leather holsters common to gun-slingers, the navel chakra gives direction to the survival and pleasure-seeking impulses of our two, lower vortexes. As such, self-esteem, confidence, self-worth and our ability to make decisions are found in the navel chakra.

Its energy waxes and wanes with greater or lesser degrees of self-mastery. An employee who all day must bow to the wishes of his employer may become a dangerous driver on his way home from work, because he is finally in complete control of something --- his car --- and vents his blocked sense of power on fellow drivers. The most common cause of "road rage" occurs in drivers taking their personal frustrations out on traffic around them. Their personal power has been stymied in an important area of their lives, so they seek empowerment elsewhere. Individuals who feel they lack any real value suffer from insufficient navel chakra energy. In time, if sufficient self-respect is not restored, they either resign themselves to a slave-mentality, or go in the opposite extreme, become violent persons, who blame the world for their powerlessness. The navel chakra's well-being is centrally important, because it decides what course our lives will take. If it lacks enough vitality to make important decisions, it quickly becomes manipulated by persons of superior will-power.

Of all the chakras, perhaps the third one suffers most in the early 21st Century. People believe that they no longer exercise any decisive effect on the course their society takes. They feel powerless to really determine their national destiny, other than continuing to elect "leaders" who consistently disappoint or fail to inspire them. Young persons are especially vulnerable to the malaise of powerlessness that pervades civilization, and many are sure life in general and their own lives, in particular, are without meaning, purpose or goals. They become victims of demagogues, who play upon the uncertainties of citizens suffering from low self-esteem. These political, commercial or personal exploiters represent the navel chakra's evil extreme. They are power-freaks and tyrants dwelling entirely on the level of their third vortex. Weakness and domination are the abuses of the navel chakra. They represent its dangers, not its true function. It was designed to provide us with a measure of control over our surroundings without subjugating them. To escape submersion under a herd mentality and loss of our sense of identity, we must assert ourselves through those things that are our very own; namely, the beliefs, world-view, honor-code, and principles we determine by looking at life from the perspective of our third vortex. With its power comes discrimination, discernment, self-control, and self-discipline. These qualities do not diminish or marginalize our power, but direct it. Without them, the exercise of power degenerates into brutality and ultimate self-defeat, not self-mastery. Our sense of competition is found at the navel chakra level. In an honorable sports contest and in ethical business practices, competition is the force that makes a worthwhile contest. But its power must end where coercion and underhandedness begin.

If the natural instinct of self-defense lies coiled in the root chakra, courage is found at the third energy center --- the courage of one's convictions and the courage of self-restraint. Here, possibilities for the mystical guidance of synchronicity can begin. For it is at the navel chakra that we may decide to stay on the Right-Hand Path of safe conventionality, or follow the Left-Hand Path toward that which most inspires us and gives meaning to existence. The latter, more difficult, but self-fulfilling route is the way to synchronicity, that confirmation of living the authentic life.

Navel Chakra Character

The individual who naturally takes charge of a situation is a navel chakra personality. Remarkable examples are the men and women who assume authority but not at the expense of their humanity. They know how to take on responsibility without resorting to domination. Such persons who successfully operate from their third vortex are very much in the so-called "real world" of physical phenomena, but they do so competently and for higher purposes, often entailing a strong sense of duty toward truth, right behavior, and their fellow creatures. The navel chakra character comprises the "officer material" of this world, and not just in the military. They are the business executives, teachers, employers and self-employed of civilian society.

Strong-willed, they are filled with resolution and purpose, demonstrating powers of concentration and fortitude. Their chief motivation is not physical pleasure, but self-mastery and fulfillment. They are not self-indulgent, but self-reliant. Third vortex individuals are principled leader-types dedicated to ideological outlooks that define the world and their place in it. Inspired by such a "philosophy of life," they inspire others to follow their vision of a better future. The navel chakra person is an achiever, who values material success if it is well-earned. Self-respect and a sense of accomplishment are the qualities of such an individual, who despises all forms of laziness, and has only contempt for dishonesty or self-pity. He or she does not bemoan or avoid struggle, but embraces it as the force for attaining targeted goals.

The dark side of these noble qualities is the brute, the bully and the boss. "The abuse of greatness," wrote Shakespeare in Julius Caesar, "is when it disjoins remorse from power." If navel chakra energy is diverted inward for self-serving motives, the result is someone who enjoys power for its own sake. Natural self-mastery is corrupted by the baser instincts of the self-centered root chakra, which clings desperately to its sense of imperiled survival in the form of wealth accumulation. The navel chakra personality becomes despotic when compassion is absent from the ability to influence. Anyone relishing dictatorial control over others through terror or coercion is an invariably insecure person seeking to compensate for his or her innermost fears through another form of power, tyranny. Such an individual has never gotten past his or her first energy center with its unresolved issues of survival and security.

The teacher who betrays the high potential of her profession by unjust treatment of the children entrusted to her care, or the husband that takes out his frustrations on his downtrodden wife, are petty tyrants misusing the natural power of their third energy center. They imagine, if only half-consciously, that by focusing injurious control over their victims, they are discharging the pressures of pent-up frustrations. But attempting to ventilate such internal stress on human scapegoats never dissipates their twisted energies. Quite the opposite: it magnifies them. The despot returns again to abuse his prey in a cycle of ill-treatment from which there is no escape, save in enlightenment.

Navel Chakra Celebrity-A:
George Washington

With the successful conclusion of the American War for Independence, triumphant colonial volunteers of the Revolutionary Army passed in a victory march down the main street of Philadelphia, Pennsylvania. Huge crowds of people crowded the parade route, wildly cheering the returning veterans led on horseback by their commander, George Washington. While the band music blared loudly, and the masses of well-wishers showered the troops with praise, no one seemed to notice the uniformly mirthless facial expression worn by his soldiers, who seemed indifferent, even resentful of the adoring mob.

John Ward Dunsmore's 1907 painting of George Washington and Lafayette at Valley Forge.

They ignored the popular acclaim focused on them, and marched straight to their barracks, where their spokesman, Colonel Lewis Nicola, confronted General Washington with a grim proposition. The officer began by recalling the hardships of the past war, made desperate less by the British, than because the fledgling U.S. government failed to adequately provide troops with clothing and medical supplies.

While statesmen dined comfortably in their luxurious mansions, warriors of the Continental Army were starving and freezing to death, or unable to defend themselves from the enemy for lack of sufficient ammunition and weapons.

Their sufferings at Valley Forge arose primarily from the disinterest of politicians more interested in fighting for their seat in Congress. Infantrymen often lacked even the most crude accommodations, because the majority of their fellow countrymen --- the very people they were fighting and dying for --- refused to aid them. In fact, only about a quarter of the American people supported the Revolution. Another quarter opposed it, while half were indifferent to its outcome, one way or the other. The form of self-rule envisioned by revolutionary idealists could not be expected to survive a majority apathetic or hostile to liberty. In view of these appalling truths, Nicola concluded, the quality of a leader is more important than the kind of political system that runs a country. History showed, he said, that good men have been known to arise from bad systems, and good systems often produce bad leaders. It was the man that mattered, not the governmental form. That being the case, the Colonel said he was speaking for his comrades by nominating George Washington for king of the United States.

One glance at the serious faces of the veterans showed the General that Nicola had indeed spoken for them. They were ready to install Washington as undisputed monarch, by force of arms, if necessary.

The destiny of a nation was at stake. He need only bow his head in ascent to have dissolved the constitutional republic and become the unchallenged master of America. At this critical stage in our country's development, real power lay not with Congress, but in the hands of a freshly victorious Continental Army.

From ancient times, virtually every man given the opportunity handed to George Washington accepted the mantle of dictatorship. But he was not like any other man. In a sympathetic but firm voice, he agreed with his men that their treatment at the hands of politicians had been shameful. For years, he belabored Congress for funds to pay the back-salaries owed his soldiers. The hostility and disinterest shown their revolutionary sacrifices by the majority of the American masses was disheartening. But the second part of the revolution, he said, was to win these people over to the principles of liberty for which they and their comrades had long suffered. Thus, with determination tempered by mildness, he softened the anger of his listeners, and declined their offer to crown him king. Although they were largely unconvinced by his arguments, they returned peacefully to their homes more out of deep respect for their General than his logic.

Washington eventually did become the national leader they hoped for after he was elected their first president. He ruled with authority, but not unjustly, and thus epitomized the healthy, properly balanced naval chakra --- conjuring all the power it was capable of generating on behalf of high ideals at the service of his fellow Americans. His life exemplified the working nature of our third energy center; namely, that the more freely we give it to others, the more powerful it becomes, and the more harmoniously it functions in relationship with our other chakras.

Navel Chakra Celebrity-B:
Joseph Stalin

Christened Joseph Vissarionovich Dzhugashvilli in 1879, he changed his name to "Stalin" (from the Russian word for "steel," stal) after becoming an ardent Communist. The name was characteristic of a man without a soul, just as some persons come into this world missing a thumb --- in other words, minus any empathy for his fellow human beings. In fact, he was born with a deformed, withered arm, for which he nurtured deep-seated feelings of inferiority and revenge, like Shakespeare's Richard III. In this, he shared a fundamental commonality with all humans who become the embodiment of high-frequency evil; namely, their insatiable malevolence is drawn from deeply irreconcilable feelings of profound personal inadequacy. To compensate and over-compensate for such low self-esteem, they feel fully justified in practicing the most radical villainy against their fellow creatures.

Nikolai Khrushchev, Stalin's very own "Butcher of the Ukraine," wrote that the Marshal was fond of repeating, "the death of one person is a tragedy; of a million, a statistic."[1] According to the *Encyclopedia Britannica*, "Stalin's political victims were numbered in the tens of millions." [2] American scholar, George F. Kennan, described Stalin's "incredible criminality, a criminality without limits." [3] To the U.S. specialist on Soviet affairs, Robert Ĉ. Tucker, Stalin was a 20th Century Ivan the Terrible, who "probably exercised greater political power than any other figure in history."[4] For example, compared with the seventy-five hundred men and women working for Nazi Germany's Gestapo in 1939, Stalin employed nearly fifty times that number at the same time --- three hundred sixty-six thousand secret police operatives, most of them used to spy on the Russian people.

He was actually a mediocrity of limited intelligence, defined only by his insatiable appetite for personal power and prestige. Despite that virtual omnipotence, Stalin was a chronic paranoid constantly fearful of conspiracies lurking in every corner. Politically shrewd, he was a bore in everything else, with no interests beyond his own control of the state apparatus. As his biographer explains, "His main motive was, presumably, to maximize his personal power." It portrays him as "short, stocky, black-haired, fierce-eyed, with one arm longer than the other, his swarthy face being scarred by smallpox contracted in infancy. Physically strong and endowed with prodigious will-power, he early learned to disguise his true feelings and to bide his time; he was implacable in plotting long-term revenge against those who offended him."[5]

He was a heavy drinker and chain-smoker; whose only pastime was the belittling of close associates in public at prominent social gatherings. Khrushchev wrote that, when meeting Stalin, anyone who allowed their gaze to stray from his was suspected of plotting against him and thereafter summarily executed.[6]

With the sudden German attack on Soviet Russia in 1941, Stalin flew into a helpless panic. "Everything Lenin built for us," he wailed, "is lost forever!"[7] As the Axis' advance continued throughout that summer, he went on an extended binge, locked inside his remote *dacha*, leaving the USSR utterly adrift. Although the German invasion had begun on 22 June, Stalin was too drunk to make a public address until 3 July; even then, he could hardly mumble in a low monotone voice that inspired nothing but defeatism. His alcoholic sabbatical must have done him some good, however, because he eventually sobered up enough to personally lead the defense of Moscow, the following winter. Cynically discarding the Marxist rhetoric by which he had lived all his life, he suddenly portrayed himself as a larger-than-life Slavic nationalist. The hypocritical pose worked, and millions of until-then demoralized Russians rallied to the successful defense of their homeland.

For the rest of the war, he proved a superb warlord, less because of any strategic abilities --- of which he possessed none --- than for his ruthless reorganization and leadership of the Soviet military. Faced with the wholesale demoralization of his armed forces through unrelieved defeat, he stiffened the country's resistance by instituting a system of Red Army commissars, who quite literally stood behind the Russian soldiers, pistols at the ready, to kill any man who wavered.

To Stalin's credit, he had already brought Russia into the industrial age --- albeit at the expense of more than ten million murdered peasants in the Ukraine, the *kulak*s --- and now he transformed her factories into gigantic munitions plants geared for total war in a matter of months. Stalin established Soviet battlefield tactics which ignored all strategy for attacks of men and materiel only when the opponent could be overwhelmingly out-numbered, regardless of the always heavy casualties incurred by his soldiers. Sometimes these mass-assaults worked; often, they failed, invariably with the wholesale destruction of Russian men and machines.

Stalin's loathing for his own mentors climaxed in January 1953, with the infamous "Doctors' Plot," in which he accused the country's leading physicians of conspiring to murder top Soviet officials. His denunciation was the pretext for yet another great purge of senior associates. But just before it could begin, the Marshall was murdered with a black-jack to the back of his skull wielded by the dictator of his own secret police (the NKVD), Laventri Beria. Joseph Stalin died the way he lived --- like a gangster.

His life demonstrated how the dynamics of our naval chakra, if continually turned inward upon the ego, can transform it into a monster of hideous proportions. Edgar Cayce, America's "Sleeping Prophet" during the first half of the 20th Century, stated that the greatest force in the universe is not electricity or atomic energy, but spiritual power.[8] Like all power, it is neither intrinsically virtuous nor evil. Its utility depends entirely upon the morality of whoever wields it. In itself, a sword is not a good nor bad object; it may either save someone's life or become a murder weapon, depending on how it is used. So too, our navel chakra.

Greek Navel Chakra Deity:
Atlas

He is a titan, one of the giants who long ago fought the gods for control of the world. Having lost that primeval struggle, Atlas was condemned to forever support the sky on his shoulders. His name in Sanskrit means "the Up-Holder." Although a prisoner of the victorious Olympians, Atlas still exercised tremendous power, because he could cause untold catastrophe to our planet, if ever he allowed the heavens to fall.

His right knee imprints the Earth in the middle of the world, while he holds aloft the star-studded Zodiac. Thus, like the navel chakra, Atlas possesses great strength, enough to distinguish the lower world of the base energy vortexes from their higher counterparts, which are nonetheless connected through his conjoining imagery.

Japanese Navel Chakra Deities:
Koku Bosatu and Hotei

In India, he is known as *Akasa-Garbha*, the "Navel of the Sky," or "Nucleus of the Universe," the twelfth *Bodhisattva*, or "Buddha of Compassion." Koku Bosatu grants strength of purpose and courage of its fulfillment to anyone who devoutly petitions him.

Hotei, a Being of Happiness, one of the Shichi Fukujin, is also known as the Wagon Priest, because he sits in an old cart drawn by boys. In sculpted representations of the god, emphasis is on his prominent navel, with its chakra of personal control. All these images underscore Hotei's identity with the third vortex.

A Navel Chakra People:
The Romans

They did not set out to conquer the world. For hundreds of years, they were forced to defend their city from the depredations of invading peoples. After generations of struggle, Rome emerged as the dominant power in Italy. They then found themselves threatened by barbarians beyond the Italian peninsula. As their city and its provinces grew in wealth and culture, its defensive perimeters continued to widen.

With military success, the Romans came to believe their mission was to civilize all humanity. They began imposing their lofty principles of legal justice and representative government, which had so blessed their sophisticated society, on foreign peoples who instinctually resisted the imposition of a fundamentally alien civilization. In their arrogance, the Romans assumed that their way of life was the best, and must be grafted, against the will of others, if need be, onto every other culture, regardless how incompatible with Latin mores.

For a time, this enforced *Pax Romanum* appeared to have succeeded, as the Roman World stretched from Britain to the Near East. But by the early 4th Century A.D., cracks were beginning to show, as nationalist movements tore the Empire in every direction, and Rome herself, too weak through self-indulgence to impose her diluted will, began to deteriorate. Over the following decades, her imperial dream turned into a social nightmare. The decay of all virtues originally responsible for the Roman way of life, increases in violent crime, collapse of the economic infrastructure, decline of legal, military and political systems swelled into an escalating chaos that eventually unraveled the whole fabric of civilized existence.

When today we walk among the ruins of the Forum, Coliseum or *Circus Maximus*, these marble bones of ancient Rome are our clues to a people's abuse of their national navel chakra. So long as its energies were directed toward their own culture, it grew to become the marvel of human history. But when they began to impose their values on others, for whatever high-minded purpose, they set in motion those internal forces that condemned their civilization to death.

A Navel Chakra Animal:
The Lion

The lion is king of the beasts not only because it is physically strong and swift. Its success depends as much for its sense of balance and grace under stress.

It embodies qualities of intent, discernment, strategy and will. The creature attacks only after carefully assessing its target and surrounding situation. Ruthless in the performance of what it was designed to do, the lion nonetheless forms affectionate "prides." In these close-knit groups, the animal displays a tender regard and care of its own kind. In myth, the lion symbolizes the all-conquering sun.

The Navel Chakra Age:
Adolescence

A Navel Chakra Profession:
The Sea Captain

The Navel Chakra Gland:
The Pancreas

Blockage of the navel chakra can result in poor digestion, ulcerous conditions, and pancreatitis (inflammation of the pancreas), because this organ is responsible for secreting digestive juices into the small intestine. The pancreas, which controls the level of sugar in the blood, is vital to life for the hormone insulin it produces. Persons who feel powerless often experience severe stomach pains caused by their blocked third energy-center adversely effecting the pancreas, an example of the mind-body relationship, a very real connection between spiritual and physical health.

Navel Chakra Food:
Meat

Navel Chakra Gemstones:
Amber, Moonstone, Topaz

Amber is associated with the navel chakra's color, yellow. Moonstone is said to have a calming, or "waning" effect on the higher intensity energy of the third vortex. Topaz was regarded by 17th Century Arabs as the gem of the Constellation Leo, re-affirming this chakra's leonine qualities.

Navel Chakra Metal:
Iron

Navel Chakra Incense:
Cedar

Navel Chakra Icon:
A Sword

Navel Chakra Color:
Yellow

The color of the all-conquering sun, ancient Rome's *Sol Invictus.* In ancient China, yellow was the color of the imperial family.

Navel Chakra Function:
Energy

The Navel Chakra Issue:
Will

The Navel Chakra Goal:
Control

A Lesson the Navel Chakra Needs to Understand:

True power resides not in controlling events, but allowing them to happen. The greatest victories we can ever win are those over ourselves, because they make possible all subsequent success.

The Navel Chakra's Negative Aspect:
Tyranny

The Navel Chakra's Positive Aspect:
Self-mastery

Chapter 10

The Heart Chakra Person

While our first three chakras are absolutely necessary for existence, they nonetheless belong to the beast in us all. Persons who only live at these levels are not fully-fledged men or women. They are just beings interested in survival, physical pleasure and power, and therefore no different from other animals who operate primarily or exclusively in these basic energy centers. Insects, for example, are strictly root chakra creatures, as are some humans. At the heart chakra, however, we begin to move into the realm of humanity. It is distinguished from its lower counterparts by a quality unlike the ego; namely, feelings of affection for living things outside ourselves.

The position of our fourth energy center is mid-point in the chakra system. Below it lie our physical needs to survive, procreate, and control. Above stand our ability to express ourselves, perceive the hidden forces of life, and connect with the spiritual power that drives our personal destiny. The heart chakra, being centrally located between these other vortices, is situated at a kind of crossroads, where it can process and harmonize their sometimes contrary vitalities. Its chief quality, compassion, can ameliorate the excesses of the lower three chakras, all the better to control them, or damp down tendencies of intellectual egotism which threaten the upper trio. Genuine modesty and unaffected humility arising from commiseration for one's fellow creatures are the hallmarks of the heart chakra. They give meaning to the expression, "heartfelt."

The fourth vortex is not activated by any intellectual process of the conscious mind, but springs instinctually from the soul itself. In the European medieval Grail epic of Parsifal, he grows up in the deep forest minus any contact with the outside world. Later, when he shoots a swan just for sport, he is shown the animal's death agony, and remorse wells up in him for the first time. Parsifal is described as "the pure fool made wise through compassion," and he is, therefore, the only kind of person able to find the Grail, that classic symbol of spiritual attainment.[1] So too, the quest for a truly meaningful life is alone available to an open-hearted human being.

Heart chakra energy diversifies into every form of love. Like any other chakra, however, it has its light and dark aspects, and must perform in a balanced manner to function properly. If it is made to dominate another energy-center, the fourth vortex degenerates from its original purpose. For example, someone may become so besotted with the notion of universal, undifferentiated love that he or she undermines the root chakra's survival instincts. These persons make victims of themselves by dispensing love to individuals who grasp such opportunities for exploitation. Love was not designed to be passed around like any cheap commodity. On the contrary, it is the most precious emotion we know, and must be used with careful discernment, or else we may be abused for our unappreciated gift. We must love, but we must love wisely. That is the guiding principle of the heart chakra.

One begins by loving the most difficult person in the world to love, because we know all the secrets of that individual better than anyone else. Many find loving themselves hard to achieve, because they are unable to distinguish between compassion for oneself and egotism. The latter is an unbalanced view of who we are, because, like all magnifications, it is a distortion of reality. Narcissus so admired his own reflection on the surface of a pool that he fell in love with himself. However, his mirror image was an illusion, the reversal of his real identity. Love of oneself is not a deformed panegyric to our virtues and accomplishments, but honest compassion for our human condition, which we share with the rest of mankind.

We may look into a mirror and not like what we see. But if we visualize ourselves as we were in the past, as an innocent child or newborn infant, we are less inclined to judge ourselves so harshly. Proper love of oneself is centrally important to our love for others. We cannot be expected to love someone else if we have a low opinion of ourselves. From a balanced appreciation for ourselves, love may radiate outward in concentric circles of affection. Loving those closest to us, in our immediate family, is natural, because our bonds with them are tied through the primal root and sacral chakras. The next concentric ring extends in respect and friendship, variations of love, to members of our local community. The next wider circle embraces men and women of our blood, language and culture through patriotism, devotion to our own people, in whom our national identity is anchored. Beyond our compatriots are the inhabitants of other lands, to whom we owe deference and courtesy. Then there are all those fellow creatures, who share the Earth with us and deserve our respect and compassion.

Love, as well as death, is the great healer. And activation of the fourth energy-center sets in motion fundamental influences for wholeness. "According to tradition," as the prolific experts on medieval spirituality, Tim Wallace-Murphy and Marilyn Hopkins, explain "the awakening of the heart chakra brings an increased ability to direct the life-force, especially for healing. This concern and increased ability to act for others cannot be awakened until the aspirant has overcome all egotistical sense of self. It is the meeting-place of the divine and the human, where the spiritual and the material are in harmony. When this centre is fully open, the candidate is empowered to act for the benefit of all humanity."[2]

So long as one concentric ring of love does not intrude on another, but a balance of affection is evenly maintained among them, our heart chakra energy flows out of our fourth vortex like the ripples equidistantly spreading from a pebble dropped on the surface of a calm body of water. The influences on others we set in motion through our love must be no less gently effective. If we knew every sorrow all humanity suffers, we would immediately perish of grief. If we knew each joy that delights all living things, we would die instantly of happiness. It is sufficient that we recognize the sorrows and joys of those in our experience to share with them our compassion and good will.

Heart Chakra Character

Non-judgment is a quality of individuals characterized by their fourth vortex. It is not that they simply "love" everyone on principle, but rather they understand that their fellow humans are a complex mix of contrary forces that sometimes results in less than perfect behavior.

When we are confronted by someone committing an act of cruelty or injustice, we naturally condemn that person, because from our perspective he or she appears wicked and unfair. But imagine if that wrongful action were somehow frozen in time, enabling to see all the preconditions that lead up to the crime in question. Suppose we could scrutinize every act of malice, harshness and inhumanity the perpetrator himself suffered over the years, from earliest childhood. Some of these troubles may have been far more painful than anything we experienced in our own lives. We would then regard them as inter-related causes that progressed, one following the other, to the commission of a deplorable action. Evil deeds endured through the past form links in a chain of behavior culminating in some heartless deed.

Such a higher vantage point would reveal the long, personal history of hurtful events that push the perpetrator onward to further iniquities. Such deforming events do not excuse wickedness. But our recognition of them does mitigate our hatred of such persons by under-standing the causes that determined their negative behavior, and forms the basis of our compassion for anyone who sabotages their own life through wrongdoing. None of the great teachers of higher morality, including Buddha and Jesus, promised their followers they could or should escape the consequences of their own misdeeds. They did, however, preach that a compassionate understanding of the causes of criminal deeds was preferable to revenge.

The heart chakra person may possess this lofty perspective of human behavior to a degree no greater than anyone else. Yet, he or she does not need to actually recognize every detail of the cruelty or injustice that went into the formation of a wrongful individual. It is enough for them to presume the existence of such preconditions. People are not bad in themselves, but become so through the occasionally powerful negative forces and circumstances which mould them. Persons acting on the impulses of their fourth energy center possesses an inner calm and generosity of spirit others naturally turn to in times of stress and difficulty. They are naturally sympathetic without being patronizing or superior. The radiance of an open heart chakra illuminates the world around it.

Heart Chakra Celebrity-A:
Mother Teresa

Born Agnes Gonxha Bojaxhiu, in Skopje, Macedonia, in 1910, she was the daughter of an Albanian grocer, who saved his money so she could join, at eighteen years of age, the Catholic Institute of the Blessed Virgin Mary, in Ireland. To her surprise, just six weeks after her arrival, she was transferred to India as a teacher. Appalled by the unforeseen magnitude of the squalor and privation there, Agnes requested from her superiors permission to work among the poverty-stricken residents of Calcutta. She saw at once, however, that what the suffering Indians needed most urgently was not Catholic dogma, but health care.

After completing studies in nursing at a British hospital, she moved into the slums, where she petitioned the municipal authorities for a pilgrim hostel. They provided her with a building near, appropriately enough, a temple dedicated to the goddess of life and death, Kali. There she founded her order, the Missionaries of Charity, in 1948, and was henceforward known as "Mother Teresa," after her favorite saint. Word of her work spread beyond India, and sympathetic volunteers came to assist her from various parts of the world. She put them all to work in dispensaries and outdoor schools built with international contributions. Eventually adopting

Indian citizenship, she and all her Indian nuns wore the sari as their identifiable habit.

Over the years, they opened numerous clinics serving patients who were blind, aged, crippled, terminally ill and afflicted with leprosy. In fact, Mother Teresa built a leper colony near Asansol, called Shanti Nagar, or the "Town of Peace". During his 1964 visit to India, Pope Paul VI gave her his ceremonial limousine, which she immediately raffled off to help financially support Shanti Nagar. Henceforward, offers to relocate in modern, even luxurious hospitals reached her from around the world. She ignored them all, preferring to administer, as she had always done, among the sick and starving of Calcutta.

A recipient of the Nobel Peace Prize in 1979, Mother Teresa was invited several times thereafter to visit United States Presidents at the White House. While being honored at a state dinner by Bill Clinton, she profoundly embarrassed the President and his followers by publicly condemning his abortion policies in no uncertain terms.

Untempted her whole life by promises of wealth, fame or power, Mother Teresa died shortly before the end of the 20th Century upon which she made an indelible mark. In true love of her fellow human beings, she acted entirely out of her heart chakra. By equating her own well-being to service for suffering humanity, she was so busy doing work that brought her a sense of fulfillment, that she never paused to wonder whether or not she was happy. As such, her life is an example of the tremendous potential inherent in this energy center to transform both our outer and inner worlds for the better.

Heart Chakra Celebrity-B:
Cleopatra

Marc Antony was the third member of the imperial triumvirate, together with Octavian and Lepidus, that ruled the world after Caesar's assassination, in 44 B.C. Although disliked by most of the cultured and privileged classes for his ribaldry and blunt manner, as a real soldier he was much beloved by soldiers, with whose swords real power lay. He liked to eat, sing, march, hunt, get drunk, party and joke with his comrades, sleep in the open on the cold ground under his robes, as they did, while participating alike in all their common joys and privations. Antony was a skilled field surgeon, and personally administered to the wounds or illnesses of his men, even those of the lowest rank. Yet, his fellow officers revered him as "the most experienced commander living."[3] His generosity to the troops increased proportionately to his ever greater acquisitions of political power, and, in time, he eventually began winning support among some senators, who imagined he might make a popular front for their own agendas.

Cleopatra Testing Poisons on Condemned Prisoners by
Alexandre Cabanel.

During Antony's tour of the Near East, he summoned Cleopatra VII, the Queen of Egypt, to answer charges of complicity in the murder of Julius Caesar. She arrived as he commanded, but in a radically unexpected fashion that made him forget his accusations. Cleopatra came sailing up the river Cydnus, in Cilicia, today's southeastern Turkey, on a gigantic barge, more like a floating theatrical stage. The queen lay ensconced under a gauzy canopy of golden cloth dressed as Venus, the goddess of love, while boys painted to resemble cupids fanned her with ostrich-feathers. Huge, purple sails and silver oars propelled the immense vessel, its decks populated by beautiful attendants dressed as sea nymphs. The entire stern was sheeted in beaten gold, and great clouds of incense, together with the music of flutes, fifes and harps, wafted to the shore, attracting great crowds of astounded on-lookers.

The effect of this incredible spectacle on Antony was powerful. All his life, he had shown many positive, valiant, even superior traits. But from early youth, he also exhibited a weakness for occasionally excessive self-indulgence. Although his willingness to share the good times with as many friends as possible somewhat mitigated the worst effects such behavior might have on his reputation, his philandering with married women and drunken excesses offended even his closest associates. A particularly humiliating instance took place, when, after an all-night drinking party, he vomited in full view of a large crowd while trying to give an important public speech.

Happily, these lower tendencies were beginning to recede, as he waged the war against Caesar's assassins and during the execution of his governmental responsibilities, which he took very seriously. People began talking of his eventual rise to emperor. His popular following was great and growing. But Cleopatra resuscitated the man's weaknesses, plying him with the greatest sex he had ever known, sumptuous banquets of boars and peacocks on gold and silver plates, followed by rounds of raucous parties awash with liquor, all amid scenes of luxury unrivaled anywhere else. She constantly flattered him and commanded all Egypt to do the same, appealing to his ego on a royal and national scale.

Yet, in the midst of this on-going Bacchanalia, he was shocked back into reality by a dispatch from Rome. His wife, Fulvia, had engineered an armed revolt against his co-regent, Octavian. Her intentions were less political than marital. She hoped that insurrection would cause her husband's break with and return from Cleopatra. He immediately took ship for home, but was informed *en route* that Fulvia had died of an illness incurred while she was on her way to their reunion. Proceeding to Italy, he was met by Octavian (now Caesar Augustus), who blamed him for none of his late wife's indiscretions, urging him instead to take up the fallen reigns of good government on behalf of Roman unity, still uncertain after the civil war. Antony's better nature responded to Augustus, and the two men formed a triumvirate with their comrade, Lepidus, who took charge of Africa. Caesar administered the Western World, while Antony controlled the East.

To solidify their bond, Antony married his friend's older sister, Octavia. She was in all respects an ideal

Roman woman --- beautiful, highly cultured, family-oriented, strong, honorable, responsible, generous and pious. Octavia exercised a gently salubrious effect on Antony, dispelling his old wildness and nurturing his nobility of soul. She genuinely loved him, and he at least deeply honored and respected her. So long as her higher influences surrounded his daily life, Marc Antony's virtues and popularity grew hand-in-hand, and the world seemed headed toward a *Pax Romanum* in which he played a significant role. When word reached Cleopatra of his marriage to Octavia, she collapsed in grief. She had planned to transform Marc Antony into her instrument for greatness, just as she had Caesar.

She had not long to wait, however, before the broken thread of her web would be reknit. The Parthians, a militant people in control of the Middle East, were rattling their sabers again. But Antony, afraid he might yield to temptation if he ventured too near his former lover's sphere of influence, sent Ventidius to restore order. Unfortunately, his general was unable to cope with the situation, so he went in person, taking with him Octavia and their new-born daughter as safeguards against his own behavior. While traveling through Greece, they learned that the crisis was more serious than anticipated. Octavia and the child returned to Rome. In Syria, he drilled the two legions Caesar sent him for a major military confrontation, while simultaneously dispatching envoys to sound out the Parthians on a diplomatic solution.

Memories of Cleopatra, however, began to haunt his every dream and waking hour. They eroded his will-power and good intentions. He wanted to return home to his wife and daughter, but duty prevented him from leaving Asia. Torn between devotion to Octavia and lust for the Queen, he at last gave way to his baser instincts. When Antony's fellow countrymen learned that he not only acknowledged three of Cleopatra's children as his own in public, but, without even notifying the senate, had the unmitigated effrontery to parcel out mostly independent kingdoms to his own, underage children, they finally recognized that he and his Egyptian Queen were uniting the East against Roman Civilization. Her total manipulation of Antony, now her willing slave, had become obvious, and both sides prepared for a clash of arms.

During the war's major naval confrontation near Actium, the engagement was not yet decided, when Cleopatra's flagship, the *Antonias*, abruptly hoisted sail and fled in the company of sixty warships. The men of Antony's fleet were paralyzed with disbelief, but not their commander. He jumped ship into a galley to pursue Cleopatra, abandoning his command without a word of explanation. The battle and the war were lost. Catching up with her, Antony came aboard and crouched in the bow of the ship named after him, hiding his face in his hands.

The downfall that inevitably caught up with both of them is among the most famous tragedies in history. Cleopatra had loved Antony, as Shakespeare wrote of another self-destroyed lover, "if not wisely, then too well."[4] She had smothered him with affection, appealing to his weaker side, while undermining his natural nobility. She was not the last of persons whose love overwhelms and ruins their beloved. Heart chakra energy is perhaps the most beautiful power in the universe. But like all energy, it must be balanced, or it becomes devastating.

Greek Heart Chakra Deity:
Persephone

The young daughter of Demeter, or Mother Earth, was alone picking flowers one day, when a huge black chariot drawn by enormous ebony stallions flew from the mouth of a mountain-cave. They were driven by a giant swathed in sable robes, who wordlessly scooped up the astonished Persephone before she realized what had happened. The horses galloped back into the cave and down a long, twisting tunnel that led to the Underworld.

The giant courteously introduced himself as Hades, the Lord of the Afterlife. Here, in this subterranean realm bearing his own name, he presided over the souls of the dead. He apologized for abducting Persephone, but explained that he was very lonely, and asked her to be his queen. She would bring some much-needed light and gayety to his somber kingdom. Hades owned all the precious jewels of the world, and these he promised would be hers forever, if only she would consent to be his royal bride.

But Persephone refused, and demanded to be reunited with her mother at once. Hades respectfully promised to return her to the surface, although only after she was his guest in the palace for a short time. He would let her reconsider his proposal of marriage, and if, after a few days, she still refused to become his queen, he pledged to bring her home.

But as time passed, Demeter, in her grief, forbade all crops to grow until she saw her daughter again, and the prayers of starving humanity rose to heaven. Zeus, king of the gods, heard their lamentation, and vowed to solve the problem. He sent his messenger, Hermes, with orders to Hades: "Return the girl!" By that time, however, Persephone felt compassionate for poor Hades, who had tried unsuccessfully to win her with the untold riches of his realm. She agreed to become his bride after all. But she knew that her absence was responsible for a worldwide drought only her return could end. So, she agreed to remain with her mother half of each year. The other half, she spent with her husband in the Kingdom of the Dead, where she eased the sorrows of departed souls, and softened the otherwise grim heart of her husband.

Thus, the ancient Greeks explained to their children the change of the seasons, as every six months Persephone returns to the Underworld. In both places, she brings light and life through the heart chakra energy of her compassion for both the living and the dead.

Japanese Heart Chakra Deities:
Aizen-Myo-o and Daikoku

Guardian of pilgrims on the True Path to enlightenment, Aizen-Myo-o is the personification of the Spirit of Love. Through him alone is spiritual illumination possible. He is envisioned as a benevolent sentinel, who protects kind-hearted persons from harm.

The fourth Being of Happiness, one of the Shichi Fukujin, Daikoku is shown in sacred art as a man sitting on bags of rice. A pouch of jewels on his shoulder, he holds a magic hammer capable of granting every wish. A golden disk of the sun over the center of his chest identifies Daikoku with the heart chakra, which, like his magic hammer, is the source of all wish-fulfillment.

A Heart Chakra People:
The Minoans

Certainly, no people during the present epoch of international materialism may be characterized by the heart chakra. Even over the long panorama of human history, very few cultures seemed to exhibit those qualities of compassion and fellow-feeling associated with the fourth energy center. Only one possible example may qualify, a sorry commentary on Man's unwillingness or inability to create society based on his innate capacity for love.

The Minoans were a highly sophisticated, prosperous people who occupied Crete and other Eastern

Mediterranean islands more than thirty five hundred years ago, and were remarkable for a singular lack of aggression. Their great cities, like Knossos and Phaistos, were the only population centers in the Ancient World not surrounded by defensive walls. The Minoans fielded no standing armies, and their navy was more a coast guard to combat piracy than a military institution.

They engaged in no wars, but channeled their national ambitions through trade with neighbors in Greece, Egypt, throughout the Aegean World, and into Asia Minor. This non-belligerent attitude was reflected by their religion, in which a bountiful Earth Mother goddess was worshiped as the central figure. In every other contemporary Bronze Age culture, military values were extolled as the supreme national virtues. The Minoans prospered for many hundreds, perhaps even a thousand years or more, until sometime during the 15th Century B.C., when Homer's militant Achaeans, known to archaeologists as Mycenaean Greeks, invaded Crete and subdued its benevolent civilization.

While perhaps the lone specimen of an advanced people applying the energies of its folkish heart chakra in the so-called "real world," the Minoans are still an example of the long-term, spiritually and materially abundant society that can be built on good will.

A Heart Chakra Animal:
The Dog

Man is not the only organism designed with a chakra system. All sentient beings possess fundamentally similar energy centers. Even the lower creatures --- insects and bacteria --- have a root chakra, the source of their will to survive. The higher up the evolutionary scale life rises, the more complex it necessarily becomes; hence, the need for more developed vortexes. The dog, for cxample, unquestionably lives through chakras much the same as ourselves. This comparison led the Classical Greek mathematician and philosopher, Pythagoras, to conclude that human souls were able to reincarnate in the bodies of animals, and vice versa.

In any case, dogs are able to communicate themselves, in however limited a fashion, by way of their throat chakra, and perceive non-physical subtleties with their brow chakra. We do not know if they operate a crown chakra to connect with spiritual dimensions, but it seems unlikely that they would not possess the ultimate vortex, since they clearly own the other six. But it is in the powerful function of their heart chakra that they particularly excel. The dog's renowned qualities of companionship and loyalty unto death exemplify the fourth energy center, and demonstrate our spiritual kinship with man's best friend.

The Heart Chakra Age:
Young Adulthood

A Heart Chakra Profession:
Nursing

The Heart Chakra Gland:
Thymus

Consisting of a knot of tissue in the middle upper chest, the thymus effects infant development and growth by regulating the assimilation of mother's milk. With the onset of puberty, this function ceases to operate, and the thymus becomes a center for the harmonization of all chakra energies, thereby helping to define the heart chakra as a physiological integrator. The thymus controls the production of infection-fighting white blood cells. Blockage of the fourth energy-center can lead to cardiovascular problems, including heart failure, because love is essential to life.

Heart Chakra Food:
The Apple

In Danish, German, and English folklore, together with West African voodoo, the apple is known as a love charm. In Old Irish myth, the Celtic hero, Conle, was captured and marooned on a barren island by the Queen of the "Land of the Living," a kind of fairy-realm. She kept him alive by throwing him a wondrous apple that, no matter how much he ate of it, it never diminished. But it also filled Conle with love for the fairy Queen.

The ancient Greek myth of Atalanta told how she lost a foot-race with her suitor when he dropped an apple to distract her. The price of her defeat was her marriage to him.

Frey, the Norse god of sunshine, peace, prosperity and fruitfulness, sent eleven apples as a love offering to the beautiful Gerda of Jotunheim, the realm of the giants. In old Scandinavia, apples were used as tests of chastity, fading when their owner was unfaithful. According to Cirlot, the apple is symbolic of marriage, because it signifies the totality a man and woman achieved by uniting their separate identities in holy matrimony. [5]

Heart Chakra Gemstones:
Tourmaline, Malachite, Serpentine

Of the five different kinds of tourmaline, only one ("Brazilian emerald") is heart chakra-green. Some are green at one end and pink at the other. Tourmaline is mostly found in the United States (California and Maine), Russia (the Ural Mountains), Madagascar, and Sri Lanka, where it derived its name from a French corruption of the Singhalese *tohramalli*, for "carnelian." Green tourmaline is most identified with the heart chakra, because this gemstone, when subjected to physical pressure, produces an electrical charge in a process known as piezoelectricity. Similarly, the fourth vortex, when activated, generates power to illuminate the world around us.

Malachite has been prized since the beginning of recorded history. From the earliest days of their civilization, the ancient Egyptians operated malachite mines between Suez and Sinai. They regarded it as a sacred stone associated with Isis, the love-goddess, and her brother, Osiris, the god of regeneration. Its green hue is supposedly the precise color tone of the heart chakra. Malachite is alleged to have a magnifying effect on the fourth vortex.

Usually green with streaks of white, serpentine signifies the snake-like chakra energy entwining its way upward around the spine, reaching the heart level. Traditionally, serpentine is alleged to provide the love instinct with a proper sense of direction, and prevent it from being misled by delusions common to passion.

Heart Chakra Metal:
Copper

Medieval astrologers and alchemists associated the metal with Venus, the Roman goddess of love. Much earlier, copper was symbolic of the Phoenician love-goddess, Astarte.

Heart Chakra Incense:
Rose

In Greek myth, roses were invented as gifts of the gods to shower down on Aphrodite, when she first emerged from the sea. Medieval Christian tradition reported that roses were white until one was kissed by Eve in the Garden of Eden. The flower blushed red, and has been so colored ever since.

Heart Chakra Icon:
A Hot-Pink Rose

Heart Chakra Color:
Green

The fourth band in the rainbow, it is a color borne by the descendants of Mohammed, whose chief principle was love of God. Cirlot mentions that green is associated in Western European traditions with sympathy.

Heart Chakra Function:
Balance

The Heart Chakra Issue:
Love

The Heart Chakra Goal:
Sharing

A Lesson the Heart Chakra Needs to Understand:
We cannot love everyone equally; true love is hierarchical.

The Heart Chakra's Negative Aspect:
Loss of identity

The Heart Chakra's Positive Aspect:
Compassion

Chapter 11
The Throat Chakra Person

For a human being, it is not enough that he or she merely survive, enjoy pleasure, have a measure of power, and feel love. The psychic vitality of these forces must be properly vented, else it builds up subconscious pressures that seeks an outlet in one or more of the first four chakras, a task for which they were not designed. This basic function belongs to the fifth vortex. It operates as a kind of emotional safety-valve for the over-flow of energy. But it does more than channel the primal drives of our lower power-centers. The throat chakra is also the sounding-board for our intellectual and spiritual impulses. As metaphysical writer, Ambika Wauters, points out, "It acts as a bridge between our feelings centered in the heart chakra and our thoughts focused in the brow chakra."[1] It is our means by which we communicate with our fellow creatures. And we must eventually disclose everything significant to us, one way or another, or we suffer for our self-censorship. As Nietzsche observed, "All suppressed truths become poisonous."[2]

All creative and performing artists are throat chakra personalities, because they live for self-expression. Writers, clowns, painters, basket-makers, violinists, acrobats and the rest of their colleagues experience life through the operation of their fifth vortex. But it is not restricted to an artistic elite, even though it finds its highest fulfillment in their work. The majority of less gifted persons are no less in need of articulating the forces molding their destiny. The throat chakra does not limit human expression to speech and artistic eloquence. A ditch-digger may communicate his deepest feelings in the manner he wields his shovel, or a housewife in the way she uses a broom to sweep the floor. The method by which we express ourselves is irrelevant to its facility. Often, our throat chakras are activated for us by artistic experiences, which articulate significant inner forces we feel are part of our deepest being, our soul, but do not otherwise understand. A statesman who publicly says what many people believe likewise opens their throat chakras.

Most importantly, the fifth vortex exists to put us in accord with the spiritual order of the universe. We achieve this grand purpose by simply expressing the truth --- our truth. It may not be what anyone else believes, and might even be violently opposed. But if we refrain from somehow communicating it, we undermine the organizational ground of our being. The uncaught perpetrators of serious crimes often turn themselves over to law enforcement authorities, even if the consequences of their surrender may be severe punishment, because the increasing, internal pressure of living with a suppressed truth becomes intolerable.

Throat Chakra Character

Well-spoken individuals are among the most obvious examples of the throat chakra personality. But eloquence is not confined to words. Communication takes many forms, some of the most effective being the subtlest. Like its fellow vortexes, the fifth energy-center has the potential for good or evil. The orator who inspires his followers to action on behalf of a noble truth uses the power of the throat chakra for a positive purpose. If he were to abuse its power by misleading them for selfish agendas not in their real interest, he degenerates into a demagogue. The power of words is great. In Egyptian myth, Thaut, a deity associated with the throat chakra, was believed to have brought physical reality into existence with a single word. From him, doubtless, the Jewish author of the Old Testament received the opening line in Genesis: "In the beginning was the word." These mythic allusions do not overstate the power of speech.

Adolf Hitler devoted an entire chapter (Volume 2, Chapter 6) of his book, *Mein Kampf*, entitled, "The Significance of the Spoken Word," to the political potential of public speaking. Certainly, it was primarily through his forceful oratory that he was able to transform an obscure, seven-member organization into a mass-movement with many millions of followers. The spoken word has the ability to cause pain or to heal. The comfort persons suffering from any manner of physical distress receive from someone speaking to them in soft tones of compassion and encouragement is well known. The same Egyptian Thaut who brought the material world into existence with a single word was also regarded as the god of medicine.

The throat chakra personality is recognizably creative or receptive to creativity. All talent and appreciation for creativity lie within it. Individuals who give themselves over to the fifth vortex may lead lives of deep personal fulfillment by following their bliss, but they can also lose their way by a confusion of goals. For example, if someone pursues the creative potential of their throat chakra in the certainty that others will inevitably recognize and reward their labors, they have missed the point of the fifth energy-center. Its purpose is not to satisfy root chakra yearnings for material security, but to express one's own truth in the most personal and effective form. When we truly believe in some creative action and dedicate ourselves to its expression, all that needs matter is that we strive to develop it. The issue of its recognition and other root chakra criteria for "success" must be of complete indifference. Even if we understand the intent of our throat chakra, and follow it, the danger nonetheless exists that we may grow so self-absorbed in our beloved work that we become oblivious to the needs of the rest our energy-centers, which atrophy as a consequence. Such persons become self-consumed egotists.

If the throat chakra individual has something of worth to say to others, he is articulate. If he speaks only of himself or uninspiring matters, he is loquacious. In either case, the creative impulse of such persons is always readily apparent. They are usually excellent workers, because they love their labor for its own sake. They rise fast and high to the top of their chosen profession, and inject a sense of artistry into everything they do, regardless of the nature of the task involved. They tend to be somewhat narrow in their outlook on other aspects of life, because they view the world exclusively through the filter of their all-consuming endeavors. But they have strong will-power for its realization, and make possible the expression of often exciting truths with the potential to positively transform the gamut of experience from a single individual to all humankind.

Throat Chakra Celebrity-A:
Luciano Pavarotti

He was perhaps the most famous public performer during the last decades of the 20th Century. Although opera as a popular medium had been in long, slow decline since the end of World War Two, Luciano Pavarotti singlehandedly revived general appreciation for this moribund art-form in thousands of out-door and auditorium concerts around the world. His audiences were made up primarily of persons who knew nothing of classical singing and even thought they hated it. Yet, he won their enthusiastic acclaim, and, in the process, enriched their lives in ways they never knew existed.

His accomplishment was not exclusively generated by the natural beauty of his voice, which was considerable, nor through the formidable power he used to support it. And he had contemporary rivals, like Placido Domingo and Andrea Bocelli, who were no less vocally gifted than he. But they never came close to achieving the extra-operatic global triumph he won. The secret of Pavarotti's success could be found in what lay behind the beautiful voice. In each piece of music he performed, he insinuated nuances of meaning his listeners mostly recognized subconsciously. They responded with loud ovations to his art, because he knew how to aim his subtle inflections at regions of their souls neglected by other singers. He brought forth from his audiences, regardless of their differing cultural backgrounds, responses they intuitively recognized as true, and they were wildly grateful.

Pavarotti was a master of artistic eloquence. He knew how to call upon the huge power of his energy-center to produce meanings that rode on splendidly modulated tones into the depths of his listeners' psyches. In so doing, he set up a resonance between his throat chakra and theirs, which sympathetically vibrated with the power of his fifth vortex. He thereby set their souls in harmonic motion, providing them with a common experience that was nevertheless mystical.

Throat Chakra Celebrity-B:
Maria Callas

Some persons begin as a caterpillar and emerge later in life as a butterfly. Thus was the transformation of an obscure New York girl of Greek origins, Maria Anna Sofia Cecilia Kalogeropoulos, into Maria Callas, the world's greatest Italianate soprano of the mid-20th Century. And, like the butterfly, she did not live long.

Two attributes began to characterize Maria as she entered her teenage years. She was developing a naturally beautiful voice, but her body tended toward obesity. A famed singing teacher, Elivra de Hidalgo, told her young pupil that she possessed an extraordinary vocal ability, but her weight problem would forever bar her from dramatic roles in opera. In 1945, at just twenty-one years of age, Maria made her stage debut in Athens, Greece, to mixed reviews. The critics wrote highly of her powerful, engaging voice, but were unsparing in their sometimes brutal comments about her ungainly figure. Humiliated and infuriated, she literally starved herself into shape, while engaging in a rigorous physical exercise regimen. Only the resilience of youth prevented her from permanently damaging her health. But in the arduous process of making herself presentable on the stage, she damaged her psyche. An inherently strong-willed woman, Maria was so determined to conquer the operatic world, she confused her physical survival with personal conquest.

Two years after her mortifying debut, a tall, surprisingly svelte woman appeared in *La Gioconda*, in Verona, Italy. Her voice was bigger and stronger than before, but this time laced with an inflection of aggression that gave her interpretation of the title role a dramatic power never seen until then. Her performance was an explosive success, and her career was not only assured, but rose to levels of popular and professional acclaim rarely experienced by any artist. Maria Callas had been born. Throughout the decades of the 1950s and '60s, she was the most sought-after opera singer on Earth, center of the most lavish productions, and the highest paid performer of her era.

She so identified with the roles she impersonated, that virtually nothing else in life meant anything to her. She lived almost exclusively for her art, and was at the same time keenly aware of her natural propensity to gain weight. Even the merest hint that she was getting heavier would dethrone her from her position as reigning queen of the opera stage. These pressures may have made life difficult for her, but they continued to add a dramatic edge to her performances unknown to any other soprano.

Singing is an athletic undertaking, however, subject to age and eventual decline, like any physical endeavor. During the early 1970s, Maria's voice began to show signs of deterioration. She still starred in all the biggest roles, but audiences knew she was cutting back on her powerful delivery just to get through each part. In time, her vocal range shrank below performance level, and even she was forced to admit that the incomparably high standards she had set for herself were no longer attainable. She passed into retirement, then began to slip into emotional depression. Her colleagues urged her to teach, to impart something of her fabulous life to younger singers, who would so greatly benefit from her art and experience.

But she was never interested in other people. Her career was the only thing that ever mattered. Her total identification with it made her the brightest star of her day, transforming her from an over-weight Greek-American in New York City to the most famous soprano in the world. All her energy-centers had been suborned to the service of her fifth vortex. Now, unable to activate her throat chakra upon which all the others had been forced to depend, Maria Callas slipped deeper into emotional depression, and died of grief at just fifty-three years of age.

Greek Throat Chakra Deity:
Hermes

As the throat chakra conveys our thoughts and feelings, so Hermes is the messenger of the gods. His name means "hastener," for someone who moves with great speed. Hermes is himself the divine patron of oratory and eloquence. In exchange for the lyre, which gave Apollo musical expression, Hermes received the Caduceus. Entwined with a pair of snakes, this was a golden staff surmounted by the image of a winged sun. Both serpents represented spiritual power rising along the human spinal column until it reached the top of the head, where the soul's enlightenment and freedom took place. As such, the Caduceus exemplifies the chakra system.

It adorned the Greek healing temples of Asclepius, Hygeia (from which the English word, "hygiene", derives) and Panacea (the modern Western term for a cure-all, "panacea"), and has been used ever since as an international emblem of the medical profession, because the Caduceus is the mystical symbol of healing. Indeed, the synchronization of all human energy-centers is the spiritual basis for physical and emotional health. But the Caduceus predated even Hellenic Greece, an indication of the chakra system's profound antiquity. The Sumerians knew the Caduceus as the "Emblem of Life," and were responsible for its earliest known image in the Middle East on a Gudea libation cup more than four thousand years old. It appears in even older Egyptian temple illustrations depicting the soul's transition to the Afterlife.

Strangely, this complex symbol was similarly revered on the other side of the world in Aztec sacred art, suggesting some important, although forgotten connection between the Old and New Worlds during prehistory. The Old Testament Caduceus appears in Genesis as the Tree of Life in the Garden of Eden, but its serpent-imagery was inverted and demonized by the Hebrew author into man's "fall" from God's grace, not his harmony with God's creation.

Hermes' possession of the Caduceus demonstrates that he is the mythic figure most identified with the entire chakra system, wherein he personifies its fifth vortex.

Japanese Throat Chakra Deity:
Raiden

He is thunder, the impressive voice of the heavens. His potency prevented the Mongols from invading Japan during 1274, when he dispersed and mostly sank their huge fleet. In sacred art, Raiden is depicted in anthropomorphic form enthroned on a cloud, from which he hurls lightning bolts at the enemy. He therefore personifies the tremendous power of speech and its ability to sear words into the human heart.

A Throat Chakra People:
The English

A folk capable of producing William Shakespeare would alone seem to merit description as a people of the fifth vortex. But when are added to the Bard of Avon's name the likes of Shelley, Keats, Byron, Milton, Goldsmith, Tennyson, Dryden, Pope, Housman, Blake, Wordsworth, Chaucer, Herrick, Browning, and a host of others no less illustrious, then an extraordinary national voice begins to be heard. Every people has its own poets, novelists and playwrights. But none have made the global impact achieved by English literary artists. Their works are as well known in all other languages, as they are in their native tongue.

No other country has exerted such a powerful influence on world literature. And no convincing conventional explanations for England's uniquely rich literary legacy exist. Far more importantly, she is an example of what becomes of a people who emphasize its cultural throat chakra. By providing a supportive environment, where expression is nurtured, England's men and women of letters are encouraged to reach the kind of literary greatness that has become their country's national heritage. When other peoples similarly access the expressive powers of their collective fifth vortex, they find their own counterparts to Shakespeare and Shelley.

A Throat Chakra Animal:
The Whale

Heavier even than the greatest dinosaur, the whale is the largest living organism the world has ever known. It is also one of the most intelligent and mysterious creatures. Among its outstanding traits is an ability to communicate over hundreds of miles through complex vocalized patterns that mostly still baffle cetologists after many years of research. The animal does not make random sounds, but actually sings notes repeated in sequence and other extended periods of time. So obvious was the musical quality of whale-song, that the eclectic Armenian-American composer, Alan Hovhaness, wrote a symphonic piece for orchestra entitled, *In Praise of Great Whales*, that included recordings of the creatures at sea.

Metaphysically, the whale signifies the powerful voice of the subconscious (the ocean depths).

The Throat Chakra Age:
Maturity.

A Throat Chakra Profession:
Art

The Throat Chakra Gland:
Thyroid

The fifth vortex's connection with the physical body is through the thyroid. Located below the larynx, or "voice box," it secretes hormones vital to metabolism and growth. Blockage of the throat chakra results in decline or loss of speech, inarticulation, stunted metabolic development, even throat cancer.

Throat Chakra Food:
Water

It signifies clarity of expression. Among her divine attributes, Benten is the Japanese goddess of clear water.

Throat Chakra Gemstones:
Turquoise, Aquamarine, Azurite.

Known since ancient times as the "Stone of Mercury" (the Roman Hermes), turquoise derived its name from the Turkish trade routes which carried the greenish-blue gem from Persian mountain ranges. It is particularly favored by Pueblo Indians of the American southwest, where they make offerings of turquoise to Earth Mother by burying pieces in the ground during the initial construction of a *kiva*, a semi-subterranean shrine used for religious purposes.

Aquamarine is said to clear the throat chakra for truth-telling, and is the gemstone associated with the goddess Benten.

Azurite exerts a powerful effect on the fifth energy-center for persons engaged in debates, arguments or making public speeches. As such, it is sometimes referred to as the Orator's Stone.

Throat Chakra Metal:
Mercury, or quicksilver

Throat Chakra Incense:
Snapdragon

Williams writes that the fragrant essence of snapdragon was developed by the mystery schools of Lemuria for improved speech. [3]

Throat Chakra Icon:
A Trumpet

Throat Chakra Color:
Light Blue

The fifth band of the rainbow, it was used in temple art by the ancient Egyptians to signify truth --- *Ma'at* --- from which the modern Western European expression, "true blue," derived.

Throat Chakra Function:
Healing

The Throat Chakra Issue:
Expression

The Throat Chakra Goal:
Communication

A Lesson the Throat Chakra Needs to Understand:
He is most convincing who is himself most convinced.

The Throat Chakra's Negative Aspect:
Gossip

The Throat Chakra's Positive Aspect:
Eloquence

Chapter 12
The Brow Chakra Person

Pursuing our heart's desire by opening the fourth vortex to an Authentic Life encourages the appearance of meaningful coincidences. But our sixth vortex is the real synchronicity chakra, because through it we detect the subtleties of our destiny. The brow chakra is sometimes referred to as our Third Eye, a reference to the Wisdom Body, a system of knowing outside rational thought, consisting of feelings or intuition. But the brow chakra includes our conscious mind and imagination, our ability to analyze and discern, as well as psychic awareness.

Its Third Eye aspects are clairvoyance, clairaudience, telepathy, intuitive medical analysis, remote viewing, psychokinesis, aura-reading, visions, precognition, premonition, prophesy, omen-reading, and related sensitivities. The human aura is a subtle light generated by the chakras and corresponding to the same colors associated with each vortex. Persons able to see an individual's aura can determine his or her spiritual, emotional, or physical health by examining it for brightness and strength. Their ability is just one feature of an opened brow chakra.

Its existence was recognized in ancient Egypt. Common representations of the pharaohs in temple art and sculpture invariably portray them wearing a golden headband stylized in the image of a cobra protruding over the center of the brow. Known as the *uraeus*, as cited above, it was nothing less than a self-evident depiction of the king's tremendously powerful sixth vortex.

As the land's first high priest, he had been intensely trained in the occult arts at Egypt's mystery schools. Pharaoh needed all the information he could process in order to successfully govern so magnificent an enterprise as Nile Civilization, and his mastery of clairvoyance, telepathy and the rest were part of his royal stock-in-trade.

He needed all his faculties, intellectual and psychic, to hold the throne. Indeed, the brow chakra comprises both the left and right halves of the brain, but may become so unbalanced on one side or the other that the neglected half atrophies. Such an imbalance most often occurs these days in favor of the left brain, that mental headquarters of our computing and analyzing talents. Its preference for facts instead of truths is decided by modern society's obsession with root chakra materialism. The right brain is the seat of our artistic nature, which also warehouses all our psychic gifts. This explains why artists are traditionally thought of as "superstitious," because it is impossible for them to separate their aesthetic from intuitive powers. Ideally, the brow chakra is an even balance between both hemispheres, allowing us to move through life simultaneously aware of the inner and outer dimensions which make up a more complete reality.

It is this heightened awareness that stimulates the "loftier" energy-centers to action. Through the ethereal inflections perceived by our penultimate vortex, the intrinsic quality of our crown chakra for spiritual enlightenment may be recognized and put into concepts or images we can understand. Signs of illumination envisioned by our brow chakra inspire the fifth energy-center to give them expression, to put them into at least a semblance of a recognizable form, as much for our own good, as for others. If we struggle with our root chakra, enjoy our sacral chakra, exercise control through our navel chakra, love from our heart chakra, express ourselves in the throat chakra, and are inspired by our crown chakra, then we see through our Third Eye.

Inner sight is important, because, without it, we cannot see the significance of our being. Yet, so many humans are blindly groping through existence, trying to feel their way for what they imagine are their "basic needs." The brow chakra is vision. It enables us to recognize the genuinely important aspects of our lives, to see beyond the values set before us by others, and find our own.

Brow Chakra Character

The brow chakra individual appears wise to the less enlightened, but if he is indeed wise, he considers himself a student with everything to learn. Twenty-four centuries ago, Plato declared that the only thing one man can really teach another is how to remember everything he forgot at birth.[1] A sincere

253

humility is evident in the Greek philosopher's statement, and persons with a well-balanced Third Eye know that the best they can offer their fellow human beings are not instructions or orders, but observations. They do not set themselves up as authoritarian experts. The most effective teacher is the man or woman who creates a bond of common sympathy with his or her listeners. When the Dalai Lama insists that he is just a simple monk, he immediately establishes a rapport with his listeners.

The brow chakra's pit-fall is intellectualism, snobbery. Persons with a balanced intelligence understand that everyone is on his or her own path toward enlightenment and self-illumination. Some are further ahead than others, but that is the only difference; the ultimate goal is the same for all. Only the fool thinks he is better than someone else because he is ahead of that person. Even so, you cannot walk the path to self-realization for someone else, any more than someone can walk your path for you. In Ireland's ritual mound known as New Grange --- a five thousand, two hundred-year-old stone structure some thirty miles north of Dublin --- a ceremonial corridor allows only one visitor at a time to pass through to its central chamber, a kind of Neolithic holy-of-holies oriented to sunrise of the Winter Solstice. Its message is clear: "You are born alone, you die alone, and you are reborn alone. Only you can traverse the path to enlightenment."

In a similar vein, the American Indian, Black Elk, said that he climbed the highest mountain at the center of

254

the world, where he experienced a powerful vision. The summit to which he referred was Harney Peak, in South Dakota.[2] Of course, the tallest mountain on Earth is Napal's Everest, not Harney Peak. That is a fact. Black Elk added, however, that the center of the world is any place where we are uplifted by a metaphysical encounter. That is a truth. Facts can be proved. But it is less important to test a truth than to grasp it. Facts are physical details; truths, spiritual vision. The Third Eye is able to make that distinction.

Brow chakra persons are witty, intelligent, and intuitive. They are exceptional conversationalists, because they are good listeners. But they are less willing to accept things at face value, because their superior powers of observation have taught them that unseen forces are often responsible for visible results. Their values in life are primarily intellectual, cultural, and spiritual, with less emphasis on, even occasionally disdain for the society of commonplace concerns. Mundane survival, transitory physical pleasures, vulgar personal power, even the heart chakra's propensity for shallow romance, bore them. Their natural allies are the throat chakra, through which they express the artistic, scientific or metaphysical issues that enliven the sixth energy center, and the crown chakra, from which they derive their highest inspiration.

Brow Chakra Celebrity-A:
Leonardo da Vinci

Statue of Leonardo da Vinci in Ambroise, central France.

Perhaps the single greatest polymath in history, the life and works of Leonardo da Vinci are famous around the world. No one before or since him excelled as the supreme master and most imaginative innovator of so many disciplines: painting, sculpture, architecture, literature, human anatomy, foreign languages, the staging of public festivals, weapons' technology, civil and military engineering. He was a pioneer in modern scientific illustration, aviation, submarine development, and the construction of armored vehicles. His Mona Lisa and Last Supper are the best-known paintings on Earth.

For Leonardo, subconscious truth and conscious fact, representing the right and left brains, respectively, were not at odds with each other, but combined in his own Theory of Knowledge. This was a synthesis of art and science, in which his art was scientifically executed, while his science was artistically developed. His genius, then, was a result of a perfectly balanced mind, wherein both sides of his awareness worked together for unified purposes. His noted biographer, L.H. Heydenreich, commented that Leonardo's universality was "a spiritual force that generated in him an unlimited desire for knowledge, and guided his thinking and behavior."

To him, "sight was man's highest sense organ, because sight alone conveyed the facts of experience immediately, correctly and with certainty. *Saper vedere* ('knowing how to see') became the great theme of his studies of man's works and mature creations." Heydenreich insists that Leonardo's genius was based on tremendous powers of observation.[3] In other words, he powered up his brow chakra to a phenomenal degree. It almost literally vacuumed up illimitable details and subtleties his consciousness then ordered into mosaics of great art and scientific vision.

Despite the unprecedented energy of his mind, he knew that there was more to living than painting the Leda, or building the working model of an airplane five hundred years before the Wright Brothers flew at Kitty Hawk. Leonardo had many friends, relished their company, fell in and out of love, enjoyed traveling, and was an amiable, gregarious man. He never exercised his genius at the expense of his humanity. Especially adored by his students, they knew that he regarded the arts and sciences, not as intellectual pursuits in themselves, but means to the glorification of the holy spirit; service and enlightenment for his fellow man. When he died at age sixty-seven, he was as much beloved for his kind heart as his mighty brain. His life demonstrated that the heights of intellectual accomplishment may only be achieved through perception through our brow chakra of the spiritual forces which underlie all visible phenomena.

Brow Chakra Celebrity-B:
Nikola Tesla

Of humble Serbian origins, the twenty-eight-year-old man migrated to America with four cents in his pocket, during 1884. The next year, George Westinghouse, head of Pittsburgh's gigantic Westinghouse Electric Company, bought the patent for Nicola Tesla's invention of alternating current. The young immigrant had made the incredibly quick transition from pauper to multi-millionaire, because he was obsessed with discoveries in electricity. Nothing else in life interested him. He was himself a powerhouse of mental energy, his every waking hour concentrated on invention for its own sake. Even the practical uses his finds might make were of use to him only in so far as they interested backers for new projects.

**Portrait of Tesla by Hungarian princess,
Vilma Lwoff-Parlaghy.**

An intensely driven man, Tesla fused every energy-center into the sixth vortex, then focused the accumulated force of all chakras into his conscious mind, which fairly exploded with new concepts. He had harnessed his entire being to the genius of the Third Eye, which glowed with an incandescent genius. The vortex of his brow chakra spun ever faster and brighter, while the other etheric "wheels" of his personality spun like lesser gears in an over-heated dynamo. The results were spectacular, but his life became a flame that burned with too brilliant an intensity. His biographer describes the inventor as "quite impractical in financial matters. An eccentric, driven by compulsions and a progressive germ phobia, Tesla had a way of intuitively sensing hidden scientific secrets and employing his inventive talent to prove his hypotheses. Tesla demanded much of his employees, but inspired their loyalty."[4]

He had very few close friends, and chose to distance himself from all personal relationships. Although physically attracted to women, he had no time for them, and never married. Tesla's restless, fervid brain was a pressure-cooker of far-out ideas his obsessive will-power wrenched into reality. He was a man far ahead of his own time and beyond ours; even today, scientists comb his personal papers for ideas. In 1891, he invented the Tesla Coil, still used in television sets and numerous other electronic instruments. Two years later, he astounded the late 19th Century when his electrical system illuminated the World Columbian Exposition at Chicago, the first mass-illuminated display in history. Its dramatic success led to his installation of the first electrical generator at Niagara Falls.

In 1898, Tesla declared he could operate an unmanned boat by electrical impulses beamed across open water. The announcement was universally condemned as a mad boast, until his pilotless model performed perfectly in a pool before thousands of astonished on-lookers at New York's Madison Square Garden. He had invented and demonstrated the first remotely controlled vessel. Advancing rapidly from this "toy," he lighted two hundred lamps without wire connections from twenty-five miles away. The following year, he moved to Colorado Springs, where he established a new laboratory. In it he produced electrical flashes over forty feet long.

While in Colorado, Tesla made what he considered the most significant find of his career. He said that his radio receiver had received signals from an advanced civilization on another planet. Like his remote-controlled boat, his statement was received with derision. But this time, he had no means of demonstrating his discovery. He lacked any means for recording the outer space transmissions, and, when they stopped being broadcast for no apparent reason, he was left without proof.

Returning to New York in 1900, he undertook construction of his most ambitious project. With a $150,000 advance from financier J.P. Morgan, Tesla began working on a huge tower powerful enough to send photographic images and written messages around the world instantaneously --- all this nearly one hundred years before the internet was born. In the middle of this project, a financial crisis struck the U.S. economy, and Morgan suddenly withdrew his promised support, leaving the great tower half-finished. Its failure marked the turning-point in Tesla's life. Fixated as Tesla had always been on his experiments, he had no business sense, and his ideas were routinely stolen from him, ending up under someone else's patent. With the 1929 stock market crash, he lost all his money, spending the rest of his life in solitary impoverishment. He was no less engrossed in his scientific plans, but from now on they would go no further than the scraps of paper on which he sketched them.

On 7 January 1943, Nikola Tesla died alone and penniless in the single, shabby room of a low-rent hotel in New York City. News of his death revived memories of the virtually forgotten inventor, and hundreds of people, including three Nobel Prize winners, turned out for his funeral.

Feeding every energy of mind and body to his sixth chakra, Tesla had starved the rest of his vortexes. The resultant man was a powerfully creative intellect with incredible vision, but his conscious connection with the spiritual source that drove his brain was cut off. Even his personal survival abilities had been stunted. Tesla's dilemma was the imbalance of internal forces, which his precursor, Leonard da Vinci, had learned to harmonize. By subduing those forces to a single chakra, Tesla set a tragic example of the pitfalls inherent in favoring one vortex, no matter how lofty, at the expense of all the rest.

Greek Brow Chakra Deity:
Athene

The goddess of wisdom, she sprang grown to an adult and in full dress-armor from the brow of Zeus, king of the gods. Athene thus epitomized the power of thought to emerge fully developed from the brow chakra. In keeping with her sixth vortex associations, she was also the divine patroness of literature and the arts.

Japanese Brow Chakra Deities:
Fudo-Myoo and Fukurokuju

An "Unshakable Spirit," Fudo-Myoo is the Guardian of Wisdom, who personifies the virtue of perseverance.

Fukurokuju is the sixth of the Shichi Fukujin, the Beings of Happiness, and associated with the brow chakra, because he is the divine patron of sagacity and insight.

A Brow Chakra People:
The Germans

Known as the "Nation of Poets and Thinkers," Germany has produced more world-class composers and philosophers than any other land in modern history. Not only their numbers, but their influences have determined the course of Western Culture. Leibnitz, Hegel, Kant, Schopenhauer, Nietzsche, Spengler, Heidegger are only some of the more famous names on the roster of bench-mark theoreticians who have shaped the thinking of humankind for the last several centuries.

So too, the worlds of opera, symphony and chamber orchestra could not exist without Bach, Handel, Beethoven, Schubert, Wagner, Brahms, and the hundreds of composers and performers, whose accumulative achievement was the driving force behind musical innovation and evolution. The

Germans are an example of the godly heights in thought and creativity possible when a people acts out of its activated brow chakra.

A Brow Chakra Animal:
The Owl

This creature perched on Athene's shoulder as her faithful animal companion, not because of its stereotyped image as a wise-looking old philosopher, but rather for the owl's extraordinary night vision. Its unsurpassed ability to discern even small, far-off details in the dark signifies wisdom, which is able to see through the darkness of ignorance. According to an authority on Native American symbolism, Jamie Sams, the owl is also associated in tribal traditions with another, highly developed quality of the brow chakra; namely, clairvoyance.[5]

The Brow Chakra Age:
Middle Age

A Brow Chakra Profession:
Science

The Brow Chakra Gland:
Pineal

Some investigators believe the Third Eye is located in the pineal gland, a tiny organ shaped like a pine-cone near the front of the brain. Rene Descartes, the French philosopher, referred to the pineal gland as a place where body and mind converge, and called it the "seat of the soul."[6] Although physicians are not certain of its biological function, they generally concur that it operates as a kind of internal clock indirectly affected by sunlight. For example, a new-born infant is able to sense light through its forehead, suggesting that humans once had a more highly developed Third Eye which has devolved over tens of thousands of years. Interestingly, some reptiles actually grow a third light-sensitive organ at the middle of their heads.

With nightfall, the pineal secretes melatonin, a hormone that regulates other glands related to sleep, and stimulates the regenerative qualities of the mind and body. Blockage of the brow chakra creates mental confusion, migraine headache, and sleeplessness. Taking daily doses of melatonin (about three milligrams) as a vegetable food supplement regulates sleep without causing drowsiness. It is especially helpful when traveling through different time zones.

Brow Chakra Food:
Fish

Long regarded as "brain food" in various cultures, the fish likewise symbolizes abundance taken from the subconscious (water). The Japanese Benten, also associated with the brow chakra, is likewise symbolized by a fish.

Brow Chakra Gemstones:
Lapis, Specrolite, Sugalite

Probably the most valued mineral in the Nile Valley, lapis is a dark-blue stone the ancient Egyptians equated with *Ma'at*, or "Truth", the central tenet of their religious beliefs. Although deified as a goddess, it was an ethical principle upon which all Egyptian life was based. *Ma'at* was the perceived universal law of the cosmos, where "Truth" was attained through balance and harmony. As such, Egyptian judges wore lapis-lazuli adornments as badges of office. Ra, the Egyptian god of the brow chakra, had hair of lapis-lazuli.

Specrolite is alleged to bring out the competitive edge in intellectual contests, while sugalite has a quieting effect aiding contemplation and consideration.

Brow Chakra Metal:
Silver

This white, ductile metal has been used for thousands of years in the creation of bells, because it was believed to give them a purer, clearer "voice" or tone. The same belief went into the manufacture of trumpets, the most famous being the fifteen ceremonial silver horns of the British Crown. The instruments are only sounded on the most special occasions, such as the conclusion of world wars. A period of outstanding Latin literature, from 14 to 180 A.D., was known as the Silver Age. The early 19th Century Silver Fork School in English literature included writers such as Bulwer-Lytton. The pre-Islamic Chakra System persisted in Moslem spirituality as the seven levels of heaven, the penultimate degree corresponding to the brow chakra, being silver.

The bones of Ra, the all-seeing eye of Egyptian myth, were made of silver. In China, parents still hang a silver locket around their children's' neck as protection against evil spirits. The modern European practice of crossing a Gypsy's palm with silver to enable her prophetic visions derives from the same practice known in ancient Greece, at the temple at Delphi, where the Pythia predicted the future. Even today, in the West, a person of inherited wealth is said to have been born with a silver spoon in his or her mouth, another ancient expression that equates spiritual riches with speaking the truth.

Brow Chakra Incense:
Lavender

The noted English herbalist, William Turner, described lavender as a "comfort to the brain."[7] In Roman times, it was used to scent public and private baths in the belief that its fragrance cleansed the mind, just as water cleaned the body. Lavender was also employed medically for head ailments, and reputed to cure such sixth vortex-related problems as dizziness and migraines.

According to Williams, Lemurian adepts of their spiritual mysteries developed comfrey to stimulate the brow chakra, particularly telepathy.[8]

Brow Chakra Icon:
A Telescope

Brow Chakra Color:
Dark Blue, or Azure

The penultimate band of the rainbow, "the color of the rarefied atmosphere, of the clear sky, stands for thinking."[9]

Brow Chakra Function:
Alertness

The Brow Chakra Issue:
Observation

The Brow Chakra Goal:
Perception

A Lesson the Brow Chakra Needs to Understand:
There is more to be perceived than our limited powers of perception are able to perceive.

The Brow Chakra's Negative Aspect:
Arrogance

The Brow Chakra's Positive Aspect:
Revelation

Chapter 13

The Crown Chakra Person

Twin currents of life-energy enter through the base of our spine in the root chakra and through the top of the head, respectively, in our crown chakra --- not unlike the negative and positive poles of a galvanic battery. We live because our lives are powered by these forces of Mother Earth and Father Sky. That energy coming from above is our direct, personal connection to the Compassionate Intelligence that interpenetrates and organizes every aspect of existence. The force of this Universal Mind is the electrical current of our soul.

The compulsion felt in our crown chakra is to know spiritual power through mystical experience. We crave such an event, because our identity as something other --- something more --- than a physical being may only be revealed by contacting with divinity. This is the perennial Search for God --- getting in touch, literally, with divinity.

If we do not exercise our muscles, our body grows weak. To strengthen the mind, we read and think. The soul is no different, in that it may only be felt if something moves it. Spiritual feeling may be achieved through the inspiration of art or human courage; compassion or empathy. These emotions are beyond the rational intellect, because they are hallmarks of the passionate soul, not cold reasoning.

Persons occasionally feel a pleasing light-headedness, as though something were gently rising through the top of the head, when they are emotionally affected by an artistic or mystical experience. In Western paintings of Christian saints, they are almost invariably identified by a luminous halo encircling the head. The same kind of halo-like identification is found in Asian sacred art depicting the Buddha and other enlightened beings. We actually feel our crown chakra flex when we experience the light-headedness generated by high moments of inspiration. So too, the halos found in Occidental and Oriental portrayals of enlightened men and women represent the activated crown chakra energy synonymous with elevated states of spiritual illumination.

Michelangelo's *Creation of Adam*

Together with the brow chakra, the Seventh Vortex is the energy-center of synchronicity. Meaningful coincidence is detected by the Third Eye, then felt in the crown chakra, through which synchronicity connects with some spiritual reality responsible for it. When observing the world through the Seventh Vortex, life is experienced as an inter-related spiritual experience. The sacred dimension of existence becomes clear, engendering in us a natural reverence for and kinship with other living things. As Pond points out, "Once we align with the Divine, all life is a spiritual path."[1] This state of sacred awareness is not confined to high moments of inspiration or flashes of revelation, but is a kind of lens through which we constantly view our changing surroundings.

In the activated crown chakra, we establish our own, direct connection with the divine. In this intimate relationship, there is no need for priests, churches, gurus, or well-intentioned intermediaries of any kind. The Cathedral of God is not some building, however materially splendid, but one's own crown chakra.

In the Medieval European epic of the Holy Grail, when the knights decide to begin searching for this image of spiritual enlightenment, they agree to enter the forest, each making his own path, where none existed before, because they considered it shameful to follow someone else's way. Here is dramatized the crown chakra's lone quest for that one-to-one relationship with the Compassionate Intelligence, to become its co-creator in building the universe. Every person, no matter how humble, co-creates with the Universal Mind in pursuing his or her destiny; i.e., "following their bliss", doing what gives their lives the greatest significance and self-fulfillment. Where their love is, there is God. When an individual begins to move above his or her first three chakras, beyond the world of occasional concerns, they rise from the temporal toward the eternal. They realize that experiencing the mystical in life is the real religious adventure. Referring to the crown chakra, Jung declared, "Religion is a defense against a religious experience."[2] In doing so, he argued that institutionalized dogmas have reduced spirituality to concepts and ideas, which short-circuit the transcendental experience. All this manifests in the radiant higher conscious of the unfolding crown chakra, when a direct connection with spiritual reality is recognized.

The more awakened our crown chakra becomes, the deeper we feel that the most important thing in life is connecting with spiritual reality. It can become an obsessive, even intoxicating quest in which we may neglect our purpose for having been born in the material world; namely, to achieve our maximum personal potential through a working balance of all our energy-centers, which are the various inflections of our soul.

The danger of crown chakra power are its inherent possibilities for fanaticism. An example might be a religious cult known as Jainism. Its adherents follow the doctrine of *ahisa*, or non-injury to all living creatures. While unquestionably a noble concept, Jain practitioners of ahisa go so far as to wear veils over their mouths when drinking, to prevent any small insect from being ingested. They call out to housewives for bedbugs, which are thrown on the naked, exposed bodies of pious followers presenting themselves as compassionate sacrifices for the hungry parasites. Jains will not eat a fruit until it has rotted and fallen from its tree. Still others refuse to move from a particular spot, lest they inadvertently crush some unseen insect. Such extreme behavior in the name of ethical purity is a denial of all the other vortexes comprising our spiritual identity.

The true function of our crown chakra is not to over-ride and negate all our other centers, but to channel divine energies that inspire our life and direct it toward enlightenment through the activity that most gives us a sense of meaning and purpose.

Crown Chakra Character

Individuals living through their seventh vortex are characterized by an inner tranquility that radiates outward. They have a calming effect on others, and seem self-mastered or "centered". There is a quality of serene awareness about them. Crown chakra persons are gentle and trustworthy. Although their powers of perception are outstanding, they are non-judgmental, more ready to forgive than condemn. They would rather suffer injustice than seek revenge, not because they are weak, but due to their moral objectivity. While they embrace certain spiritual guidelines, they are open to other beliefs, from which they may learn something applicable regarding their own views, and allow everyone the right to their opinions in all matters.

Persons chiefly motivated by the ultimate energy-center may sometimes be difficult for others not at the same level. The world of everyday concerns, even survival, is significantly less important than spiritual matters, and interests them relatively little. Crown chakra persons have the greatest paranormal abilities, but they are the least inclined to use them --- in front of others, at any rate --- because they know that such powers are gifts to be properly appreciated, not abused in selfish displays of egotism. Of the other chakra personalities, the crown fears death least of all. He or she knows that losing the physical body is an inevitable part of our growth process, just as the caterpillar throws off its clumsy, grotesque form to take flight as a magnificent butterfly.

Earth is a beautiful, terrible place, but there are other levels of consciousness to visit, and, if we must "shuffle off this mortal coil" to reach them, so be it. Death is a door through which we pass many times. This recognition imparts an inner calm to the crown chakra personality that translates into real courage. Such individuals are more inclined to not only experience greater instances of synchronicity, but to unhesitatingly heed them. Indeed, their whole lives are interpretations of meaningful coincidences and omens inflected throughout the subtleties of everyday life. Crown chakra awareness is extraordinarily perceptive, and applies spiritual observations to the soul's development.

Unhappiness is a sin against physical life, which is more fleeting than we realize, so reasons the person living through the seventh energy-center. But our earthly existence is just a phase in our much longer history. Such conclusions are unavailable to the other six vortexes. Assurance and conviction come only through the force of a spiritual reality pouring into an opened, receptive crown chakra.

Crown Chakra Celebrity-A:
The Dalai Lama

In 1933, the 13th Dalai Lama --- the secular and religious leader of the Tibetan people --- died. His body was embalmed at the Potala, the royal palace in Lhasa, the capital of Tibet. There it was placed in state facing south. Some time later, monks praying in front of the mummified corpse were surprised to notice that the head had turned of its own accord to the northeast. This change was acknowledged as an omen for the general direction in which the next Dalai Lama would be found. But no search could be undertaken until the appearance of another confirming portent. This occurred a year and a half later, when the regent of Tibet dreamed of finding the reincarnated Lama.

He led a ten-day expedition to a sacred lake, where the monks fasted and prayed for several days. They also gazed into the crystal-clear waters, where they saw the vision of a three-storied temple with a golden roof. Nearby, to the east, a simple peasant farmhouse with unusual, blue-colored eaves was part of their vision. The monks began traveling in search of such a place. After several months, they did indeed find the temple envisioned in the lake. To conceal their identity, the monks dressed as beggars and went door to door in the village located east of the temple. At a farmhouse with blue eaves, a woman carrying her young son in her arms was visited by one of the distinguished monks. He had been the 13th Dalai Lama's closest friend. When Bstan'dzin-rgya-mtsho, the little boy, saw him, he reached out with his hand and grabbed the monk by the collar, asking, "Don't you remember me?" Then, as he reached for the monk's prayer beads, the boy exclaimed, "These are mine! Why do you have them?"

Several weeks later, the regent and his followers returned to the blue-eaves farmhouse and placed a rosary, walking-stick and drum on a low table. The three items had all been the personal possessions of the late 13th Dalai Lama. These were placed alongside better-made copies from which the child was asked to choose which belonged to him. Unhesitatingly, he picked out the originals, and the monks declared Bstan dzin-rgya-mtsho the reincarnated Dalai Lama.

Today, he remembers his past lives while dreaming, but places relatively little emphasis on reincarnation. "What is past," he laughs, "is past". Even so, all the Dalai Lamas for the last 600 years are regarded as physical rebirths of the compassionate "Buddha-to-be". The divine bodhisattva Avalokiteshvara is a highly evolved soul who postpones his own nirvana by voluntarily reincarnating in the material world to help others achieve enlightenment. In his relation to the question of reincarnation, the more compassionate our actions today, the more positively we develop as sentient beings, now and in times to come. When the Buddha was asked about reincarnation, he similarly responded by saying that our present circumstances were in large measure determined by our past lives, just as our future incarnations are presently being fashioned by our behavior in this life.

While the 14th Dalai Lama's fame continues to soar in the outside world, he is the most reviled man in the Peoples Republic of China. Government officials there have condemned him as the worst "enemy of the people" since Chang Kai-shek. Chinese armed forces overran Tibet in 1950, and the Dalai Lama fled to India, where he still resides at the center of a refugee colony in Dharmasala. Since his relocation, the Dalai Lama has become the most unique of all his predecessors, because he alone has been forced by historical circumstances into world prominence. Earlier Lamas were reclusive and remote, secluded behind the imposing walls of the Potala palace. One of our time's best-known public figures, he is also the most visible representative of Tibetan Buddhism.

Paradoxically, among Buddhism's central tenets is the concept of non-attachment. The term means letting go of everything that binds us to the physical world. All material is transient, according to the doctrine of non-attachment; only spirit is eternal. The Dalai Lama has been compelled to bring this concept from theory into reality, because he is confronted with the greatest lesson in non-attachment: the loss of his country, the holy land of Tibet. He consistently refuses all calls for armed resistance against the occupation authorities, while presenting himself as "a simple monk", who would prefer studying esoterica in the arcane Gelug school of Tibetan Buddhism.

While certainly true, such a self-portrayal masks the subtler energies of the ultimate weapon; namely, spiritual power. Tibet might pass away, as have other nations during the past and others in the near future. Its disappearance as a state could be the ultimate exercise in non-attachment the Dalai Lama and his followers might have to endure. But he and they believe in a Universal Mind that pervades existence, and oversees the world with an infinite compassion.

Their focus is not political, but on that cosmic consciousness from which all enlightenment derives.

The Dalai Lama ideally personifies the crown chakra, not only because he has attained high levels of mental purity through a lifetime of self-discipline and spiritual dedication. Fate demands that he simultaneously deal, on a daily basis, with the physical survival of his people and the material reality of their refugee existence in the outside world. For all his high-powered spirituality, the 14th Dalai Lama is firmly grounded by current events. He best exemplifies the crown chakra personality through his soul's developing connection with the Universal Mind, together with his strong sense of commitment to the mundane world in which he was born. His life is a superior balance between the titanic forces of exceptional illumination and extraordinary responsibility.

Crown Chakra Celebrity-B:
Jim Jones

Beginning around 1960, James Warren Jones was generally regarded as one of the most charismatic preachers the American Middle West had ever known. With degrees from Indiana University and Butler University, he was a mainstream evangelist with the Christian Church/Disciples of Christ. But his fiery oratory was uncommonly effective. So much so, he rapidly established a devoted congregation in California, where he built the "People's Temple". This was an inter-racial mission for the sick, homeless and jobless residents of America's most prosperous state.

Most of Jones' congregation were poor blacks, many of them suffering from a variety of illnesses, including alcoholism and drug addiction. He found that his empathy for these unfortunates was so deep, that they sometimes seemed to be cured when he prayed with and for them. Such experiences exhilarated him, as he felt spiritual power descend from heaven, through his hands, and into his lamentable parishioners. According to Jones' biographer, "He preached a 'social gospel' of human freedom, equality and love, which required helping the least and the lowliest of society's members. Later on, however, this gospel became explicitly socialistic, or communistic in Jones' own view. The hypocrisy of white Christianity was ridiculed, while 'apostolic socialism' was preached."[3]

Jones won widespread acclaim in California's Democratic Party, for which he became an important fund-raiser and close confidant of numerous liberal politicians, such as Governor Jerry Brown. In time, Jones felt he had become a spiritual power unto himself. He claimed to heal the incurably sick, speak telepathically with extraterrestrial beings from other planets, and predict the future. All this he conveyed to his followers, who were absolutely convinced he was a manifestation of Christ-consciousness.

Gathering up his congregation of around a thousand persons, he relocated the People's Temple to Guiana.

It was surrounded by four thousand acres of dense jungle, and part of a new religious center known henceforward as Jonestown. Here was established an agricultural cooperative under his personal authority and direct supervision. While administering to his flock, Jones developed his theory of "translation". In essence, it held that he should take his congregation with him to another planet set aside by one of his extraterrestrial friends, because the Earth was doomed to perish soon in an atomic holocaust. The "translation" from this planet to the next could be achieved by way of Jones' tremendous spiritual powers, but only through the mechanism of mass-suicide. He openly discussed the new theory with his followers, some of whom strenuously objected, but reconsidered their initial objections after having been physically tortured by Jones' more fanatically devoted parishioners.

Jim Jones during 1970, when he gleefully envisioned the justifiable destruction of the United States in nuclear war.

Word of these excesses leaked back to some of his political friends in the United States, who could not believe their hero was capable of such behavior. Perhaps some incorrigible individuals were seeking to blacken his good name. Accordingly, in November 1978, U.S. Congressman Leo Ryan flew down to Guiana, where he was given a royal welcome at Jonestown by its illustrious founder. The politician was favorably impressed and about to return home with glowing reports of the communal center's inter-racial harmony, when he was timidly approached by sixteen of People's Temple followers, who begged Ryan to take them with him. They told of Jones "translation" theory, and feared for their lives. Although he did not believe their story, he promised to wait at the airstrip, where his private plane would return them to the United States. The next day, November 18, his new passengers prepared to board their flight out of Guiana, when Jones' bodyguards suddenly appeared, firing automatic weapons. In moments, Congressman Ryan and four other persons were shot dead.

Back at the People's Temple, the Reverend Jim Jones announced that the moment for "translation" to another, better planet of peace had arrived. He would heal them all, including himself, through suicide. His spiritual powers, he promised his followers, were so great, they could transcend death, bearing their living souls across time and space to their own world. Although a few of his adherents fled into the jungle at this news, most obeyed his command. Shooting resumed, while poison injections were liberally administered. Two hundred seventy-six children were killed, mostly by drinking soft-drinks laced with cyanide. An additional 638 adults died, among them, their megalomaniacal pastor.

It is easy to dismiss Jim Jones as a simple lunatic. But there was nothing simple about this man. Nothing in his early life, or even a few years before his death, suggested insanity. He no doubt began his religious career as a sincere, if exceptionally intense young man, who projected his consciousness through his seventh vortex. He generated so much crown chakra energy, it drove him mad. Instead of allowing himself to become the vehicle for spiritual power, he hoarded it for himself in perhaps the ultimate blasphemy, because he tried to withhold that power from God. The result was a twisted mind and a toxic soul that poisoned not only himself, but nearly a thousand other people to death.

Greek Crown Chakra Deity:
Apollo

One of civilization's grandest mythic conceptions, Apollo is the Olympian patron of human culture, healing, music, poetry, and the fine arts. He is envisioned as an anthropomorphic image idealized into superhuman form, personification of the folkish soul of Classical Greece.

He battled a subterranean monster for control of the location where he wished to create his most hallowed temple. At Delphi, above the Gulf of Corinth, Apollo overcame Python, the monstrous serpent-guardian of the place, which was already a sacred site located in utter darkness within the bowels of the Earth. The mighty creature's body was cast into a deep crevice. There it rots forever, emitting fumes which, if inhaled by a particularly gifted priestess, enable her to hear the prophecies, always couched in metaphor or riddle, Apollo shares with mankind through her. This myth encodes the core meaning of his godhood. His solar identity was a poetic metaphor for enlightenment. Python's conquest represented the victory of spiritual illumination over the powerful forces of dark ignorance, whose nauseating decay was transformed into the sweet fragrance of prophetic truth. In his gift of prophecy, the sun-god Apollo's nature is aesthetic, hence his patronage of beauty, the cultural means by which we obtain his blessings. In him, aesthetic and spiritual catharsis are one and the same mystical encounter.

Persons affected by these super-charges of the soul occasionally experience a lightness of being, a pleasant physical sensation, wherein something palpably felt but unseen seems to gently rise from and above, although still connected to, the top of the head. This is the crown chakra ascending out of our physical body toward the source of eternal life (divinity), because the seventh energy-center has been properly activated through a genuine mystical event.

In addition to the rest of his divine duties, Apollo is the god of healing, a natural gift he gave to Hermes, who developed it into the practice of medicine.

Apollonian therapy is more shamanistic than medical, however, and depended, not on potions or surgery, but spiritual regeneration, the underlying cause of all health. Here Apollo exemplifies the intimate, inextricable connection between body, mind and soul forming the chakra system, particularly in the seventh major vortex. To energize it is to unleash all the curative potential of which the human body is capable of generating. Even today's materialist physicians realize that the best service they can render their patients is to facilitate as much as possible the body's natural recuperative powers.

Late Roman Era statue of Apollo

As Edgar Cayce, the most famous American psychic of the 20th Century, insistent in "life-readings" uttered during his numerous trance states, "There can be no physical healing without spiritual healing."[4]

Japanese Crown Chakra Deities:
Amaterasu and Bishamon

Amaterasu is the supreme solar divinity. Interestingly, various peoples assign different genders to their mythic conception of the sun. To the Germans, it is feminine, while the French regard it as masculine, even though both are kindred folk of the same Indo-European family. Such fundamental differences demonstrate the individual inflections a people make in their spiritual relationship to the great light-giver of our solar system. To the Japanese, that source has always been female. Her name means the Heavenly Shining One, whose title is Omikami, the Great Goddess. The center of her worship is headquartered at Ise, location of Japan's foremost shrine, where Amaterasu manifests herself in the celestial mirror she used to admire herself at Heavenly Rock Dwelling, thereby allowing sunlight to brighten the world after a period of extended darkness.

She is the Japanese people's own mythic expression of a universal phenomenon. On a literal level, Amaterasu dispels nighttime with her light, while, on a metaphorical level, she scatters the darkness of the mind with enlightenment. Appropriately, her symbol is the mirror. "Hand mirrors," such as the one Amaterasu held, "in particular, are emblems of truth", according to Cirlot. The goddess's connection between the physical and spiritual worlds is exemplified in his description of the mirror as "a symbol of the imagination---or of consciousness---in its capacity to reflect the formal reality of the visible world". He goes on to point out that the mirror is "the instrument of self-contemplation, as well as the reflection of the universe ... it takes the mythic form of a door through which the soul may free itself 'passing' to the other side."[5]

Thus, the mirror signifies Amaterasu's connecting function between this world and the next --- the link connecting us through the crown chakra between our material body with the spiritual dimension. This mirror relationship was defined nearly twenty centuries ago by the Roman philosopher, Plotinus: "Matter serves as a mirror upon which the Universal Soul projects the images or reflections of its creations, and thereby gives rise to the phenomena of the existence we see and touch."[6] Complimenting Amaterasu's mirror are Western folk traditions portraying the Land of Departed Souls as a hall of mirrors. The mirror's symbolic associations with the soul suggest chakra imagery in the taboo against breaking a looking-glass; to do so meant that the soul had been shattered, bringing seven years of bad luck, corresponding with the seven broken vortexes.

The forces of dark ignorance are driven off by Amaterasu's illuminating truth, as depicted in this traditional illustration.

Bishamon is the last of the Beings of Happiness, the Shichi Fukujin. He personifies the crown chakra, because he grants affluence --- not material wealth merely, but the far more valuable riches of spiritual illumination.

A Crown Chakra People:
The Tibetans

Like human population groups everywhere, they have their educated classes, their farmers, artisans, commercial businessmen, civil and religious leaders. What distinguishes the Tibetans, however, is the extraordinary level of social harmony they experience through class collaboration. This cooperative attitude is generated by their unique form of Buddhism, which they universally follow, and the tragedy of their lost homeland they all share in common. Both the Buddhist ethic and historical event combine to provide modern Tibetans with a collective worldview from the perspective of their crown chakra. It is this mutual outlook that enables them to cope with their national disaster, while allowing them to go through life as a joyful experience.

Their seventh vortex is the violet-colored lens through which they see the world. It screens out the materially transient, morally trivial and spiritual inessential, but highlights the real values of existence --- right understanding, thoughts, speech, efforts, livelihood and concentration. These pathways translate into compassion for our fellow creatures, service to others, and enlightenment for ourselves. A crown chakra viewpoint permits them to feel compassion, even sympathy for their oppressors, because the Tibetans believe in the consequences of karma. It is the evolutionary result of an intentional act, a metaphysical extension of Newton's Law: "For every action there is an opposite and equal reaction." In other words, whatever we do with intention in this life generates evolutionary consequences.

Other peoples who suffered persecution have chosen a permanent status of victimization to enlist sympathy for themselves at the expense of perpetual hatred from their enemies. Their ego is so mired in the lower chakras with feelings of revenge, they have utterly cut themselves off from all the potential of their higher selves. Meanwhile, the Tibetans, who regard the ego as adversary, accept their national calamity as an opportunity for spiritual evolution beyond enmity through right understanding and true compassion.

A Crown Chakra Animal:
The Eagle

Among Native Americans, eagle feathers are regarded as the most sacred of all healing tools. In North American tribal traditions, the bird represents an advanced state of grace bestowed by the Great Spirit. In the Pima Indian story of the deluge, their ancestors were warned of the impending cataclysm by God impersonating an eagle. In Greek myth, the king of the gods, Zeus himself, often assumed the guise of an eagle. The ancient Indian *Rig Veda* tells how the sacred soma drink was brought to mankind by the spirit of God in the form of an eagle. In the Mahabharata, Garuda is an eagle-like manifestation of the sun, or light, associated with the triumphant illumination of the Crown Chakra.

The Golden Eagle

The Crown Chakra Age:
Old Age

A Crown Chakra Profession:
Philosophy

The Crown Chakra Gland:
Pituitary

Believed by some students of chakra energy as the actual location of the crown chakra itself, the pituitary may be the seat of human super-consciousness, our paranormal potential. DeLong describes this gland as a "receiver tuning in to the high cosmic Universal Energy, as well as psychic energy".[7] He writes that this spiritual dynamic enters through the top of our head through the hypothalamus area of the brain into the pituitary. It operates as a kind of transformer for raw, spiritual energy, which is released into other parts of the brain, generating various psychic phenomena.

Crown Chakra Food:
The Peach

In China, the peach tree is especially venerated for ling --- the soul substance or spiritual force --- it contains. In England, peach-wood is traditionally used for the manufacture of divining rods, because it is believed to feature spiritual properties similar to the Chinese ling. The ambrosia which granted the gods immortality was made from peach juice. The heavenly realm in the west ruled by the great goddess, Hsi Wang Mu, was a peach garden, where the gods themselves were reborn. If, in the afterlife, the soul of a man or woman ate a peach from the world tree, they would be granted three thousand years of perfect health, and could perpetually renew their youth, so long as they continued to eat the sacred peaches. In Taoist imagery, an old man emerging from a peach symbolizes immortality.

Crown Chakra Gemstones:
Amethyst, Sapphire, Quartz Crystal

In Greek myth, Amethyst was a young priestess of the moon-goddess, Artemis, to whom she dedicated her virginity. One day, Dionysus, the god of drunken ecstasy, saw Amethyst as she was gathering flowers alone in the forest. He proposed his sudden lust to her, but she ran from him. He pursued the girl, and was gaining on her, when she prayed to Artemis for help. "Rather let me die pure in my vow to you," she cried, "than let me be violated!" As she continued to run, she felt her body become heavy. Her pace slowed, and her arms and legs seemed to meld into her torso.

When Dionysus finally caught up with Amethyst, he was astonished to see that Artemis had granted her prayer. The chaste priestess was being changed. As the transformation was nearing completion, he was overcome with sorrow and remorse, and poured an offering of sacred wine over the white stone, which absorbed the liquid. Thus, was created the gemstone named after the woman who preferred death to impurity and dishonor.

"Sapphire" is a Hebrew corruption of the Babylonian *sappur*, or "holy blood", referring, from very ancient times, to its association with the Supreme Being. Kunz alludes to it as "sacred and the gem of gems". He describes a specimen in London's South Kensington Museum in the late 19th Century that "appeared a rich blue color by daylight, but turned violet, resembling an amethyst" by artificial light.[8]

It is alleged to attract divine favor, and was used by medieval European sorcerers to hear and understand the most obscure oracles. The Asteria, more commonly known as the Star Sapphire, is the

Stone of Destiny, because, as one's perspective of the gem changes, a bright star pattern appears, formed by the three crossbars that internally traverse it. According to William Henry, the Stone of Destiny was originally in the possession of Thaut, the Egyptian deity of wisdom, who placed it, "along with the other power tools", inside the Great Pyramid of Giza during its construction, which the god oversaw.[9]

The gemstone is several times identified in the Hebrew bible with God. The Ten Commandments received from the Lord by Moses were engraved on tablets of sapphire. In Revelation, the high-priest's breastplate contained a sapphire, and an entire foundation of the New Jerusalem was literally paved with sapphires. Ezekiel i, 26 describes God's throne as having the appearance of sapphires. In Exodus xxiv, 10, Moses and Aaron claim to have seen him thus seated, a road paved with more sapphires under his feet. The Book of the Angel Raziel was inscribed on a sapphire, which was given to Adam, who passed it on to Enoch, the Hebrew equivalent of the Egyptian Thaut. Previous to the Great Flood, Noah was given a sapphire, which instructed him in building the ark.

Quartz is associated with both the sacral and crown chakras because the mineral is synonymous with joy; the former is physical pleasure; the latter, spiritual happiness. The purity of quartz crystal has long been associated with the purity of the soul while in the presence of the Supreme Being. The mineral is traditionally used in *scrying*, or the ability to experience paranormal visions by gazing into a clear crystal. These visions may include remote viewing, prophecy, or glimpses of the Afterlife.

Crown Chakra Metal:
Gold

According to Cirlot, "gold is the state of glory", "a symbol of spiritual evolution" in the Buddhist Great Work every human should endeavor to achieve. [10]

Crown Chakra Incense:
Lotus

Williams tells how Lemurian adepts distilled fragrance of the lotus to help open their initiates pituitary gland. Maria Leach, editor of *Funk & Wagnall's Standard Dictionary of Folklore, Mythology, and Legend*, describes the lotus as having been associated from ancient times with "divinity, superhuman birth, spontaneous creation, eternal generation, immortality and resurrection, purity and spirituality, the essence of enlightenment"[11].

Crown Chakra Icon:
A Jewel

Crown Chakra Color:
Purple, Violet

Crown Chakra Function:
Understanding

The Crown Chakra Issue:
Spirituality

The Crown Chakra Goal:
Enlightenment

A Lesson the Crown Chakra Needs to Understand:
Although we are spiritual beings, we nonetheless live in the so-called "real world".

The Crown Chakra's Negative Aspect:
Irresponsibility

The Crown Chakra's Positive Aspect:
Spiritual connectedness

The Chakra Deities
Each one of our seven major energy-centers is embodied in a corresponding divinity. It may even be said that these supernal entities are themselves the powers that drive the vortexes. But there are also mythic images that deify the chakra system in its entirety. They are personifications of the complete soul, not its individual inflections or aspects. These godly conceptions reflect the belief in various cultures that the rainbow, in effect, is God's chakra. In terms of natural science, the rainbow is not "physically real", but an optical effect as an image in the eye of the beholder, back to the sun, at a particular time and place. In other words, someone looking in the same direction from a different position will not see the rainbow. It will be exclusively visible to an observer standing at the right location and moment. This meteorological explanation perfectly describes the metaphysical occurrence of synchronicity, which may be

experienced only by occupying the intersection of a specific time and place.

The goddess Iris holding the Caduceus is depicted on a mid-5th Century B.C.E. Greek vase.

To the Greeks, Iris was the goddess of the rainbow, all the colors of the chakra united into a single spectacular phenomenon, just as the human soul attains its true glory in the empowerment of all its energy-centers. She brought communications to mankind from the gods, just as the seven major vortexes bring spiritual illumination to individual human beings. According to Leach, "she was the joiner and conciliator who restored the peace of nature".[12] Here, too, we see opposing forces resolved in the spiritual unity of the properly balanced chakras Iris epitomizes.

Benten is sometimes portrayed in sacred art as a beautiful Japanese goddess with four pairs of arms. Two hands are united in prayer, but in the other six she holds a wheel, bow, arrow, key, sword and jewel. Although symbols of various meaning, they simultaneously parallel each of the major chakras. The wheel is obvious enough as a chakra, or "wheel", and specifically refers to the labor human beings endure as part of their root chakra to make a living in society. Sexual tension in the sacral chakra is exemplified by her taut bow, while the sword, represents personal power implicit in the navel chakra. The arrow signifies direct experience, the brow chakra's salient characteristic, while jewels commonly embody the enlightenment concept implicit in the crown chakra, which unfolds like a lotus to reveal its precious blossom. A famous example is the Tibetan Buddhist mantra, *Om mani padme aum* --- "The jewel is in the lotus."

Benten is the divine patroness of language, eloquence, the arts and music, the means by which catharsis, or "illumination" may be obtained. She is also the only female member of the Beings of Happiness, the Shichi Fukujin, individually associated with the chakras. Emphasizing the goddess's chakra association is her portrayal in sacred art riding on a serpent. The monster was devouring children before she subdued it. The serpent's sword was taken away to be used thereafter as the emblem of the third vortex. Her conquest of this dangerous creature signifies the raw, potentially destructive power of uncontrolled chakra energy to "devour" our sacral capacity for happiness (as symbolized in the child victims) --- an energy positively ventilated in and empowering the fifth vortex Benten herself embodies.

Chapter 14

How to Connect
with the Seven Chakra Types

"Everything that lives is caught in the grip of an inexplicable power which forces it to do its part in a great, predetermined scheme."
—Ignatius Donnelly, 1881[1]

The first chakras were invented by the god of wisdom, Shiva, who gave them to Vishnu, creator of the universe, as weapons against demons. This ancient Hindi myth metaphorically describes the power of living energy-centers to combat the inherent savagery and negative drives against which all individuals struggle. Because these lower urges are fundamental to human nature, they can never be entirely overcome. At best, all we are able to do is lean toward the good. We may win battles against our innate capacities for negativity, but the war is a life-long struggle. Whenever Buddha fought with evil monsters, he never destroyed them, but gave them useful jobs, usually as guardians of Right and Truth.

Regarding ourselves in terms of chakras helps to us to know who are, because, in the aggregate, they comprise our complete sense of identity. We begin to comprehend the source of behavior and the drives that form personality. The same perspective may also afford a realistic appreciation of others, since the character of every man and woman is made up of the same seven points of psychological reference.

Individual dissimilarities appear in the different stress or accent they place on them. We all have and use --- consciously or not --- these vortexes, but each of us with a different emphasis that defines our individual identity.

No single vortex is the soul itself. Rather, each energy-center is one of its component parts. A definition of the individual soul might be a particular combination of all the major chakras. The previous seven chapters described these vortexes and their symbolic imagery. Merely reading about them may increase awareness of our chakras, but in this chapter a simple exercise is presented to tap their symbolism of the specific energies each vortex possesses. The chakra system may be equated to the power-plant of an automobile. For an engine to perform properly, each of its pistons must fire in harmony. If one piston is out of sync, the whole engine runs rough, the other pistons must work harder to over-compensate, and the car's performance falls off. The same applies to our seven major chakras. If only one is not functioning as it should, the quality of life declines.

The exercise described here is analogous to an engine tune-up, wherein the timing is balanced. It is a simple breath-meditation-visualization designed to accommodate synchronicity. By opening our energy-centers, we arrive at an inner still-point, a serene space where we become aware of the previously overlooked subtleties of our surroundings. The fast pace of modern life is distracting. But calming the conscious mind by activating and coordinating the chakras uncloses our sense of perception to the hitherto unseen nuances of meaning that permeate our lives. Such insights may spotlight critical areas of our personality or the personalities of others, including our and their emotional or medical health problems. Mere recognition of these issues triggers a kind of chakra energy for healing.

Sanskrit for the "vital power" that pervades all living things, *prana* enters through the crown chakra from the Sun and the root chakra from the Earth, radiating outward from our bodies to connect with all the elements of the universe. This life force animates and interacts with these two vortexes and all those in between, while drawing *prana* into their cores, like the funnel of a whirlpool. They connect with us physically and psychologically through a particular adrenal gland corresponding to each chakra, as described in the previous chapters. By raising the level of this "vital power" through our energy-centers, they are vivified and opened. The Yoga practice of *pranayana* comprises complex breathing exercises and postures specifically aimed at manipulating and intensifying this force to help achieve higher levels of consciousness. As Rosalyn Bruyere, who researched the human electromagnetic field at UCLA, observes, "Breathing is the way of accessing *prana*."[2] The method defined here likewise employs a breath technique, but is a much simpler version designed for everyday use.

Its fundamental purpose is to empower our energy-centers by raising the "serpent power" that lies coiled at the base of the spine in the root chakra. The Sanskrit term, *Kundalini*, also means "spiral power." When ascending to each vortex, it enlivens and opens the chakra to awaken all of the energy-center's hidden capacities. Adepts at raising the *Kundalini* power sought to create a personal union between the self and the infinite. While the potential for such a union certainly exists, the goal of synchronicity meditation is to make ourselves as receptive as possible for meaningful coincidence, the mystical experience of our times --- to render our spinal columns lightning rods for flashes of illumination from the heavens. The *Kundalini* experience enables us to feel more alive than we may have ever felt before, because it ushers in sudden increases of energy, dispelling all the negative aspects of the chakras and electrifying their positive qualities, resulting in euphoria, even catharsis.

Kundalini's symbol is famous, but less often appreciated for its original, real identity. The Caduceus is a staff entwined by two snakes and surmounted by the image of a winged sun. This highly visible emblem of medicine and medical practitioners is recognized world-wide, and may be found on Classical Greek statues of Hermes or on the tomb walls of Pharaonic Egypt. The staff signifies the human spinal column, up which the twin serpents (*Ida* and *Pingala* in Hindu tradition) form coils around the major energy-centers, while rising toward the sun, the symbol par excellence of enlightenment. The soul then takes wing into illumination --- mankind's highest destiny. This is the implication for the Caduceus carried by Hermes, the messenger of the Olympian gods, beings of eternity. In Egyptian tradition, Thaut, the god of wisdom and medicine, held the Staff of Life.

The Caduceus is not only the supreme representation of spiritual growth, but forms one of the most powerful meaningful coincidences of all time. Heinrich Zimmer, the German mythologist, traced its origins back to Mesopotamia, more than forty-eight-hundred years ago, and was sure it was older still, because the Sumerians seem to have imported it from a previous civilization. How remarkable then, that the Caduceus appears to represent the DNA strand discovered only in the last half of the 20th Century! Both signify the building-blocks of all organic life, the spiral pattern of their energy-form, that, in the words of Wallace-Murphy and Hopkins, "programs all development and evolution. Both the Caduceus, with its four complete loops on either side of the staff, and the DNA spiral, represent the number eight, which, since ancient times, has been held to symbolize eternal, spiral motion, the supreme signature of the universe."[3] In other words, the Caduceus and DNA helix are indeed identical in form and implication. How could anyone have even suspected human DNA so many thousands of years ago? Yet, parallels between the ancient spiritual symbol for life and its modern scientific discovery are undeniable.

No less modern was a universal principle at the core of pharaonic Egyptian religion. *Ma'at* means "straight", right, true, truth, genuine or righteous. Sometimes in temple art, *Ma'at* was portrayed as a goddess, really a variation of the more famous Isis, holding an ostrich feather in her right hand or worn in her head-band. Isis was worshiped as the founder and mistress of a mystery cult, in which the rebirth and eternal life of the human soul was made possible through initiation into her secret doctrine. She was originally a mortal woman who solved the enigma of immortality, saving herself from death and restoring her dead husband, Osiris, to life eternal. "Cannot I, by the sacred name of God, become a goddess of like rank to Ra in heaven and upon Earth?," she asked herself.[4] The "sacred name of God" she used to become immortal was *Ma'at*. Occasionally, in religious representations, the upright feather took the place of her head whenever she personified this concept. More commonly, her feather stood alone to signify perfect balance, which the ancient Egyptians believed was the true and ideal state of all creation.

To them, *Ma'at* was the physical and moral law of the universe, and its central position in their belief system explains why church and state were inextricably bound together during dynastic times. The equipoise of contrary forces and their harmonization was good not only for society as a whole, but for every individual, as well. The only alternative was chaos, the precursor to destruction. *Ma'at* was a harmonious relationship between the inner and outer man or woman, the reconciliation of mind, body and soul. Only in such a state of being could true happiness be found and human beings function properly. Yet, there were gradations of *Ma'at*. Perfect harmony was regarded as a fleeting moment, like a whiff of perfume passing on the breeze. It was to be ever sought for, however, because *Ma'at* was the only real peace in a natural world of perpetual struggle.

Ma'at lies in that breathless moment before an ostrich feather, balanced upright on the tip of its quill, falls one way or the other. *Ma'at* moments occur in meditation, in the pure stillness of a meadow, in the catharsis of great art, in the mutual recognition of love. A state of *Ma'at* may be reached when all of one's seven major chakras are turning freely and energetically. It is the closest Man may come to perfection in an imperfect world. As such, *Ma'at* is the zone for synchronicity. The thrill of otherworldly awe engendered by a meaningful coincidence is not unrelated to the bliss experienced in moments of *Ma'at*. The two phenomena are inflections of the same mystical experience.

Ma'at sets the stage or clears a space in time for synchronicity to occur, almost as a precondition. Although it may take us unawares, *Ma'at* can also be achieved deliberately through meditation or an aesthetic encounter. Although they allow meaningful coincidence to manifest itself, they do not guarantee its appearance. In any case, the bliss associated with *Ma'at* represents an arena for synchronous events to shape the on-going mystery of our lives.

Less mysterious is the application of that remarkable comparison to our daily lives. When Kundalini energy connects with the root chakra, stress is reduced, releasing certain chemicals into the bloodstream, calming emotions related to physical existence. Reaching the sacral chakra, sexual pleasure is strengthened, and our natural capacity for joy broadens to include everything in our vicinity. At the naval chakra level, stamina and vitality improve, while stomach ailments vanish in a rush of self-mastery. When Kundalini power touches the heart chakra, compassion radiates outward, replacing judgmental reactions with fellow feeling. As it reaches the throat chakra, the body's almost infinite capacities for self-healing become active. Pain decreases, the cells rejuvenate, and the aging process slows down, because hormonal secretions of the endocrine glandular system, set in motion by the thyroid, balance all the other glands.

At the brow chakra, Kundalini energy highlights all psychic abilities, opening the Third Eye to all forms of paranormal powers, including observation of the auras which surround all living things. The aura is energy radiating from our chakra system, and corresponds to the same color scheme. Being able to "see" the human aura --- the degree of its brilliance --- is an assist to health, because the aura's relative luminosity is an indication of a particular chakra's strength or weakness. Attaining the crown chakra, Kundalini stimulates spiritual growth, the real goal of mankind.

But these are the side-benefits of a chakra meditation whose chief purpose is encountering a mystical experience through meaningful coincidence.

General Synchronicity Meditation

Silence is a prerequisite for any meditation. We must have quiet in order to hear the music of the spheres. Sequestering oneself for perhaps twenty or thirty minutes in surroundings free of as many disturbances as possible is essential. Ideally, meditation should be performed at a "sacred site;" in other words, a location associated with a spiritual milieu. Such places may be temples, shrines, churches, or a harmonious environment in a natural setting. Their local energies can contribute mightily to the success of any meditation.

But a quiet corner of one's own home is more usually practical and comfortable. The hallmark of Synchronicity Meditation is simplicity. The meditator is not required to sit or lay in any specific position. Personal comfort should determine the proper posture. Begin by closing the eyes, then take a deep breath through the nostrils. Hold it for seven counts, then exhale slowly through the mouth, as though blowing out a candle. Repeat twice more. The object of this breath exercise is to lower the heartbeat, which, in turn, slows the flow of blood to the brain, allowing for a calm state of mind.

Breathe normally, inhaling through the nose, exhaling through the mouth. With each exhale, count your breaths from one to seven, then back from seven to one; from one to fourteen, and fourteen back to one, and so by sevens in this forward-backward-forward pattern as high as forty two. Meditators may not wish to count that many breaths, but they should strive for a minimum of half that number. Sometimes, persons meditating in this number sequence experience the physical sensation of slowly rising when they count their breaths upward, and gently descending as they count down. The feeling is nothing less than the soul rising and falling to the spiritual rhythm being created by the meditator. In any case, this exercise is intended to clear the mind of all the psychological dross and mental static we accumulate during the normal course of our everyday lives in the so-called "real world." It is important, therefore, that we do not allow our thoughts to drift into material concerns during meditation. Counting our breaths helps keep our attention focused. Visualizing may be of some assistance. With every inhaled breath, imagine breathing in golden sunshine, filling every internal aspect of the body. Imagine black soot or a shadow with every exhalation. Distractions are quite common and do not ruin a meditation, unless they are yielded to. If the count is lost, resume where it may have been left off. The actual number of breaths counted is not as important as the time spent doing so. If distracting thoughts persist, a simple command usually works: "This is my own time. I will deal with this problem when I am finished here."

When the meditator has finished counting breaths, he or she should visualize a pure-white snake coiled inside the base of the spine. Now imagine a stationary wheel in the same area of the body. This is the root chakra. As the name of a deity identified with this energy-center is spoken out loud, the wheel is seen to spin faster and faster, until it resembles a whirling vortex. As the meditator exclaims "Hades!," or "Ebisu!," a red glow emanates from the rapidly rotating wheel. The white snake slowly uncoils itself to become an identical pair of serpents, which rise into the red radiance of the twirling root chakra. These snakes are the *Kundalini* energy, as represented in the ancient Caduceus and today's DNA double-helix. The meditator then visualizes the same procedure for the other six chakras, each in its turn, one after the other, with their corresponding colors and deities.

After the twin serpents have risen into the crown chakra, take a deep breath through the nostrils, while crossing the arms in front of the chest, open palms touching the shoulders. Hold the breath in this position for seven counts. Then exhale gently through the mouth, while slowly unfolding both arms as though they were wings. Envision all the electrified colors of the rainbow-chakras streaming outward in a brilliant display from the torso. Repeat this seven-count breath gesture twice more.

Immediate consequences of the meditation may include feelings of "centeredness," inner calm, tranquility, and mental clarity. The longer-range goal of creating sensitivity to meaningful coincidence (and, in fact, all manner of mystical experience) is in the process of attainment. Practitioners should not expect instant results, but must realize that the spiritual path is a life-long undertaking. Patience, persistence and humility are the real keys to success in meditation. With each breath-count, the meditator's soul grows stronger, just as the athlete's body becomes more powerful with every weight he lifts. But the strength of the soul is transparency to transcendence --- openness to enlightenment through synchronicity.

Specific Synchronicity Meditation

The general mediation just described uncloses our perception of meaningful coincidences while attracting them. It stills the mind, making our power of perception receptive to understanding their significance, even interpretation. But something more finely tuned is needed to access a particular chakra --- to connect with its unique energies, either in ourselves or others.

A specific meditation begins with the same breathing techniques presented in the General Meditation. The difference takes place after the breath-count is completed. Instead of uncoiling the *Kundalini* serpent to enliven every chakra, our new objective is to direct *prana* at a specific vortex. Somewhat more preparation is therefore needed for deliberate concentration. The physical images described in each chakra now become tools for drawing upon the singular energies of an explicit center. If, for example, the meditator targets his or her heart chakra, the presence of its own symbols will become part of the experience. Photographs, illustrations or statuettes of Mother Teresa, the goddess Persephone with her flowers, or Daikoku of the Shichi Fukujin, with a sun-disk over his breast, comprise the proper setting for the meditation. Appropriate symbolic objects may join the scene. These include a rose, an apple, something made of copper (or the metal itself), and the associated gemstones --- tourmaline, serpentine or malachite. The fragrance of rose incense completes the ritual environment.

To be sure, these chakra meditations are rituals if we understand that ritual is the reenactment of myth. Myth, in turn, is a metaphor pointing beyond its own image to a mystery or truth. Myth is a discourse between the conscious and subconscious mind, symbolic of spiritual powers within ourselves and the world around us. These energies that operate throughout the universe are personified by deities chosen to embody our various chakras. Thus, myth is not a historical fact, but dramatizes something meaningful to one's inner life. Such a truth is in the nature of a revelation which can only be experienced, not explained. To give it literal interpretations reduces its value.

The function of ritual is to dramatize the myth, to make it live for those in possession of it, and thereby identify with divine power, the ultimate mystical experience that gives meaning to our existence as individuals and as a species. Even so, not all of the images associated with a particular vortex are required for a successful meditation. They should be regarded as nothing more than tools, means to an end; i.e., getting into the unique energy patterns of a certain energy-center.

In meditation aimed at accessing a specific chakra, the meditator commands the *Kundalini* serpent power to rise from its lair at the base of the spine. It then ascends as a pair of white snakes into the desired vortex. In the case of the heart chakra, attention is directed to the thymus, which releases its own kind of *prana* related to matters of love and compassion, as much for others as ourselves. The same opening and closing of the crossed-arms-over-the-chest gesture is used to conclude the meditation.

By thus freeing the energies of a particular vortex, we not only come to understand and recognize its singularity, but tap into the forces of its very being. If so, then some observers have wondered, "Do other animals have chakras?" The question is tantamount to asking, "Do other animals have souls?"

Answers may be found in general human relationships with certain creatures. Dogs, cats, horses, goats, lambs, etc. have been common household pets in most cultures for thousands of years. Snakes, lizards, turtles, etc., less so. Spiders, scorpions, ants or beetles, least of all. Feelings of affection for a grasshopper or mosquito are rare, but human compassion is commonly aroused if we find one caught in a spider's web. Doubtless, arachnida and insects operate on at least the first three chakras for survival, reproduction and dominance. That they possess the remaining four energy-centers of compassion, self-expression, insight and spiritual connectedness seems unlikely. Their lack of these vortexes may explain why humans are generally unable to relate to them on the same level as other animals.

In addition to the root, sacral and navel chakras, our fellow mammals are undoubtedly compassionate, expressive and insightful. We do not know if they have a spiritual connectedness, as we do, but it seems logical that they should, since they possess all the rest. The naturally close relationship between dolphins and whales with humans undoubtedly suggests some kind of shared energy. Yet, we commonly develop similar affection for certain non-mammals, especially birds, which show every sign of owning at least three of the top four chakras. We have seen that certain animals may be associated with each of the seven major chakras. The snake, cat, lion, dog, whale, owl and eagle epitomize and exemplify, respectively, the root, sacral, navel, throat, brow and crown chakras. Recognition of our inner energies among creatures forms a basis for fellow-feeling and compassion, thereby raising our own spiritual nature to higher levels of empowerment and self-discovery.

Chapter 15

Understanding Human Types through Synchronicity

"When we try to pick out anything by itself, we find it hitched to everything else in the universe."
—John Muir[1]

Synchronicities connect with each of the Human Types. While each type can experience the full range of meaningful coincidence, particular synchronous events themselves may elucidate each one of the seven personality divisions. Synchronicity is fundamentally a form of guidance that enters into the personal lives of every human being. Even if we knowingly discard it, at least part of its influence nevertheless enters our subconscious. A typical example was recounted by the California poet, Miriam Hohf. "Many years ago, when I was a small child living in the Pennsylvania countryside," she remembered, "I took long walks by myself across the fields and into the forest, listening to the birds and talking to the rabbits and squirrels. I never felt afraid and deeply loved all the trees and animals. But on one otherwise beautiful, sunny day, my surroundings felt different somehow.

"Everything was absolutely calm and motionless. Just when I approached the edge of the forest, however, a gust of wind suddenly arose, loudly rustling the leaves. I stopped and listened to them, because I felt they were speaking to me. They seemed to be saying, 'Go away! Do not come into the woods today! There is danger here! Danger! Not safe to play here today! Go away!' For the first time, a chill of fear ran through me and I fled, almost in tears. I did not visit the forest again, too afraid to return.

"About a week after my experience, mother told me about a terrible story just published in the local paper. It seems that on the same day the leaves spoke to me the body of another little girl was found by the police. She had been brutally raped before being murdered. Did the spirits of the forest warn me in the rustle of their leaves?"

Miriam's experience was a root chakra synchronicity. She was aware of an otherworldly quality in the stirring of the leaves that warned of danger. For some time prior to this meaningful coincidence, she was innocently developing a personally spiritual rapport with the forest, so much so, she eventually grew so in tune with it, the very leaves seemed to speak to her. Such experiences, for all their sense of wonder, are common for persons who strive to live in harmony with natural forces. The feeling of identification can become very strong and close, actually to the point of melding with the mystical force that underpins all natural phenomena.

Common to nature-based spirituality around the world is the belief that nature is the physical expression of God; hence, the closer man comes to nature, the nearer he approaches divinity. While living alone for some years in a beautiful forest, I sometimes felt so inwardly serene that I could "just let myself go" sometimes, and gladly dissolve into the natural surroundings. I later learned of the same feeling experienced by other people who lived by themselves in the general vicinity.

Another example of a root chakra synchronicity, appeared in the June 1999 issue of *Omni* magazine, concerning Henry Z. Jones, Jr., a genealogist from San Diego, California. While researching a group of German families who emigrated to New York in 1710, "I had no reason to think I was related to any of those eight hundred seventy-four families," he said. "Totally at random, I picked one name, Dietrich Schneider, for my researcher in Germany to track down."[2] When he received the report some months later, Jones was shocked to learn that he was a direct descendant of Dietrich Schneider.

In *Synchronicity and You*, I mentioned that persons interested in their ancestry seem almost inevitably involved in synchronous events that assist them with research. After interviewing three hundred colleagues who shared their own synchronous events with him, Jones concluded in his book, *Psychic Roots: Serendipity and Intuition on Genealogy,* that meaningful coincidences definitely assist investigators trying to learn about their family histories. He cited the rather typical example of another genealogist who was searching without any success among the stacks of a library for some documentation about her 18th Century relative, when she was suddenly struck on the head by a book that had fallen from a high shelf. She opened the book to find precisely the reference to her ancestor she needed. Looking for one's "roots" is unquestionably part of the root chakra personality. Someone who needs to feel connected on a fundamental level with their origins is energizing their first vortex. As described later, some meaningful coincidences connect subconscious dreams with our waking consciousness. But the following case exemplifies a sacral chakra synchronicity.

In 1995, a man being unsuccessfully treated for clinical depression dreamt about Rita Muller, a woman he had not thought of since he last saw her, some thirty years before. Their brief relationship had represented one of the few personally fulfilling moments in his life. Later that afternoon, he enjoyed hearing a Beethoven quintet being broadcast over the radio, which he far more often listened to in the evenings. When the performance concluded, he was surprised to learn from the announcer that one of the players was Rita Muller, a name he never encountered outside his affair three decades before. His sacral chakra synchronicity affirmed that his innate capacity for physical happiness still existed. Based on this self-awareness, his therapy at last began to make progress in overcoming his depression, which originated in his previous conviction that he had lost all potential for joy.

Synchronicity sometimes elucidates our lives in mysterious ways that at once strengthens our character and sensitizes our soul. A case in point was shared with me over national radio by a woman who called into the station over which I was being interviewed in summer 1999. She told of her own, life-changing synchronicity that began for her when she was a young girl in Nebraska nearly fifty years before. When only fifteen years old, Nora was told by her family doctor that she would suffer total blindness in a few years. Further testing confirmed that no preventive surgery could save her sight. She naturally slipped into deep depression, but was unfortunately not supported by most of her own family members. They were emotionally unequipped to deal with such a tragedy, and virtually ignored Nora.

Sinking deeper into despair, she was consoled by only one person, her Swedish immigrant grandmother, Ulla. The old lady was comforting but forthright. She told the sorrowful teenager she had to face up to the inevitability of going blind. "But when one door closes, another one opens," Ulla said. "Other abilities will increase in power. Very often, people who lose one sense get stronger in others. Some who can no longer see eventually find they have developed superior hearing." Above all, the grandmother stressed personal independence. "From now on, and as time progresses, you must learn to think and act more and more for yourself. Be independent! Then you will succeed, no matter what you do or what happens to you."

Thanks to Ulla's moral support and cheerful encouragement, Nora weathered her youth ever shrouded in darkness, until complete blindness overcame her by her twentieth birthday. Following her grandmother's advice, she worked hard at becoming independent in all things. So capable did she eventually become in directing her life that she rose to the top of a profession requiring exceptional hearing abilities. In terms of worldly success, her personal accomplishment was great, but in striving to fulfill Grandmother's goal of self-reliance, Nora lost whatever spiritual values she might have once had, and tended toward atheism. In time, Ulla passed away, but Nora never forgot her emphasis on independence. Some years later, Nora's high-paying salary finally allowed her to purchase the best seeing-eye dog money could buy. The directors of an exclusive breeding and training kennel in upper-state New York put her name on a long waiting list after taking a personal suitability test. She would be informed later when an animal would become available. The trainers named their animals and determined to whom they were given.

Nearly a year passed before Nora was informed by the kennel directors that a seeing-eye dog had been selected for her. They sent her a long computer print-out listing the dozen or so dogs assigned to their prospective owners. The names were what might expect --- Rex, Spot, Lad, and so forth --- all save the one allocated for Nora. The female German Shepherd had been given an exceptionally unusual name, "Ulla." Almost faint with astonishment, Nora read over the dog's pedigree: It had been born on July 4th, Independence Day. This double-synchronicity produced nothing less than a transformational effect on the blind woman. It seemed as if all the sorrow and struggle of her adolescent and adult life had been suddenly suffused with high meaning and a sense of purpose. In a single moment of mystical connection between completely separated elements, Nora's cynicism regarding any spiritual possibilities had to give way before the mystical possibilities open before her. This dog with her Grandmother's name and theme of independence had already begun to lead her out of the darkness, in more ways than one.

Nora's potent meaningful coincidence suggests she is a navel chakra person. She sought control over her life, but went to the extreme of acquiring independence at the sacrifice of her mystical relationship with the forces that brought her into being. The nature of the synchronicity she experienced was likewise concerned with self-mastery, but only through blindly trusting a fellow creature who led Nora toward spiritual enlightenment. Her meaningful coincidence dealt with matters of self-control, and is therefore defined as a third, or navel chakra type experience.

During the spring of 2000, a recently married man brought his wife's engagement ring back to the store from which he purchased it for refurbishing. While the ring was being cleaned and some recorded music played in the background, he engaged in small talk with the store clerk. The newlywed had just told her about some beautiful blue birds that had come to roost over the window of their home, when a line from the recorded music, "if happy little blue birds fly," was heard from the old song, "Somewhere over the Rainbow." Blue birds, of course, are famous symbols for happiness, especially married bliss.

People in love commonly experience synchronicities that bind their hearts, and the man's meaningful coincidence of related elements --- the perfectly timed music about blue birds, their symbolism and appearance at the newlyweds' house, the ring, even the store at which it was purchased, etc.--- all combined and crossed-referenced each other in a single, significant moment, but only when the husband was present. It was a fourth chakra, or Love Synchronicity, that underscored the role of passion as the active ingredient in meaningful coincidence.

"When I made the track, 'Eternity'," writes Danish composer, Henrik Hytteballe, "from the album *Flow* (http://shantipublishing.com/Flow), I had a special story in mind.

"In his book about awareness, *Lifetide* (NY: Simon & Schuster, 1979), author Lyall Watson tells about being on a distant, Indonesian island, watching sea turtles coming up on land to dig holes for their eggs, and wanted very much to see a giant leatherback. So, he was taken by a local elder to a certain lagoon, where the djuru, or "wise man", began splashing his hands on the surface of the water, as though playing a piano, while singing a song in some ancient language. After about twenty minutes, a giant turtle did indeed appear. As it came closer, the djuru raised his arm, holding his palm down towards the animal. The turtle lifted its head to nip his fingers, as gentle as a calf. Then it turned and disappeared into the vast ocean.

"I see this as an example of communication beyond words between different species. I did not share Watson's account with the producers at Real Music, the company that released my album, but for the 'Eternity' track, they included the image of a turtle swimming under the sea, just as I had wordlessly envisioned it."

In response to Henrik's email, I told him how his video was "well-timed to the death of an old friend, who died about the same day you sent 'Eternity'. Her passing and its arrival form a synchronicity, a term coined by Carl Jung to describe 'meaningful coincidence'. That is the same, wonderful phenomenon you experienced connecting the Indonesian turtle and the animal's 'coincidental' but perfectly appropriate appearance in your visual haiku. In many cultures around the world, the turtle --- because it moves from the land, into the water, back onto the land, and through the water in a continuous process --- is symbolic of the eternal soul, which similarly travels from this earthly existence, into the purely spiritual, then reincarnates in a never-ending cycle. The mechanism of synchronicity is passion --- our enthusiasm or deep interest or engagement in something that triggers meaningful coincidence and an individual's personal connection to the Creator. As He, She or It creates originally, whenever we also create something original, a kind of resonance or energetic frequency builds up between human and God, not unlike static electricity."

Synchronous events sometimes connect with our dreams, bridging the subconscious with conscious reality. For example, in February 2000, while preparing slide photographs for an evening class about "sacred sites," I chose to include a shot of a small and little-known shrine built perhaps two thousand years ago by the Mayas. It was located near the sea on the small island of Isla Mujeres, the "Isle of Women," about two miles from the coast of Yucatan. During five years of making "sacred sites" presentations, I never brought this transparency to school, nor discussed with my students the famous Crystal Skull associated with the off-shore island. The life-size representation of a female human skull, the Crystal Skull was found during the excavation of some Maya ruins. But archaeologists believe it was meant to symbolize the moon-goddess, Ixchel, whose shrine is found at Isla Mujeres. To the Mayas, Ixchel was the divine patron of all psychic powers, especially prophecy.

On nothing more than a whim, I decided to show slides of the island and the Crystal Skull at my class that night for the first time. The photo was only one of a hundred presented. After class, a woman student told me she had been shocked to see the slide of Isla

Mujeres and learn of the Crystal Skull there, because a few nights before she dreamt of visiting the same island, where she marveled at the Crystal Skull in a small temple. Previous to attending my lecture, she never suspected any connection between the great crystal artifact, the moon-goddess and the obscure little island.

Her experience belonged to a brow chakra person, whose psycho-drama (or dream) connected her irrational (or, better expressed, transrational) subconscious to the rational consciousness of a particular material object signifying just such a connection. The Crystal Skull and the deity it represents is the most perfect symbol of the woman student's awakening (as from the dream she experienced) to her innate psychic potential.

The categories of synchronicity and the Seven Human Types are not so separate that they are unable to sometimes merge one into the other. A case in point was an Ontario man who had repeated dreams of his grandfather's portrait. So far as he knew, no such painting existed in the material world. Later, during a vacation in England, he visited an old castle about which he knew nothing. Aimlessly strolling into one of its many rooms, he was astonished to see exactly the same portrait envisioned in his series of dreams hanging on the wall.

The Canadian's experience combines elements of both the dream and ancestry. But here too, the psychic power of the brow energy center, sometimes referred to as the Third Eye, was activated in a personality of the sixth chakra.

As will probably come as no surprise to the reader, several meaningful coincidences were experienced while putting together this book. Since the subject is synchronicity, one might expect it to have attracted its share of the phenomena. A particularly memorable example took place when the text was less than half-finished. I was beset by many doubts and worries, among them the fear that its composition was progressing too slowly. Suddenly, I had a strong yearning to learn how many words were written so far. I tried to ignore the urge and get on with the work at hand, but my curiosity got the better of me, and I activated the word-count on my computer. It registered twenty-two thousand, two hundred twenty-two words. This number seemed remarkable at the time because at the moment I was writing about the second chakra on page twenty-two of my original manuscript.

Repetition of the second numeral, representing as it does the sacral chakra's potential for happiness, meant that I was to put aside my worries, enjoy the writing process, and trust in the outcome of my labors. My tension yielded to a calm, centered feeling, and I resumed work with relaxed confidence. The synchronicity was of a crown chakra type, because it connected to spiritual matters associated with the seventh energy center.

A more moving synchronicity took place as I just began writing about the Greek goddess, Iris, and Benten, one of the Japanese Beings of Happiness. Both are mythic personifications of the rainbow, that most dramatic symbol of the chakra system. I was collecting my thoughts and about to write them out, when a double rainbow appeared outside my window. What a wonderful confirmation and blessing from the two lovely goddesses I was at that moment beginning to describe in terms of the human chakras! The sensation of connection with something far greater than myself made that a moment in time never to be forgotten.

It seems clear that if we can begin to think with our chakras, as it were, we may appreciate and even understand our own meaningful coincidences as true mystic experiences. Observing them through the filter of our vortex system reveals that they thread our lives into the vast interconnectedness of the universe through broad patterns of significance otherwise invisible to us. The same chakra filter may be used as a template held up before our fellow human beings to disclose the true nature of their character, their desires, strengths and weaknesses.

Afterword
Indra's Net

"The seeker must find the 'mysterious meaning' and the 'awareness of divine things' through ritual and symbols alone."
—Lucie Lamy [1]

Like many investigators of synchronous phenomena, the image of a net connecting everything in the universe came to mind during the early stages of my research, suggesting an initial title (later rejected by the publisher) for my first book on the subject: *Indra's Net.* It derived from a Rig Veda poem describing the Hindu god of creation wielding a cosmic net of inter-connectedness over all phenomena.

The image of such a metaphysical net and the title of this examination --- Synchronicity As Mystical Experience --- are succinctly combined in the words of Guido von List. A great Austrian scholar of the late 1800s specializing in Middle European spiritual origins, he had an instinct for penetrating to the mystical core of phenomena like acausal events.

Von List could have been describing Synchronicity itself, more than half-a-century before Jung coined the term, when he observed, "Chance! Actually, there is no such thing as chance, for all events, without exception, are in the great web of fate --- as warp and woof --- all well-ordered. Because these incalculable

331

influences often suddenly and inexplicably disturb our own woof of fate, these are called 'chance,' without, however, having considered a chance occurrence as something irregular or lawless (that cannot be!), but perhaps as something incalculable. The oldest Aryan mystics already recognized this, and therefore portrayed the Rulers of Fate, the Three Norns, as Weavers of Fate, who, out of the 'warp' and 'woof', weave the 'raiment of time', i.e., 'fate'." [2]

Here, von List intimates perhaps the single greatest insight provided by an appreciation of Synchronicity and its general implications; namely, identifying the Compassionate Intelligence that manifests itself in meaningful coincidence: God is the sum total of everything in the universe. If this conclusion is correct, then thinking of mankind as something separate from its Creator is profoundly erroneous. On the contrary, you and I --- our every thought, all our actions, and everything that happens to us --- are inflections of the Supreme Being, which is simultaneously within us and throughout the galaxies. We share God's identity, because "he" is accumulated existence. As the visionary, Mechtilde von Magdeburg, exclaimed as long ago as 1256 A.D., "The day of my spiritual awakening was the day I saw --- and knew I saw --- all things in God, and God in all things."[3] Her moment of inner illumination sprang from the same inspiration that caused Ireland's greatest 20th Century poet, William Butler Yeats, to exclaim nearly seven hundred years later, "Everything is blest! Everything we look upon is blest!"[4]

A temple statue of Thagyamin, the Burmese Indra, offering the seashell of infinite abundance at Myanmar's Shwedagon Pagoda, Yangon. Photo by Roger Price, https://www.flickr.com/photos/83555001@N00

The same revelation is at the heart of the Grail quest, as insightfully perceived by a modern French scholar of Celtic mysticism. Jean Markale observed that " ... when the hero of the Quest finds himself in the castle of the Grail, he doesn't know what it is, at least not during the first visit. He has not looked around himself enough to discern the multiplicity of Being and understand that this multiplicity merges together into a fundamental unity. He thus sees

333

nothing. In the same way, numerous knights who have set off on the Quest pass by the Castle of the Grail without seeing it. Without even seeing that there is a castle. For the door of the castle is always on the inside. It is the opened door to the closed palace of the king. The wisdom attained by the winner of the Quest is within the reach of everyone."[5]

In other words, the Grail Castle's inside door is the inner opening to spiritual power we all possess.

The Damsel of the Sanct Grael by **Dante Gabriel Rossetti.**

"God," then, is not some cosmically remote, impersonal, unknowable Force, nor a long-bearded judge enthroned in the clouds, holding human souls in the palm of his hand over the flames of eternal damnation. Instead, Synchronicity suggests that the Divine Mind is an intimately personal consciousness inviting us to participate as co-creators. We honor that invitation, Joseph Campbell used to say, when we live the "authentic life;" in other words, by pursuing our own, innermost truth, and striving for that which is most meaningful to us.

Whether we lead a revolution or collect stamps is immaterial, because whenever we pursue our chief passion we unloose energies across the universe our Co-Creator uses to fashion the future in ways beyond our understanding. All we need to know is that we are best fulfilled in "following our bliss," the highest command of heaven everyone hears in the holiest chambers of his or her soul. Synchronicities are the echoes of that calling. They are personal messages meant for us alone, sent from the Compassionate Consciousness. In harkening to them, we follow our high destiny, the real meaning of life.

Following one's bliss, however, is not synonymous for "doing our own thing." Living the Authentic Life is not self-gratification. On the contrary, pursuit of one's heart's desire is acting upon that which is most significant to us. Indeed, endeavoring to manifest our own inner truth often requires self-sacrifice --- the scorn and even hostility of outsiders. Essentially, synchronicity points us in the direction of and guides us down the Left-Hand Path leading toward that inner truth. Persons who follow this Road Less Traveled may have to give up the material comforts and social approval associated by majorities everywhere with "success". But they live and die fulfilled in the comforting awareness that they strove to realize their ideal, even if they failed to materialize it. Merely making the effort was success in itself. They would only have failed if they had not pursued their dream. At the extreme terminus of the Left-Hand Path stands the Crucifix -- the ultimate symbol of total self-identification with the Dream. The Ego As Adversary --- this is the principle anyone undertaking on the Authentic Life must grasp.

But in applying it, no matter what the cost in self-abnegation, he or she will feel, then know that their existence has not been in vain. They used their time to its best advantage by championing their highest potential. That is the meaning of life; namely, to manifest our own inner truth. It is the only genuine wealth which cannot be diminished by time or stolen by others. For all the sacrifices the Authentic Life demands, persons who live it never wonder why they were born, nor despair because they missed their chance to do what was really important for fear of contrary opinions, or in the name of responsibility to others. That is the fate of individuals who choose the Right-Hand Path. Such individuals eventually come to the horrible realization that they wasted their lives by rejecting their innermost truth. They sold their real identity --- their souls --- for fear of losing the comfort and security social approval promise, but do not always provide.

It is at this juncture --- where both roads meet --- that Synchronicity plays its critical role by urging us to follow our bliss along the Left-Hand Path. In accepting the divine guidance of meaningful coincidence, we are doing God's work.

What is "God's work"? Organizing order out of chaos. When we strive to manifest our ideal, no matter how apparently insignificant it may seem to others or even ourselves, we unleash prolific energies beyond our imagining, thereby participating in the organizing principle that orders the entire universe. We co-create with the Creator, who personally invites us to join in its construction. And we receive this invitation from on high whenever our lives are suddenly, unexpectedly illuminated by the miraculous flash of Synchronicity.

Endnotes

Introduction: Are We Beneficiaries or Victims of Meaningful Coincidence?

1) Hogue, John. *Nostradamus, The New Revelations.* MA.: Element, Inc., 1994.

2) Muir, Jim. "Uncanny Twist, Flag Search takes bizarre Turn in Benton". *The Southern Illinoisian.* Carbondale, 16 September 2001.

3) Aurandt, Paul. *More of Paul Harvey's The Rest of the Story.* edited and complied by Lynne Harvey. NY: William Morrow & Co., 1980.

4) West, John Anthony and Toonder, Jan Gerhard. *The Case for Astrology*, NY: Coward-McCann, 1970.

5) Thurston, Ph.D., Mark. *The Essential Edgar Cayce.* NY: Jeremey P. Tarcher, 2004.

6) Dalai Lama. *In My Own Words: An Introduction to My Teachings and Philosophy.* CA: Hay House, 2011.

Chapter 1: Applying the Mystery of Synchronicity

1) Ford, Michael Custis. *The Ten Thousand.* NY: Thomas Dunne Books, 2010.

2) von Goethe ,Johann Wolfgang, *Maxims and Reflections*, CreateSpace Independent Publishing Platform, 2011.

3) Zimmer, Heinrich. *The King and the Corpse: Tales of the Soul's Conquest of Evil.* NJ: Princeton University Press, 1971.

4) Ehrmann, Max. *Desiderata*. MA: Hard Press, 2008.

5) Thurston, op. cit.

6) Jung, Carl Gustav. *Jung on Synchronicity and the Paranormal.* MA: Hard Press, 1998.

7) Isaacson, Walter. *Einstein: His Life and Universe.* NY: Simon & Schuster, 2008.

8) Mindell, Arnold. *Quantum Mind*. MA: Hampton Roads Publishing, 2004.

Chapter 2: The Synchronicity of Numbers

1) West, op. cit.

2) *Philolaus of Croton: Pythagorean and Presocratic: A Commentary on the Fragments and Testimonia with Interpretive Essays.* MA: Cambridge University Press, 2006.

3) Upczak. Patricia Rose, *Synchronicity, Signs & Symbols*. CO: Synchronicity Publishing, 2001.

4) *Plato: Complete Works*. IN: Hackett Publishing Co., 1997.

5) Tompkins, Peter. *Obelisks*. NY: Harper & Row, 1969.

6) Guthrie, Kenneth Sylvan. *The Pythagorean Sourcebook and Library: An Anthology of Ancient Writings Which Relate to Pythagoras and Pythagorean Philosophy*. MI: Phanes Press, 1987.

7) Philolaus, op. cit.

8) West., op. cit.

9) Svensson, Horik. *The Runes*. NY: Barnes & Noble Books, 1995.

10) Plutarch. *Lives of the noble Grecians and Romans*. UK: Benediction Classics, 2010.

11) West., op. cit.

12) Thurston, op. cit.

13) Eliade, Micrea. *Patterns in Comparative Religion*. NE: Bison Books, 1996.

14) Abbot, A.E. *Encyclopedia of Numbers*. MT: Kessinger Publishing, 2003.

15) *Fate*, November, 1968, vol. 21, no. 11, issue 224.

16) West, op. cit.

17) Icie M. Marlow, *Fate*, January, 1978, vol. 31, no. 1, issue 334.

18. *Fate*, August, 1968, vol. 21, no. 8, issue 221.

19) Lionel, Frederic. *The Magic Tarot: Vehicle of Eternal Wisdom*. NY: Routledge Kegan & Paul, 1983.

20) Valla, Maria. *The Power of Numbers*. CA: DeVorss & Co., 1971.

21) Hopcke, Robert H. *There Are No Accidents*. NY: Doubleday & Co., 1998.

22) Upczak, op. cit.

23) *The Didascalicon of Hugh of Saint Victor: A Guide to the Arts*. NY: Columbia University Press, 1991.

24) Eliade, op. cit.

25) Kozminsky, Isidore. *Numbers: Their Meaning and Magic*. London: Rider & Co., 1972.

26) *Fate,* May, 1977, vol. 30, no. 5, issue 326.

27) *Fate,* November, 1976, vol. 29, no. 11, issue 320.

28) *Fate,* March, 1977, vol.30, no.3. issue 324.

29) *Fate,* November 1983, issue 404, vol. 36, no. 11.

30) *Fate,* January, 1971, vol. 24, no. 1, issue 250.

31) *Fate*, April, 1966, vol. 19, no. 4, issue 193.

32) *Fate,* February, 1971, vol. 24, no. 2, issue 251.

33) Kozminsky, op. cit.

34) *Fate,* March, 1982, vol. 35, no. 3, issue 384.

35) Kozminsky, op. cit.

36) *Fate,* March, 1967, vol. 20, no. 3, issue 204.

37) Kozminsky, op. cit.

38) Finnessey, Arthur. *History Computed*. NY: Gravelston Press, Inc., 1997.

39) Kozminsky, op. cit.

40) Godwin, David. *Godwin's Cabalistic Encyclopedia*. MN: Llewellyn Publications, 1997.

41) Cirlot, J.E. *A Dictionary of Symbols*. NY: Philosophical Library, 1962.

42) Crowley, Aleister. *Book of the Law*. NY: Red Wheel, 2011.

43) *Fate,* August, 1969, vol. 22, no. 8, issue 233.

44) Kozminsky, op. cit.

Chapter 3: Tragic Synchronicity

1) *The Wisdom of the Great Chiefs: The Classic Speeches of Chief Red Jacket, Chief Joseph, and Chief Seattle*. CA: New World Library, 1994.

2) Burman, A. "Premonitions of Death for *Titanic* Passengers". *Northhampton Chronicle and Echo*, 14 February 1998.

3) Ibid.

4) Ibid.

5) *Fate,* June 1977, vol. 30, no. 6, issue 327.

6) Allan, Tony, *Prophecies, 4,000 Years of Prophets, Visionaries and Predictions.* London: Thorsons, 2002.

7) Korovin, Igor, *Air Crash Investigations: The Worst Single Plane Crash In American History, The Crash Of American Airlines Flight 191.* lulu.com, 2011.

8) Madigan, Shawn. *Mystics, Visionaries, and Prophets.* MN: Fortress Press, 1998.

9) Steward, Reginald. "They Envisioned America's Worst Airline Disaster in Dreams," vol. xxxiv, nr. 11. *London Daily Herald*, 16 January 2003.

10) Wax, Judith. *Starting In The Middle*. NY: Holt, Rinehart, and Winston,1979.

11) Kozminsky, op. cit.

Chapter 4: Parallel Lives and a Presidential Curse

1) Wallace-Murphy,Tim and Hopkins, Marilyn, *Rosslyn, Guardian of the Secrets of the Holy Grail.* MA: Element Books, 2000.

2) *Fate,* January 1978, vol. 31, no. 1, issue 334.

3) *Fate,* September 1978, vol. 28, no. 9, issue 306.

4) *Fate,* November 1977, vol. 30, no. 11, issue 332.

5) *Fate,* August 1972, vol. 25, no. 8, issue 269.

6) Fate, December 1969, vol. 22, no. 12, issue 237.

7) *Fate,* February 1983, vol. 36, no. 2, issue 395.

8) *Fate,* January 1967, vol. 20, no. 1, issue 202.

9) *Fate,* December 1981, vol. 34, no. 12, issue 381.

10) Barmann, George. *Plain Dealer.* Cleveland, Ohio, 5 August 1976.

11) *Fate,* April 1966, vol. 19, no. 4, issue 193, "ESP Bonds of Twindom."

12) *Fate,* June 1966, vol. 19, no. 6, issue 195.

13) *Fate,* February 1967, vol. 20, no. 2, issue 203.

14) *Fate,* February 1976, vol. 29, no. 2, issue 311.

15) Walker, Barbara G. *The Woman's Encyclopedia of Myths and Secrets.* CA: HarperSanFrancisco, 1983.

16) West, op. cit.

17) Kauffman, Michael W. *American Brutus: John Wilkes Booth and the Lincoln Conspiracies.* NY: Random House, 2005.

18) *Fate*, March 1969, vol. 22, no. 3, issue 228.

19) Putrino, John, "Premonition on the President", *Fate,* July 1964, vol. 17, no. 7, issue 172.

20) *Fate,* October 1969, vol. 22, no. 10, issue 235.

21) Roberts, Josie. "U. Virginia Scholars Debate Validity of Curse of Tecumseh", *Cavalier Daily* (University of Virginia). 30 August 2000.

22) Feldman, Jay. *When the Mississippi Ran Backwards*. NY: Free Press, 2005.

23) Brinkman, Grover. *Grit magazine*. 24 February 1963.

24) Schopenhauer, Arthur. *Essays and Aphorisms*. NY: Penguin Classics, 1973.

Chapter 5: The Fate of Synchronicity

1) Trismegistus, Hermes. *The Emerald Tablet of Hermes*. NY: Merchant Books, 2013.

2) Robinson, Amos, *Fate,* April 2002, vol.55, no.3, issue 624.

3) *Fate,* March 1977, vol.30, no.3, issue 324.

4) *Fate,* November 1983, vol. 36, no. 11, issue 404.

5) *Fate,* January 1976, vol. 29, no. 1, issue 310.

6) *Fate,* April 1981, vol. 34, no. 4, issue 373.

7) *Fate,* July 1976, vol. 29, no. 7, issue 316.

8) *Fate,* December 1974, vol. 27, no. 12, issue 297.

9) *Fate,* July 1973, vol. 26, no. 7, issue 280.

10) Jay, Alan. *The Columbian.* Westminster, B.C., 9 January 1967.

11) *Fate,* April 1970, vol. 23, no. 4, issue 241.

12) *Fate,* June 1967, vol. 20, no. 6, issue 207.

13) *Fate,* April 1989, vol. 42, no. 4, issue 469.

14) *Fate,* April 1975, vol. 28, no. 4. issue 301.

15) *Fate,* September 1974, vol. 27, no. 9, issue 294.

16) Ibid.

17) *Fate,* June 1974, vol. 27, no. 6, issue 291.

18) *Fate,* November 1969, vol. 22, no. 9, issue 234.

19) *Fate,* August 1969, vol. 22, no. 8, issue 233.

20) *Fate,* August 1969, vol. 22, no. 8, issue 233.

21) *Fate,* October 1969, vol. 22, no. 10, issue 235.

Chapter 6: We Are The Children Of Meaningful Coincidence

1) Berkeley, George. *An Essay Towards a New Theory of Vision.* NY: BookSurge Classics, 2004.

2) Cirlot, op. cit.

Chapter 7: The Root Chakra Person

1) Stoker, Bram. *Dracula.* NY: Top Five Books, 2014.

2) Hoffman, David E. *The Oligarchs: Wealth And Power In The New Russia.* NY: Public Affairs, 2011.

Chapter 8: The Sacral Chakra Person

1) Pond, David. *Chakras for Beginners.* MN: Llewellyn Publications, 1999.

2) Baker, Jean-Claude. *Josephine: The Hungry Heart.* NY: Cooper Square Press, 2001.

3) *Goodness had nothing to do with it: The Autobiography of Mae West.* NY: Prentice-Hall, 1959.

4) Noonan, George C. *Classical Scientific Astrology*. AZ: American Federation of Astrologers, 2005.

5) Cirlot, op. cit.

6) Kunz, George Frederick, Ph.D. *The Mystical Lore of Precious Stones.* Volume 1, CA: Newcastle Publishing Co.,1986.

7) Ibid.

8) Cunningham, Scott. *The Complete Book of Incense, Oils and Brews.* MN: Llewellyn Publications, 2002.

9) Ibid.

10) Williams, Mark R. *In Search of Lemuria, The Lost Pacific Continent in Legend, Myth and Imagination.* CA: Golden Era Books, 2001.

11) Cirlot, op. cit.

Chapter 9: The Navel Chakra Person

1) Khrushchev, Nikita Sergeevich. *Khrushchev Remembers.* NY: Little Brown & Company,1970.

2) Encyclopedia Britannica, Macropedia, vol. 17, *Joseph Stalin.* Chicago: Encyclopedia Britannica, Inc., 1981.

3) Kennan, George F. *The Life of Joseph Stalin*. NY: MacMillan & Co, 1973.

4) Tucker, Robert C. *Stalin As Revolutionary, 1879-1929: A Study in History and Personality* (Vol. 1). NY: W. W. Norton & Company 1974.

5) Ibid.

6) Khrushchev, op. cit.

7) Kennan, op. cit.

8) Thurston, op. cit.

Chapter 10: The Heart Chakra Person

1) von Easchenbach. Wolfram, *Parzival*. NY: Penguin Classics, 1980.

2) Wallace-Murphy, op. cit.

3) Plutarch, op. cit.

4) Shakespeare, William. *Othello*. NY: Simon & Schuster, 2004.

5) Cirlot, op. cit.

Chapter 11: The Throat Chakra Person

1) Wauters, Ambika, *Chakras and their Archetypes*, CA: The Crossing Press, 1996.

2) Nietzsche, Friedrich, *Thus Spoke Zarathustra*, NY: Penguin, 1972.

3) Williams, op. cit.

Chapter 12: The Brow Chakra Person

1) Plato, op. cit.

2) Neihardt , John G.. *Black Elk Speaks: Being the Life Story of a Holy Man of the Oglala Sioux.* University of Nebraska Press, 1988.

3) Heydenreich, H. *Leonardo da Vinci,* volume 2. NY: Grosset & Dunlap, 1954.

4) Hunt, Inez and Draper, Wanetta W. *Lightning in His Hand, The Life and Story of Nikola Tesla.* NY: Alfred A. Knopf, 1964.

5) Sams, Jamie and Carson, David. *Animal Medicine Cards.* NM: Bear & Company, 1988.

6) Sanderson Haldane. Elizabeth, *Descartes, His Life and Times.* MA: Adamant Media Corporation, 2004.

7) Turner, William. *The Names Of Herbs.* London: English Dialect Society, 1881.

8) Williams, op. cit.

9) Cirlot, op. cit.

Chapter 13: The Crown Chakra Person

1) Pond, David. *Chakras for Beginners.* MN: Llewellyn Publications, 1999.

2) Jung, C.G. *Modern Man in Search of a Soul*. NY: Harcourt Harvest, 1955.

3) Reiterman, Tim. Raven: *The Untold Story of the Rev. Jim Jones and His People.* NY: Tarcher-Perigee, 2008.

4) McGarey, William A. *The Edgar Cayce Remedies*. NY: Bantam, 1983.

5) Cirlot, op. cit.

6) Hadot, Pierre. Plotinus or the Simplicity of Vision. University Of Chicago Press, 1998.

7) DeLong, op. cit.

8) Kunz, op. cit.

9) Henry, William. Quoted by Farrell, Joseph P. *The Giza Death Star.* IL. Adventures Unlimited Press, 2002.

10) Cirlot, op. cit.

11) Leach, Maria. Funk & Wagnall's Standard Dictionary of Folklore, Mythology, and Legend. NY: Harper & Row, 1984.

12) Leach, Ibid

Chapter 14: How to Connect with the Seven Chakra-Types

1) Donnelly, Ignatius. *Diaries*. Minnesota Historical Society, 1881.

2) Bruyere, Rosalyn L. *Wheels of Light.* NY: Simon and Schuster, 1994.

3) Wallace-Murphy, op. cit.

4) Witt, R.E. *Isis in the Ancient World* MD: Johns Hopkins University Press, 1997.

Chapter 15: Understanding the Chakra Types through Synchronicity

1) Muir, John. *Nature Writings*, NY: Library of America, 1997.

2) Jones, Jr., Henry Z., *Psychic Roots: Serendipity and Intuition on Genealogy*. NY: Genealogical Publishing Co., 1999.

Afterword: Indra's Net

1) Lamy, Lucy. *Egyptian Mysticism: New Light on Ancient Knowledge.* London: Thames and Hudson, 1981.

2) von List, Guido. *The Secret of the Runes.* translated by Stephen E. Flowers, Ph.D. VT: Destiny Books, 1988.

3) von Magdeburg, Mechtilde. *The Flowing Light of The Godhead.* CT: Martino Fine Books, 2012.

4) Ellmann, Richard. *Yeats: The Man and the Masks.* NY: W. W. Norton & Company, 2013.

5) Markale, Jean. *The Templar Treasure at Gisors.* translated by Jon Graham. VT: Inner Traditions International, 2003.

References

Anger, Kenneth. *Hollywood Babylon II.* NY: E.P. Dutton, 1984.

Cayce, Edgar. *Atlantis, The Edgar Cayce Readings,* Volume 22. Virginia Beach, VA: Association for Research and Enlightenment, Inc., 1987.

Cheney, Margaret. *Tesla, Man Out of Time.* NY: Simon & Schuster (Touchstone), 2001.

Imel, Martha Ann and Dorothy Myers. *Goddesses in World Mythology.* UK: Oxford University Press, 1995.

Joseph, Frank. *Synchronicity and You, Understanding the Role of Meaningful Coincidence in Your Life.* MA: Element Books, 1999; re-published as *The Power of Coincidence.* London: Arcturus Books, 2009.

Karagulla, Shafica, M.D., and van Gelder, Dora. *The Chakras and the Human Energy Fields.* IL: The Theosophical Publishing House,1989.

Knappert, Jan. *Pacific Mythology, An Encyclopedia of Myth and Legend.* London: Diamond Books, 1992.

Lash, John. *The Seekers Handbook, The Complete Guide to Spiritual Pathfinding.* NY: Harmony Books, 1990.

Lippman, Theo, Jr. "Do Candidates Recall Zero-Year Curse?" *The Baltimore Sun.* 18 August 1999.

Synchronicity as Mystical Experience

MacKenzie, Donald A. *Myths of China and Japan.* NY: Gramercy Books, 1994.

Markale, Jean. T*he Grail, The Celtic Origins of the Sacred Icon.* translated by Jon Graham. VT: Inner Traditions International, 1999.

Morford, Mark P.O. and Lenardon, Robert J. *Classical Mythology*, Second Edition. New York: Logman, 1970.

Ovason, David M. *The Secret Symbols of the Dollar Bill.* CA: HarperCollins, 2004.

Stewart, R.J. *The Underworld Initiation, A Journey Towards Psychic Transformation.* UK: The Aquarian Press, 1985.

Stricherz, Vince. "End of a Presidential Tradition", WA: *The Seattle Times.* 20 January 1989.

Willis-Brandon, Carla, Ph.D. *A Glimpse of Heaven, The Remarkable World of Spiritually Transformative Experiences*. MA: Adams Media, 2004.

*"Top 10 Freaky Coincidences in History",
https://www.youtube.com/watch?v=ES6BGxpBD-4*

*"10 Most insane coincidences in history",
https://www.youtube.com/watch?v=j-QTV-vXHX4*

76363743R00215

Made in the USA
San Bernardino, CA
11 May 2018